Jesse
LIVERMORE

WORLD'S
GREATEST
STOCK
TRADER

Richard Smitten

JOHN WILEY & SONS, INC.

New York • Chichester • Weinheim • Brisbane • Singapore • Toronto

Published by John Wiley & Sons, Inc.
Published simultaneously in Canada.

This publication is designed to provide accurate and authoritative information in regard to the subject matter covered. It is sold with the understanding that the publisher is not engaged in rendering professional services. If professional advice or other expert assistance is required, the services of a competent professional person should be sought.

Library of Congress Cataloging-in-Publication Data:
Smitten, Richard.
    Jesse Livermore : world's greatest stock trader / Richard Smitten.
       p. cm.—(Wiley investment series)
    Includes index.
    ISBN 0-471-02326-4 (pbk. : alk. paper)
       1. Livermore, Jesse L. (Jesse Lauriston) 1877–1940.
   2. Stockbrokers—United States—Biography. I. Title. II. Series.

HG4928.5.L58 S655 2001
332.64'5'092—dc21
[B]   2001026187

Printed in the United States of America.

10 9 8 7 6 5 4 3

This book is dedicated to my father, Louis Smitten. Without him there would be no book. He is a man who has done close to the impossible: He has balanced worldly success with spiritual success.

In 1923, seven men who had made it to the top of the financial success pyramid met together at the Edgewater Hotel in Chicago. Collectively, they controlled more wealth than the entire United States Treasury, and for years the media had held them up as examples of success.

Who were they? Charles Schwab, president of the world's largest steel company, Arthur Cutten, the greatest wheat speculator of his day, Richard Whitney, president of the New York Stock Exchange, Albert Fall, a member of the President's Cabinet, Jesse Livermore, the greatest bear on Wall Street, Leon Fraser, president of the International Bank of Settlement, and Ivan Kruegger, the head of the world's largest monopoly.

What happened to them? Schwab and Cutten both died broke; Whitney spent years of his life in Sing Sing penitentiary; Fall also spent years in prison, but was released so he could die at home; and the others Livermore, Fraser, and Kruegger, committed suicide.   Donald McCullogh,
Waking from the American Dream

The steps of a short sale are defined as a sale of stock you don't own, in anticipation of a drop in price. Stock is borrowed from your broker for delivery to the purchaser. Later, stock is purchased in the open market and returned to the broker to complete the transaction. In other words, the stock is sold first then bought later, hopefully at a lower price. This is the reverse of a normal buy-first, sell-later transaction.

Louis Smitten, speculator

Contents

Preface

There is nothing more difficult to take in hand, more perilous to conduct, or more uncertain in its success than to take the lead in the introduction of a new order of things.

Niccolo Machiavelli

WHEN I WAS 13, MY FATHER TOLD ME ABOUT THE GREAT-est stock trader who ever lived, Jesse Livermore. I sat and listened as my father informed me that Livermore had set a new standard for the trading of stocks. Fascinated, I began reading about Livermore before I was 14.

I did not know that 40 years later Livermore and I would have a date with destiny—or that I would devote more than a year of my life to investigating his life. I did not know that I would ultimately get to know him as well as anyone ever did get to know him.

Livermore was a person of great secrecy, mystery, and silence. He strove to control his emotions and thereby overcome the human frailty of passions that we all suffer from. Above all, he wanted to beat the game, solve the puzzle, best the stock market.

Many readers will be familiar with Jesse Livermore under the name Larry Livingston, from the best-selling book *Reminiscences of a Stock Operator* by Edwin LeFevre, a financial journalist. First published in 1923, *Reminiscences of a Stock Operator* is the fictionalized biography of Livermore. There is no question that *Reminiscences* is one of the best financial books ever written. Generations of traders, investors, and market watchers have turned to it for insight into the strategies of a great trader and for understanding of crowd psychology and market timing.

After reading *Reminiscences* and Livermore's own book, *How to Trade in Stocks,* I realized that there was a lot more to Livermore's story. The published record revealed almost nothing about the real Jesse Livermore. I embarked on a two-year journey that would take me into Livermore's world—both professional and personal. I was able to interview Paul Livermore, Jesse's surviving son, who spoke for the record for the first time about his father. I also spoke to Patricia Livermore, the wife of Jesse Livermore Junior and close confidant of Dorothy Livermore, Livermore's second wife and the mother of his two children.

Just like the famous financier J.P. Morgan, Livermore suffered from great bouts of depression throughout his life. In the period he lived there were no remedies for this condition, and finally, in 1940, he ended his life by his own hand.

Livermore was quiet and secretive, yet lived a very opulent and exciting life, moving in the highest social circles. He was personally blamed for the great crash of 1929, and received numerous death and kidnapping threats. He married a beautiful Ziegfeld Follies showgirl and fathered two children, one of whom would eventually be shot by his own mother.

This book is a complete biography of Jesse Livermore, the man and the trader. It chronicles his life in fine detail and also reveals many new aspects of his groundbreaking trading techniques, which were revolutionary then and which remain revolutionary today.

There are four simple themes to this book.

First, human nature never changes. Therefore, the stock market never changes. Only the faces, the pockets, the suckers and the manipulators, the wars, the disasters, and the technologies change. The market itself never changes. How can it? Human nature never changes, and human nature runs the market—not reason, not economics, and certainly not logic. It is our human emotions that drive the market, as they do most other things on this planet.

Second, the achievement of material goals and career ambitions does not equal the achievement of happiness in life. There is no correlation between success and happiness. There is no automatic balance between worldly riches and emotional fulfillment.

Third, it is our *will* that allows each of us to accomplish our goals, not our intellect. Talent is not enough. Luck is not enough. Only the will to suffer hard work and incredible persistence leads to the attainment of the impossible. There are no shortcuts; there is no easy way. Especially, as you'll find out, in the stock market.

Finally, it is the individual, not the group, that has led to the great discoveries of humanity. The great ideas, the great fortunes, and the giant steps forward in technology, politics, and medicine have all come from individuals, not groups.

There are many ways to play the market, hundreds of theories, techniques, systems, and strategies. This book covers Livermore's approach. It reveals for the first time in one volume his secrets on how to successfully speculate and make money. A great deal of the research conducted on Livermore's life was based on interviews with his family, personal papers, newspaper accounts, and Livermore's own writings. Some poetic license was taken in recreating dialogue to paint a more vibrant picture of Jesse Livermore, the man, and his times. In certain parts of the book I have replicated conversations as they were told to me by family members.

And I think you will agree, after reading this book, that there never was another stock market speculator like Jesse Livermore.

Acknowledgments

Special thanks to Paul Livermore for his kind cooperation in going back in time in such great detail to revisit a sometimes painful past and to Paul's beautiful wife, Ann, who was so gracious with her time.

Thanks to Patricia Livermore, who also had to travel back to the years she was married to Jesse Livermore Jr. and relive so much heartbreak, tragedy, and sorrow.

Special thanks to my father for introducing me to the Livermore story when I was a young man and for his brilliant technical assistance and editing of the book. Also thanks must go to my fabulous daughter, Kelley Smitten, for her constant support and help in editing this book.

I also must thank Ed Dobson at Trader's Press for his great encouragement during preparation of the original edition of this book. Ed shares with me, and many other people, an endless fascination with Livermore's life and times.

Thanks to Debi Murray of the Historical Society of Palm Beach County for guiding me through the society's precious archives and letting me have a glimpse into Palm Beach life at the turn of the last century.

Finally, thanks to Jesse Livermore for trying to do the impossible—beat the game and master the stock market.

* *chapter one* *

The Great Bear of Wall Street

Chaos is come again.   Shakespeare, *Othello*

Early on the morning of Tuesday, October 29th, the canyons of Wall Street were thronged with thousands of excited thrill-seekers who had come to witness the anticipated carnage. Policemen on horseback and detectives in uniform attempted to keep the mob clear of the entrance to the New York Stock Exchange, but it was no use; every time they succeeded in opening a pathway, the jostling crowd immediately closed ranks again.

Inside, on the floor of the exchange, one could actually feel the tension and fear in the air as the hands of the clock crawled toward 10:00 and the opening gong. Less than a week earlier on Black Thursday, the stock market had suffered the most disastrous decline in its history, and the staggering plunge of prices on the following Monday afternoon had only increased the prevailing sense of panic.

In broker's rooms across the country, investors visited nervously and coughed and shifted their feet as they stood and stared in hypnotic fascination at the silent stock ticker, the mechanical courier that would soon deliver, with cold indifference, a verdict of survival or—more likely—utter ruin.

William Klingaman, *1929: The Year of the Great Crash*

ON THAT SAME MORNING, AT EXACTLY 7:20, NOT 7:19 OR 7:21, Jesse Livermore stood at the massive entrance to his 29-room mansion in King's Point, Long Island, waiting to see the flying-maiden hood ornament on his black Rolls-Royce. The chauffeur knew the drill, he had to enter the driveway at seven twenty. Jesse Livermore was a precise man.

A light gray fog wafted in from Long Island Sound. It accentuated the cold air, the change of seasons, and added an ominous feel to the air. As usual, the car rolled down the long circular drive at precisely 7:20 and stopped in front of Livermore. He nodded silently to the chauffeur, opened his own door, and slipped into the back seat, the newspapers folded under his arm. He placed them on the leather seats as he did every morning: the *New York Times,* the *London Times,* the *Wall Street Journal.* He glanced at the headlines again; they were basically all the same—"Stock Markets Plummet Throughout the World."

As the car made its way down the driveway, Livermore clicked on his reading lamp and pulled the side-window curtains closed. He wanted to study the newspapers in dark silence. There were no surprises in these newspapers for him. In fact, he had been waiting for these very headlines for almost a year now. He had planned carefully for this day, and he had been patient.

When the car crossed into Manhattan, the driver did not drop the window between them. Instead, he used the microphone. "Mr. Livermore, we've passed into Manhattan. You asked me to tell you."

Livermore pushed open the thick black curtain and let the light of the sun stream into the darkness of the back of the limo. He thought about telling the chauffeur to drive down to Wall Street so he could see, could feel, the atmosphere in the Wall Street canyons.

But that might somehow affect the way he played it from here on out, affect his emotions, his objectivity. Was this the bottom? Was it just a pause in a steep decline? Would confidence in the market return and stop the free fall? Should he cover his short positions? His fortune would rest on the answers to these questions, and he had long ago realized that it was what people actually did in the stock market that counted—not what they said they were going to do.

Some people might want to see the human chaos, feel the desperate financial pandemonium that occurred when the fear-devil rose up and conquered the greed-god that had appeared so strong and indestructible—but not Livermore; he wanted to stay untouched by these human reactions. He would be able to see everything clearly soon enough. He would listen to the quiet clicking verdict of the stock tickers in his office suite when the market opened for trading.

He slid the black curtain back across the window and began to study the newspapers again in the darkness. He spoke without looking up. "Harry, we'll go straight to the office."

Before the automated traffic-light system was installed, a New York City police officer would sit in a booth and operate the lights. When the Livermore limousine approached, this officer would make sure the light was green so Livermore would have no interruptions on his journey from King's Point to his office in Manhattan.

Once a week, Harry the chauffeur would retrace the route, stopping at each traffic-light booth. There he would pass out a cash gratuity to the police officer in charge for the officer's kind consideration in making sure the financier always had a green light when he passed. Livermore was a person who demanded precision.

Livermore exited his car at 730 Fifth Avenue, the Hecksher

Building. He stepped into the private express elevator that stopped on the eighteenth floor, the penthouse. Livermore demanded a straight shot to his office. He chose not to speak with anyone, if he could avoid it.

There was no name on the door of Livermore's office suite. He opened it with his key and entered the small waiting room, an anteroom where Harry Edgar Dache sat during office hours. It was difficult to get past Dache, who stood 6 foot 6, weighed 275 pounds, and was considered by the press to be pug-ugly as well as not very friendly.

At this hour, however, the office suite was empty. Livermore was always first. He opened the second door with a special key kept in a safe. Only he and Dache had the combination. Dache even supervised the cleaning people when they cleaned Livermore's offices. Many considered them the most palatial in New York City, with hand-carved arches, custom bookshelves, and walls paneled in beautiful mahogany and carved oak. Livermore had first seen this paneling in the library of an old English manor house. He had paid to have the paneling dismantled and shipped to New York, where it was reassembled in his offices.

The office suite itself consisted of an anteroom; the trading room with its green chalkboard that covered the entire wall, along with the walkway for the board men; the conference room; and finally Livermore's huge private office. The chalkboard was visible from all the rooms.

Livermore usually employed a staff of seven, six board men plus Dache. The primary job of his employees was to post stock quotes on the green chalkboards that stretched the length of the office area. Dache oversaw all activities in the office and did whatever else he was asked. The board men were sworn to secrecy and paid well. The rule in the offices was no talking during market hours. Livermore wanted no distractions while the market was open. The quotes had to be posted immediately and accurately; millions were riding.

There were several ticker-tape machines in each room. The snaking tape was like the blood that flowed through his veins. It was life itself. He was never out of arm's reach of a stock ticker. There were tickers in the main rooms of all his homes: Lake Placid, Long Island, the Manhattan apartment, the suite of rooms in the Breakers Hotel in Palm Beach, even on his 300-foot yacht.

Livermore read the numerous *New York Times* articles that he had saved from the recent editions. All the papers blamed him for the calamitous crash, personally blamed him for initiating the decline—the precipitous free fall which now seemed to have no bottom. But he believed that business—in his case, the stock market—was like war. In war, you died if you made a mistake; in the stock market, if you made a mistake, you could go broke very fast. One could die, financially, in a heartbeat.

Livermore was a serious person, and on this day he planned to do some serious business. He was impeccably dressed, as he was every day, in a handmade suit from Saville Row in London. His shirts were the latest style, made of the finest Egyptian cotton, monogrammed on the cuff. His suit hung perfectly from his slim frame, his silk tie subtly striped to blend in with it. His blond hair was combed back, parted on the left side. He used pince-nez glasses, which were perched on his nose. He wore a vest with a gold chain that spanned the pockets. On one end of the chain hung a thin gold pencil, on the other, a small golden penknife. He often fidgeted with the pen or the knife, spinning one or the other, while he was talking.

He was the most famous bear on Wall Street, a trader who was as likely to sell short as to buy long. He didn't care; he knew that stocks went down as often as they went up—but when they

declined, they did it twice as fast as when they went up, and that
was what was going on today.

He had a line out at the present time of over a million shares,
well over $100 million. It had been placed months ago, slowly,
secretly, and silently, using more than 100 stockbrokers, so nobody
could tell what he was doing. He was short the market—he had
sold stock that he would later supply, at a much lower price. He
was living up to his reputation as the Great Bear of Wall Street.

Today, he was like a lone wolf stalking the arctic tundra, looking
for prey—and looking out for other predators that might kill him.
There were plenty of Wall Street players he knew who could do
just that—end his financial life with one deadly, hammering blow.

He picked up one of the *New York Times* articles he had saved
from October 20, and read the headline: "Stocks Driven Down in
Wave of Selling." He was careful not to gloat. There was no one
who knew better than Livermore how fast things could change in
the stock market. He read on:

> In the two hours in which trading was limited on the New
> York Stock Exchange active issues passed through one of the
> wildest breaks in history. Final quotations revealed net losses
> ranging from 5 to 20 points and the aggregate depreciation in
> open market values was estimated at $1,000,000,000 (one bil-
> lion) or more.
>
> The total turnover was 3,488,100 shares which represented
> the second heaviest volume for a Saturday since the Stock
> Exchange was established. During the first half hour trading
> took place at a rate of more than 8,500,000 shares for a full
> five-hour day. The stock market community did not know
> until an hour and twenty-three minutes after the 12 o'clock
> closing gong what the final prices were, so late was the over-
> burdened ticker.

PIVOTAL STOCKS HIT

One of the stories which gained wide circulation wherever stock market tickers clicked yesterday was that Jesse L. Livermore, formerly one of the country's biggest speculators, is the leader of the bear clique that has been hammering away at the market for weeks, and that the particular weakness which developed in high priced and pivotal stocks was to be attributed, in part at least, to his activities.

Arthur W. Cutten of Chicago, the recognized leader of the bull party, watched the ticker from his hotel in Atlantic City yesterday and told close friends that nothing has developed to change his opinion about the market—that good stocks would eventually sell higher.

Reports of a struggle between Livermore and Cutten for stock market supremacy, which have circulated widely in Wall Street for the last three or four days, were discredited. Livermore is presumed to be heavily short of leading stocks and Cutten heavily long of the same group of issues. The ascendency of Livermore to the position he once held as the country's leading market operator on the bear side, after several years of eclipse, is one of the most interesting developments in the market.

The short selling which it was generally agreed was the principal factor in today's decline, served to induce further liquidation of stocks and the cumulative effect was reflected in a demoralized market in certain issues. It was plain that the market was receiving no organized support. Stocks which ordinarily have powerful backing were allowed to shift for themselves.

With stocks driving higher during the last few months following each downward reaction, the situation was ready made for Livermore. The Street stories are that he went short of a large line of issues such as: United States Steel, Montgomery Ward, Simmons Co., General Electric, American and Foreign Power and half a dozen other of the market's pivotal issues. He then initiated his familiar hammering tactics under which the market first faltered, then broke.

Cutten, the Fishers, Durant and others of the group known in Wall Street as the "Big Ten" were large holders of these particular stocks and have seen their plans and pools wrecked by what were natural economic developments, coupled with much shrewd short selling.

One of the tales started and circulated in the financial district yesterday, was that Livermore had the backing in a bear campaign of Walter P. Chrysler, who was said to be piqued because he suspected that the Chicago-Detroit group had hammered at Chrysler motors in the market, driving it down below 55 from its high of 135 this year.

The outstanding bear leader appears to be Livermore, who has regained a tremendous fortune through adroit short selling and who, temporarily at least, is regarded as being exactly "right" on this market. Cutten, who started as a grain trader, has amassed an estimated $100 million or more in the stock market during the last three years of bull markets. Cutten is the leader of the bull faction and is temporarily at least regarded as "wrong" on the market.

Mr. Cutten was in New York and watched the market from the office of the head of the stock exchange. His expressed opinion to friends is that much of the selling had been hysterical, and that he believes good stocks should be held for higher prices. He has not changed his formerly stated position about the long distance outlook. Neither has he made any statement about the market for publication. Naturally they have nothing to say about their market positions at the moment or what they have been doing in recent days.

The *Times* article had more to tell:

Jesse L. Livermore, who has been in eclipse, so far as stock market operations are concerned, for several years, has made a smashing comeback, if Wall Street reports are true. The comeback of Mr. Livermore as one of the foremost market players is another Wall Street wonder. As a boy he was a board marker in Boston brokerage houses where he developed such skill at tape reading that, despite limited capital he was barred from every bucket shop in Boston and New York. This gave him the nickname that has stuck to him through later years of the "Boy Plunger."

Coming to New York and playing the markets skilfully after long series of ups and downs he struck an extended winning streak and made a fortune of many millions. It is reported that in the current bull market he decided that stocks were too high and guessed wrong. The continued advances of such issues as General Motors, Steel, General Electric and others is said to have taken back a large part of his fortune. He was short of them all and covered time and time again. It was reported in the financial district that he was down to his large irrevocable annuities, of which he has several for himself and his family, acquired during years of earlier prosperity.

Arthur Cutten, Livermore's rival, might be mistaken for a country storekeeper. He cares nothing for conventions, appearances or customs. Shy, quiet and unassuming, he has many times sat back in the corner of a Pullman smoking room and heard casual travelers discussing his stock market feats without disclosing his identity. When not attending to his businesses, he is a gentleman farmer on his estate near Chicago.

On the other hand, Livermore is the fastidious, well-dressed man of the city. Slight and blond, and he wears his dark clothes well, rides in Rolls-Royce cars, maintains a retinue of servants, half a dozen places of residence and probably the most luxurious offices in New York located atop the Hecksher Building.

Temperamentally, the two are entirely unlike. Cutten is calm, slow of speech and not at all impetuous. Livermore is quick, nervous and excitable, given to superstitions, but willing to bet his last nickel if he thinks he is right. Livermore has been down not once, but half a dozen times. Cutten at least in the last years, has typified the bull market.

The markets of the next month or so are likely to prove wildly exciting affairs, because of the direct pull and haul against each other of a wide variety of economic factors, all of them powerful. It is now pretty certain that when stocks go up, Mr. Cutten will be there helping them along. It is equally certain that when they decline, Mr. Livermore will be in the market hammering away. There is however no personal battle between them.

"Humph, it's never personal!" uttered Livermore, as he finished the article and placed it on his desk. He and Cutten had often been trading adversaries for years now, ever since they had been young men buying and selling commodities in the Chicago grain pits.

The phone rang, and Livermore signaled to his assistant Dache, who had just arrived, that he would answer.

"Hello."

"This Jesse Livermore?"

"Speaking."

"You bastard, Livermore. This is your doing and you are going to pay. I'm broke thanks to you. No, I'm more than broke. I owe my broker thousands of dollars of margin money, but I still got my gun. I'm headed down there to blow your brains out. Next time you answer your door I'll be standing there and the next thing you know you'll be walking through the gates of hell, which is where you deserve to be you . . ."

Livermore slammed the phone down. It all sprang from these articles, picked up by every paper in the United States, blaming him for the crash. But it wasn't him. He wasn't that powerful; no one was, not even the men from the great House of Morgan. But that wouldn't stop the public from thinking he had triggered the crash and was driving it down by selling, selling, selling. He had called the *Times* and given them an interview explaining that he was not to blame, but it had not worked. No matter what, it seemed people wanted to blame him, maybe just so they could have someone to call on the phone and threaten. He reread the headline of the interview he had given that appeared in the October 22, 1929 edition of the *Times:* "Livermore Not in Bear Pool." He read on:

Jesse L. Livermore, who has been widely reported in Wall Street to have been heavily short of the market on the present break, and to be the leader of a bear pool, denied yesterday any connection with such a pool.

Mr. Livermore's statement, issued from his offices at 730 Fifth Avenue, follows:

"In connection with the various reports, which have been industriously spread during the last few days through the newspapers and various brokerage houses, to the effect that a large bear pool has been formed, headed by myself and financed by various well known capitalists; I wish to state that there is no truth whatever in any such rumors as far as I'm concerned, and I know of no such combination having been formed by others.

"What little business I do in the stock market has only been as an individual and will continue to be done on such a basis.

"It is very foolish to think that any individual or combination of individuals could artificially bring about a decline in the stock market in a country so large and so prosperous as the United States. What has happened during the last few weeks is the inevitable result of a long period of continuous, rank manipulation of many stock issues causing their prices to rise many times above their actual worth, based on real earnings and yield returns.

"The men who are responsible for bringing about these fictitious prices are the same men who are directly responsible for what is happening in the stock market today. It is unfortunate for the general public when such a condition arises that real sound investment issues have to suffer along with the readjustment of issues of least merit.

"If anyone will take the trouble to analyze the selling prices of different stocks, as for instance, United States Steel, which is selling around eight to ten times its current earnings, many other issues must look, and have looked for a long time, as selling at ridiculously high prices.

"The Federal Reserve Board through its various warnings and many expressions from very high banking authorities could not stop the market from going up, so it must be plain and seem utterly ridiculous for any sane person to presume that one lone individual could have any material effect on the course of the prices of securities."

"Fools," Livermore mumbled on finishing the interview. "Fools, to think I could have brought an entire market to its knees. Impossible!"

Perhaps he was part of the trigger mechanism, but it was a pregnant situation. Wild speculation always brought the market to its knees. He had been trading for 35 years, since he was 14 years old. He had made and lost millions of dollars. In 1929, he was at the height of his power, and he knew this was another moment of euphoria.

Livermore pondered the situation carefully. The threatening phone calls had shaken him. He was well aware of the deep psychological wounds that a loss in financial fortune could cause. He had been through it himself many times in his career. He would have to make another statement, and quickly—his family could also be in jeopardy. They had been threatened before.

He waited quietly by the stock ticker that sat on top of his massive desk. The mahogany desk was clean except for the brass-based ticker, a single pad of paper, a pencil, and a matching pair of mahogany in- and out-boxes.

By now, the office was fully staffed. Six markers were up on the boards, wearing alpaca jackets so they would not smear the chalk symbols. Each board marker wore earphones and had a mouthpiece. They were connected directly to the floor of the New York Stock Exchange. Each had a domain of stocks or commodities to administer. The ticker began to click, spitting out a strip of paper like a white snakeskin with perforated scales—the symbols of most of the companies in the United States. These stock symbols represented much of the wealth of the country.

For Livermore, reading the ticker tape was like reading the newspaper. He knew all the symbols by heart, and he had an exceptional mathematical brain that could remember all the quotes, just as a good bridge player can remember all the cards that have been played. To be doubly sure, he watched his board crew as the markers began to move under Dache's supervision, filling the length of the chalkboard with trades. Today, he paid particular attention to his stock holdings. Livermore could look up at the board and instantly calculate to the dollar where his overall portfolio stood. There was silence in the office aside from the sounds of the tickers and the chalk on the boards. There was always silence in the Livermore trading room when the market was open. There was no need for idle chatter when the market was open, and all the board men knew it.

Today Livermore's total profits plus equity were pushing $100 million. This did not change his expression. The main office phone rang again. He motioned for Dache not to answer the call. He did not want to be bothered by another threatening call now that the market was open. The calls broke his concentration; he had nothing to say to anyone, and he did not want to hear from anyone. With the market open he was like a wolf on the prowl. He could only concentrate on what he was doing. Every 1 percent move, up or down, in his portfolio meant he made or lost $1 million.

The slightest loss of attention could cost him millions of dollars. It was exactly the way he loved to trade—every fiber of his being was alive. Nothing else existed but the tape. The tape would tell him everything if he was smart enough to read it, find the hidden clues, and act on them. He was fighting the two great emotions of the stock market: fear and greed. He had a huge bet on the table.

That night he went home to King's Point and found his wife, Dorothy, and two sons, Paul and Jesse Jr., gone. The paintings had been taken down, some of the Persian rugs were gone, and the silver had disappeared. He went up to the safe on the second floor where Dorothy kept her jewels—a fabulous collection, mostly from Harry Winston and Van Cleef and Arpels. All gone.

He went into the kitchen and found the four cooks and two butlers working, preparing dinner for the family.

"Where are Mrs. Livermore and the boys?" he asked.

"They have moved into the chauffeurs' apartments sir," the main butler answered. "We have all heard about the great crash. We are very sorry, Mr. Livermore."

Livermore stared at them for a few seconds, expressionless, and walked to the apartments above the car stables. There were two chauffeurs, one for Dorothy, or "Mousie," as he called her, and one for himself, or "J.L.," as he liked to be called. The car stables were attached to the great stone mansion. He walked into the living room of the apartment, stepping over the rolled-up carpets and around the priceless works of art and antique furniture. Dorothy sat on the couch with the two boys. They were fully dressed in their best clothes.

"Mousie, what's going on? What are you doing?"

"We heard. I'm very sorry, J.L.," she replied.

"What are you talking about?"

"We heard that everybody has gone broke in the crash. It has been on the radio all day. Men jumping out of windows, shooting themselves in their offices, disappearing. Some of my girlfriends called. I'm so sorry, J.L."

He looked at her. Long seconds passed. She was beautiful sitting there with the two handsome boys, one on each side, her jewelry in a special leather case next to her.

She was his opposite: effusive, full of life, funny, instinctive. A true social animal who was at her best in the middle of a crowd of people. She would blurt out whatever was on her mind. She was a great natural comedian, and the best part was that she did not make jokes on purpose. In fact, she was often confused as to why people were laughing.

He looked down at the jewelry case. He had gone to her several times in his worst moments, his worst defeats in the market. He had taken that case to Harry Winston more than once when he was broke and needed a stake. The jewels, worth close to $4 million, were always good for a million in cash from Harry, a stake to start up again. When he went back to retrieve the jewels, after he was on his feet, he always took care of Harry with a wad of cash.

"Mousie, you and the boys come back to the main house for dinner. Bring the jewelry case."

"Oh, J.L., you need them again?"

"No. Today was the best day I ever had in the market. I closed out half my holdings. We're going to be fine. I certainly won't be needing those jewels. Now, you and the boys come along."

He turned and walked out, a smile on his face. What a day. She never failed to surprise him, to make him smile. They were having personal problems, mostly his fault due to the other women. Nevertheless, he hoped they would make it. He knew that if they divorced he would miss her very much. His eyes misted as he thought of their love. Then he shook his head to rid himself of those thoughts. He would enjoy her and the boys while they were still with him. Who knew what the future held?

The threatening phone calls stayed with him; more came in as the days passed. He needed to ward off these threats. He rang up the *New York Times* again, a newspaper that was always ready to quote the secretive Jesse Livermore. The headline of the November 13 edition read: "Livermore Now a Bull: Announces That Stocks Are Too Far Down and Some Are Sound Bargains." He read on:

Jesse L. Livermore, who for many weeks past has been enlisted on the bear side of the market and is credited with having sold-short more stocks in this plummeting market than any other single individual, announced to the *New York Times* last night his conviction that the leading stocks had been driven down too far. Although Mr. Livermore made no statement as to his own positions his statement left the presumption that he has covered his shorts and again is on the buying side of the market.

"Leading stocks with good dividend records and a certain future are on the bargain counter right now," declared Mr. Livermore. "Many of them have been driven down too far. People throughout the country have become panic stricken and have thrown their sound securities over without regard to values. To my mind this situation should go no further. There is no reason why first-class securities should be ruthlessly thrown into the market in such fashion as we have seen in the last few trading days.

We have seen within the last few days large blocks of these securities thrown on the open market by sellers, many of whom had no other reason than they had been gripped by fear."

But the calls kept coming anyway: "Livermore, you dirty liar. I know how smart you are. You say you are on the positive side of the market while you beat the prices down into oblivion. I'm coming for you. I hope you never get another good night's sleep, you miserable bastard."

And coming: "I'm coming for you. What do I have to lose? I lost everything in the market, thanks to you and your rotten friends. You think you can crush the little man, destroy my family and me with your illegal operation. You are a dead man, you just don't know it. My family suffered, now your family is going to suffer!"

And coming: "I lost my house today Mr. Livermore, what do you think about that? My house that I spent 23 years paying off.

They evicted me today. I'm out on the street like a bum, with my wife and four kids. You did it, and you're going to pay for it."

Nonstop the threats poured in over the phone, in letters, even in hand-delivered telegrams.

By December 21, 1929, Jesse Livermore had had enough. He hired his old friend Frank Gorman, a former Nassau County police officer, as a precaution. Gorman and Livermore were old friends by 1929. Livermore had used him several times in the past when things had gotten hairy. The last time, he had employed Gorman to protect him from "Boston Billy" Monaghan a notorious thief who had robbed Livermore's mansion, been caught, and sworn revenge.

Gorman immediately moved into the King's Point mansion. He accompanied the boys to school every day and became Dorothy's shadow.

Livermore maintained his routine, going in to the office every day and watching the tape, making his moves. One afternoon, Livermore walked to the window and pulled open the drapes. The view took in the bustling metropolis that was New York City in the early days of 1930. As the ticker tape slid unattended between his fingers, carrying its endless quotations—all negative, like casualty lists from a battlefield—he looked out.

He wondered how his life had come to this point. And he wondered why he was not happier. After all, these had been the days of his greatest financial success.

★ *chapter two* ★

The Back Story

The childhood shows the man
As morning shows the day.   John Milton

JESSE LIVERMORE WAS BORN ON JULY 26, 1877, IN SHREWS-
bury, Massachusetts. His parents were Laura and Hiram Livermore.
Livermore's father was a poor farmer who tried to plow a living
out of the unforgiving New England soil. Hiram Livermore lost
his first farm early in Jesse's life, and the family moved to Paxton,
Massachusetts, to live with Jesse's grandfather. Hiram eventually
saved enough money to buy some farm property in South Acton.

Livermore quickly learned what it was like to farm the rock-
filled fields of New England. Picking up large rocks the plow
brought up was his first job. Scraping out a living on a small patch
of land in Massachusetts was tough, backbreaking work that
yielded small rewards in turn-of-the-century America.

As a boy, Livermore was slender, slight, and often sick. This lead
to a lot of reading, especially of the few newspapers and magazines
that he could get his hands on. He devoured any available books
and escaped into the theater of the mind that they opened for him.

He was imaginative and intelligent, able to use deductive reasoning to arrive at logical conclusions. It did not take him long to
conclude that his boyhood dreams of success and adventure could
not be built out of punishing New England farm life.

Livermore's father was a distant, reserved man who did not show
affection easily. He ruled the household with a hard-edged, no-
nonsense attitude toward life. Livermore's mother was the opposite—loving and gentle, with plenty of time for her gifted boy.

At school, Livermore excelled in mathematics. He could finish
equations in his head and just give the answers, or find an alterna-
tive way to solve the problems given to the class. Once, he challenged a teacher to a race to solve a complex math problem. He
won. He was quickly promoted in math and given more advanced
courses to satisfy his yearning to learn more.

Mathematics was his friend; it came easily to him. He did three
years' worth of arithmetic schoolwork in only one year. He could

keep multitudes of numbers in his head, forming patterns. The numbers always yielded to his computerlike brain.

When Livermore was 13, his father explained that education was unnecessary, useless for a simple farmer's life. At the age of 14, Livermore's father yanked him out of school and handed him overalls. His father explained that he was going to be a full-time farmer and was obliged to contribute to the family welfare.

But Livermore was smarter. He appeared to comply with his father's wishes, but he actually conspired with his mother to escape. Within weeks—with $5 supplied by his mother in his pocket—he sneaked off the farm and hailed a wagon on the road headed for Boston. He knew it was the right thing to do. He needed to set out into the world and make his fortune. While he had no specific plan, he knew he was moving in the right direction.

He was still only 14 when he reached Boston and, with it, the adult world, but his life patterns were already programmed, burned into his brain. He realized the value of hard work. He had the taciturn, quiet strength and determination of so many New Englanders—people who were used to dealing with hard, unyielding soil, unforgiving weather, and financial maelstroms.

His image of men was based on his father: silent, hard-working, stubborn, distant, unemotional, determined, noncommunicative, and supreme dictators of the household. His image of women was based on his mother and the few girls that he had met at school: gentle, nurturing, intelligent, emotional, and loving. He also knew that women seemed to like him, and they were always good to him.

He realized, even at 14, that success, wealth, and fame could come directly from working with the brain, not the body. He also realized that it was action that counted, not talk—this he had learned from his father.

But it was his mother who had given him the meager finances he needed to break for Boston and a new life. He would repay her with great interest, just as soon as he could. Paying one's debts was already ingrained in him, and it is something he did all his life, no matter how long it took.

When Livermore entered Boston at the ripe old age of 14, his life was just beginning, but he would never forget the lessons he had already learned in his youth. Now, however, he needed to concentrate on his future. He confined his mother and father to a compartment of his brain, then locked that compartment tight. He could stand no distractions if he was to succeed. This ability to park his emotions, to compartmentalize, came naturally to him. He could function no matter what the condition of his emotional life. He fought all his life to keep his business and personal lives completely separate. And he almost succeeded.

At 14, he was blond, blue-eyed, slender and intelligent, with a quick flashing smile of perfect white teeth. His confidence was rock solid.

He slipped off the wagon in Boston and stood outside the Paine Webber offices for a moment, taking them in, before entering. He watched as the customers came and went. The stock tickers clicked and spit endless white trails of paper tape. The board boys moved up and down the room-length green chalkboard, like dancers on the stage. They posted stock prices as fast as the stock caller, often a customer sitting in the gallery watching the tape, could yell the current quotes at them.

The customers sat in chairs against the walls, frantically watching the chalkboard, occasionally rising to go to their brokers as though they were placing bets in a horse room. Livermore inhaled all the action: the clicking of the tickers, the clatter of chalk on the boards, and people talking loudly, excitedly. All the movement and action thrilled him. His fingers tentatively touched the glass globe of the stock ticker; it was both warm and cool to his hand. It was like a crystal ball, except if you could read its fortune you would be as rich as Croesus, the richest man in the world. He watched. People were getting rich every second based on what that impersonal tape said. He did not think about losing.

The office smelled good to him, heady, with its aroma of wood, chalk, paper and ink, of human excitement and energy, coffee brewing, and food being eaten at desks. He liked the juice—the excitement—from the second he walked into the Boston office of Paine Webber.

He was already a long way from the farm.

He was wearing a suit that was slightly too big for him. His mother had bought it large so he could grow into it. He found the manager, took a deep breath, and tapped him on the shoulder. The manager was a man in his late 40s. He looked at Livermore and saw a farm lad, a country bumpkin.

"Whadda you want, kid?" he asked, looking him over.

"A job."

"You any good with numbers?"

"Yes."

"See them kids up on the walkway postin' the numbers?"

"Yes."

"Well, we're short one chalkboard boy. A no-show." He studied Livermore. "You a no-show kinda kid? You gonna let me down?"

"No sir. I'll show."

"Alright." He smiled. "I'll give ya a shot, kid. I started that way myself, a chalkboard boy."

"Yes sir," Livermore answered.

"And look at me now, 25 years later, I'm the boss around here. Don't you ever forget that this is America, kid, where anybody can do anything they set their mind to. Now, I can't stand here blabberin' with you all day. I gotta make some money. You want the job?"

"Yes sir."

"Alright. Take off your big brother's jacket, kid, and get up there on the walkway."

"I don't have a big brother."

"I don't care whether you do or you don't. I was only ribbin' you, kid, 'cause your jacket's so big. Get up there now. Ain't you ever been ribbed?"

The manager watched as young Livermore shed his coat and climbed the ladder to the walkway. He was immediately handed a piece of chalk by one of the other boys.

"Here, kid, take this." The boy also handed him an alpaca office-coat.

"Kid? You call me a kid? You're only a kid yourself." Livermore said.

"Not up here on this walkway, I ain't no kid. I been doing this for four years." He smiled.

"Hey kid," the manager yelled at Livermore.

"Yes?" Livermore answered, fearful that he had already changed his mind about the job.

"You never asked me about the pay."

"What's the pay?" Livermore answered.

"Six bucks a week," the manager replied. "And kid, don't do that again—always negotiate. Don't just take what the guy offers you. I mighta went to seven bucks. I mean, I gave you a clue. I told you I was short a boy. You gotta take it when you can in this world. Negotiate."

"Yes sir."

The manager winked at him and went back to work.

Livermore had been in Boston for less than an hour. He had gotten a job and a free lesson in negotiating, and he had already decided to buy himself a suit that fit. He did not like being insulted about the way he dressed.

Livermore found himself a room with board near the Paine Webber offices. He was up at the crack of dawn every day and was always the first one to the offices, often waiting for the manager to arrive with the office key. He loved everything about his job. Being a chalkboard boy was like going to stock market college. He was privy to everything in the office. In the beginning it was all Greek to him, but every day something new was revealed, and he knew that if he could someday break the code and develop a system of trading, he would be rich.

Young Livermore had access to everything: talk from the brokers, from customers with tips, and from customers who played the tout sheet tacked to the bulletin board every morning. Creative theories on trading were explained to him in the dull times, on his breaks, and at lunch. The office was consumed with one thing, making money from the actions of the stock market. Everyone there was a *player.* Livermore and the other kids were an important part of it. They were moving up and down the walkway, posting the actual trades on the chalkboard.

The action on the board would become one of the keys to his later success. He quickly learned that it was never what the brokers, or the customers, or the newspapers said—the only thing that was important was what the tape said. He also observed that the tape's pronouncements very rarely matched what the brokers or the customers had predicted. The tape had a life of its own, and its was the most important life. Its verdict was final.

He loved the actual physical job of writing the quotes on the chalkboard because he had a photographic memory when it came to numbers. His memory for numbers was perfect—the yelling of the quotes from the ticker could not come quick enough for Livermore. He never fell behind in posting the quotes, no matter how fast they came. They racked up in his brain like stacked cordwood.

Eventually, he started to see repeating patterns come alive in the numbers. At night, alone in his room, he would write out the numbers for several issues from memory. He started keeping a numerical diary, and certain recurring numerical patterns emerged. He noticed that the numbers moved in consistent waves, often in smooth repeating trends. When the price of a stock started to go upward, or downward, it usually remained in that trend until some pressure caused it to reverse. The clues to this action were often in the numerical patterns.

"Stocks act in line with the laws of physics," he thought. "A body in motion tends to stay in motion, until a force or obstacle stops or changes that motion." He kept logs tracking the stocks for longer periods, and then he had another revelation: There were patterns within the patterns, and even larger patterns emerged.

He kept the diary in secret and discussed his observations with no one. He was secretive by nature. He had ultimate confidence in his mathematical ability, even at the age of 14. Besides, he was too busy posting the numbers and watching the action of the market on the chalkboard to engage in idle chatter during business hours.

Because he was working the chalkboard—listening for the shouted quotes, erasing prices, writing in new numbers hundreds of times a day, thousands of times a week—he learned to be interested only in the change in price, not the *reason* for the change. He had no time to waste trying to rationalize the action of the stock. There could be a million reasons why the price had changed. These reasons would be revealed later, after the fact. But by the time these reasons were understood, the change would already be a historical event, and it would be too late to make any money.

His notebook was neat, well-written, and precisely accurate. At 15, he began to look for repeating patterns, searching for a system, trying to identify natural mathematical laws that were operating within the market.

He had also observed that the majority of the people in the office lost money. These people seemed to be acting randomly. They had no plan, no consistent, reasoned approach to the market. They were just gambling, just like at the track, just playing hunches. One day they would play the favorites, the next day the long shots or the jockeys; or they would buy a tout sheet and play the recommendations of the tipster—random-action stock picking.

These were heady days for Livermore. He was loving every minute of his life in the markets. And he was getting paid for it!

After six months of doing his job every day, eventually making a series of paper bets in his notebook and keeping track of them, he was still missing a crucial part of the equation, and he knew it. He had yet to buy his first stock. He knew that unless he actually purchased a stock, he could never know how he would handle himself. Like a gambler who has never made a wager, it was only talk and speculation until he slapped his money down. When a trader made a bet everything changed, and he knew it. Then and only then did the trader enter the heated jungle of emotions. He knew that he would always have his intellect under control, and it was a strong one. What he did not know was whether he could control his emotions.

He had watched the customers at the Paine Webber office, and he knew it would be his emotions that would make or break him—particularly greed and fear, the two devil-emotions of the market. You either controlled them or they controlled you.

The time had come for Livermore to buy a stock, but he had very little money. Where could he buy a stock cheaply?

Livermore would later marry and have two sons, Jesse Jr. and Paul. He recounted to them, on many occasions, where he found cheap stocks: the *bucket shops*.

Nov. 6, 1928—In a darkened hospital room at the edge of Hell's Kitchen on the West Side of Manhattan, the king of easy money lay dying. Through the shadows that drifted slowly across his mind he could hear a weary voice repeating the same question again and again. "Who did it, Mr. Rothstein?" the voice asked in a disinterested, mechanical way. "Who shot you?" But Rothstein would not tell. His only response was to slowly turn his face to the wall and whisper: "If I live, I'll tend to it." Then he closed his eyes and faded away."

—William Klingaman,
1929: The Year of the Great Crash

Arnold Rothstein, known in underworld circles as "the Brain," was a genius with money. He started out as a gambler, but after a fantastic string of successes, he became an underworld king and lived like it. He was accused of many crimes, among them fixing the 1919 "Black Sox" World Series. His fortune was vast. His financial tentacles reached into every vein of American vice.

Among Rothstein's many holdings were most of the bucket shops in the major cities of the United States. A bucket shop looked like a broker's office. It had a gallery for the customers, a chalkboard to record the stock quotes, and an active stock ticker spewing out the daily trades on an almost instantaneous basis. But it was more like a horse-betting parlor than a true broker's office. At a bucket shop, traders could play the market on 10 percent margin. In other words, traders needed to have only 10 percent of the price of the stock they wanted to buy. The rules were simple: Put up 10 percent and make a bet by buying a stock. A ticket with the *buy number* would immediately be printed and given to the purchaser. This ticket would indicate the time, the price paid for the stock purchased, and the number of shares purchased. The purchaser would watch the quotes, and as soon as the stock lost 10 percent of its value, the shop moved in and quickly swept away the money. Conversely, if the stock price went up and the trader won, the trader went up to a clerk who marked the ticket stub with the price of the last trade on the stock ticker. Then the trader went to the cage window to collect the money. It was a sucker's play—the house won 95 percent of the time.

Most important for the functioning of the bucket shop, the money spent to buy the stock was never sent to the floor of the exchange. It was simply *booked* by the bucket shop; the bucket shop would hold the bet, like a bookie. Bucket-shop action was quick and fierce. Traders could buy as few as five shares or as many as the house could cover—thousands of dollars worth.

Because Livermore had no capital, no stake, it was inevitable that he would enter the bucket shops, a world controlled by the crime bosses. It was only a matter of when and how.

In 1892, when Livermore was 15 years old, his friend Billy, another board-crew kid, approached him. "Jesse, you got any money?"

"I'm eating my lunch.'

"Never mind your lunch. You got any money?"

"Why?"

"I got a tip on Steel. I need somebody to go in with me."

"How you gonna play it, Billy?" Livermore asked.

"Bucket shop. I'll run over and make the play during lunch."

"How much you need?"

"I need five bucks. I wanna buy five shares of U.S. Steel. It's selling at ten dollars."

"Just a minute." Livermore reached into his pocket and pulled out his notepad.

"What's with the notepad?" Billy asked.

"I'm reading my horoscope for today," Livermore answered. He checked the history of the trading figures on U.S. Steel in his notepad. The numbers were moving in the same pattern as they usually moved before the stock went up. He was satisfied they had a good chance. "Okay."

He handed his friend the money. Two days later he smiled as he pocketed his winnings—a pure profit of more than $3. Livermore was in the game. He was finally a player.

Livermore started to visit the bucket shops on his own, always checking his notepad for the exact price quotes of the stocks he followed, looking for patterns. He had developed a system and he stuck to it. He played both sides of the market, going long if his numbers told him to do so, or jumping on the short side if his numbers pointed to the downside. It made no difference to him.

Soon he was making more money at the shops than he was at his job. So he quit and played the market in the Boston bucket shops full time. Before he was 16, he had well over $1,000 in cash. He went home for a visit. His mother was ecstatic to have her son home; his father just shook his head in wonderment. How could a boy of 16 legally lay his hands on over $1,000 in cash?

Livermore gave half his winnings to his parents, paying back his mother. He returned to Boston with a line of over $750 and continued with what would be his life's work. He worked alone, never telling anyone what he was doing, never taking on a partner, never borrowing money. He moved from bucket shop to bucket shop so as not to draw attention to himself. This lone-wolf strategy served him well, and it fit his personality. He would act this way all his life—buying alone and in secret, selling alone and in secret, telling no one. His true thrill came from being *right*—using his brain to win, not his brawn, not his connections, not his powers of persuasion—just using pure brain power to figure out what few men could figure out: how to make money in the stock market. The thrill came from the winning, not the money, though the money was nice. The money always came if his judgment was right.

It was at this young age that Livermore earned the nickname "Boy Plunger," based on his youthful looks and large bucket-shop bets.

Just as a gambler who was a consistent winner would be barred from a casino, Livermore was finally barred from the bucket shops of Boston after his winnings had piled up. All the bucket-shop proprietors knew who the Boy Plunger was and what he looked like. He tried changing his name and wearing disguises, but they quickly saw through the deception. He tried a new strategy: losing at first and then making a big move at the end of his play. This worked only for a brief time, always ending in being told to get out and take his business elsewhere.

Livermore was killing the bucket shops. At first they had thought he was just a kid, what could he know? But soon the bucket-shop managers found out exactly how much he *did* know, right in their cash-boxes. The supreme boss in most cases was Arnold Rothstein, and he kept a close eye on his businesses. The managers had their own skins to look out for. Livermore, now banned from the bucket shops in Boston, took his theories, his system, and his stock-buying principles to the great city of New York in hopes of playing the bucket shops there. Unfortunately for Livermore, the New York Stock Exchange and the police had successfully shut down all the New York bucket shops. So Livermore would have to find new hunting grounds.

He figured that the same principles, the same system, would work in the major brokerage houses. He was sure his theories would hold up.

He was wrong.

He arrived in Manhattan with $2,500. His Boston bucket-shop stake had, at times, been over $10,000, but he had suffered a few reversals before leaving Boston for New York. These reversals bothered Livermore, so he analyzed what had happened. He never blamed the market. It was illogical to get angry at an inanimate object, like a gambler getting mad at a deck of cards. He always wanted to *learn* from his mistakes and thereby *profit* from those mistakes. There was no arguing with the tape. The tape was always right; it was the players who were wrong. He reviewed his bad trades, and the conclusions became clear to him.

His first conclusion was that he won when all the factors were in his favor, when he was patient and waited for all the ducks to line up in a row. That led him to his second conclusion, that no one could or should trade the market all the time. There were times when a trader should be out of the market, in cash, waiting.

Years later, his friend Bernard Baruch would reaffirm this early conclusion. Baruch would occasionally say, "J.L., I think it's time to go grouse shooting." Baruch would then sell out all his positions and go to the famed Hobcaw Barony, his 17,000-acre plantation in South Carolina. Its sandy beaches and salt marshes once offered the finest duck hunting in the United States—and no telephone.

Livermore, 20 years old, was in New York with some cash in his pocket, but without access to a bucket shop. So he entered the game on the Big Board, the New York Stock Exchange. He settled on working out of the offices of E. F. Hutton. The people at Hutton liked him, and his winning bucket-shop reputation preceded him. On respectable Wall Street, his nickname was transformed from "Boy Plunger" to "Boy Trader." With so small a stake, he could hardly expect to be a plunger among the big players.

At first he did well and ran up some good commissions for the brokers, but he eventually went broke. It took six months of hard work for him to bust out. Ultimately, he actually wound up on the wrong side of the ledger. He owed the broker money.

Disgusted with himself, he went to see E. F. Hutton one evening after the market closed.

"I need a loan, Ed," he said.

"How much?" Hutton asked.

"A thousand dollars."

"I'll just give you a credit in your account for a thousand."

"No, I want a loan."

"Why?"

"I can't beat Wall Street right now. I'm going back to the bucket shops. I need a stake, then I'll be back."

"I don't get it," Hutton said. "You can beat the bucket shops, but you can't beat Wall Street. How's that?"

"First off, when I buy or sell a stock in a bucket shop, I do it off the tape. When I do it with your firm, it's ancient history by the time my order hits the floor. If I buy it at, say, 105, and the order gets filled at 107 or 108, I've lost the comfort margin and most of my play. In the bucket shop, if I buy it off the tape, I immediately get the 105. The same is true when I want to sell short, especially on an active stock where the trading is heavy. In the bucket shop, I put my sell order in at, say, 110, and it gets filled at 110, but here it might get filled at 108. So I'm getting it from both sides."

"But we give you better margins than the bucket shops," Hutton said.

"And that Ed, is what really killed me. See, with the extra margin from you I could stay with a stock—not like the bucket shop, where a ten percent move wiped me out. See, the point is that I wanted the stock to, let's say, go up, and it goes down. Holding on to it longer is bad for a trader like me, because I was betting it would go up. I can afford to lose the ten percent but I can't afford twenty-five percent on margin. I have to make too much back to get my money back."

"So, all you could ever lose in the bucket shops was the ten percent because they would sell you out?"

"Yes, and it turns out that was a blessing. All I ever want to lose in any one stock is ten percent," Livermore said. "Now, will you lend me the money?"

"One more question." Hutton smiled. He liked this young man. This young man was a force to be reckoned with, a mental force. "Why do you think you can come back here next time and beat the market?"

"Because I will have a new trading system by then. I consider this part of my education."

"How much did you come here with, Jesse?"

"Twenty-five hundred dollars."

"And you leave with a borrowed thousand," Hutton said, reaching into his wallet, extracting the thousand in cash, and handing it to Livermore. "For thirty-five hundred dollars, you could have gone to Harvard."

"I'll make a lot more money with my education here than I ever would going to Harvard," Livermore said, smiling as he took the money.

"Somehow, I believe you, Jesse."

"I'll pay this back," Livermore said, pocketing the money.

"I know you will. Just remember when you come back, do your trading here. We like your business."

"Yes sir, that I will," Livermore said.

Ed Hutton watched him leave. There was no question in his mind that he would see him again.

Livermore's options for bucket-shop trading were limited. The East Coast was closed off to him, so he looked to middle America. He headed for Saint Louis, where he had heard of two huge bucket-shop operations.

He took the train, arrived in Saint Louis, checked into a hotel, showered, and headed for the first bucket shop. It was a large operation, with a trading gallery that held more than 200 people. He started slow, using a false name and playing conservatively. He traded for three days until he was singled out. He had built his $1,000 stake up to $3,800.

On the morning of the third day, he was called into the boss's office and greeted with, "Hello, Mr. Jesse Livermore. Sit down."

They had recognized him. He was told that he was banned from that bucket shop, to leave immediately.

He quickly went down to the next bucket shop, only a block away. He went up to the window and made his play.

"Fifteen hundred shares of BRT."

The clerk had just started to fill out the slip when the manager came up and stood in front of Livermore. "Your money's no good in here. We ain't the suckers here on this side of the cage, the suckers are on your side of the cage, Livermore."

"You know my name?"

"And your game." He handed the money back to Livermore.

"Listen . . ."

"No, you listen. You think I didn't just get a call from down the street about you? Now, I'm only gonna ask you one more time nice. Get the hell outta here!"

"Get outta here doesn't sound to me like you're asking," Livermore replied, taking back his money.

The next day he took the train back to New York. He visited E. F. Hutton's office. He handed back the $1,000 he had borrowed.

"You want interest?" Livermore asked with a smile.

"I'll get my interest out of your commissions. That didn't take long. Did they make you?"

"Yeah, they nailed me within four days."

"How'd you do?"

"Not great. I'm about right back where I was when I walked in here six months ago."

"So it's Harvard or Wall Street again, huh?"

"No, it's Wall Street or nothing."

"How could you have a new system to beat Wall Street in four days?" Hutton asked.

"I don't have to beat Wall Street. I have to beat myself, my emotions."

"That's the smartest thing I've heard from you yet, Jesse. Good luck."

"Luck?"

"Yes, Jesse, we all need a little luck in this life. Now let's reopen your account."

Livermore traded for several months. But when he summarized his account, he found that he had only broken even. His confidence remained high, but he still had not established a consistent winning system for playing the market as he had with the bucket shops.

Then one day a fellow named Bill Sullivan walked into the E. F. Hutton offices and told Livermore that the man who ran the Saint Louis bucket shop had made a killing on a racetrack scheme and moved to the East Coast. To avoid the New York City police he had opened a new bucket-shop operation in Hoboken, New Jersey, just across the river. Sullivan told Livermore that it was a *no-limit* house. There was no limit to the amount of stock a trader could buy or sell.

Livermore waited for Saturday to roll around before he visited the Hoboken bucket shop. On Saturdays the market was open only until 12. Inside the shop, the setup was very grand, with a full quotation board, a customer's gallery, and plenty of clerks for service. Livermore acted dumb and placed a few early orders. Then, at a little past 11, he laid down $2,000 in cash and went short on $20,000 worth of stock. The stocks plummeted, and just five minutes before the close he covered the shorts and cashed in. His profit was $6,000. He went to collect, but the clerk did not have enough cash to fully pay out. He was told to return on Monday for the rest of his money.

On Monday he showed up. Waiting for him was the same man he had last seen in Saint Louis.

"Livermore, what do you want?"

"My money."

"I told you never to trade in my establishment when you were in Saint Louis. This is New Jersey, and I don't want you trading in here, either. There's no money waitin' for you here this Monday morning."

"Give me my money," Livermore intoned.

The man looked at him for a few long seconds.

"Hey, at least I'm playing an honest game, not like your race-track escapades," Livermore continued, staring back. "If you want to trade in this part of the country, you better pay me."

A crowd had now gathered behind Livermore. He repeated, "I want my money. I played fair and square."

"You were banned."

"Not here in Hoboken. Now, give me my money!"

The man finally nodded and the clerk peeled off some $1,000 bills until Livermore had his money, the full $6,000.

"Livermore, I have a boss, a very unforgiving boss. So do me a favor and don't come back in here."

Livermore looked him in the eye, nodded and walked out. He put his money in his pocket and thought about the situation on his ride back to Manhattan.

The next day he called Bill Sullivan, the man who had told him of the bucket shop. "Listen Bill, thanks for the tip on that place in Hoboken. I need you to do me a little favor."

"How little?" Sullivan asked.

"I'll bankroll you, and I want you to go to Hoboken and make some small plays. Then when the time is right, I'll give you the word."

"What's my cut?"

"Twenty percent plus expenses, and I'll give you a thousand dollars for a bankroll."

"Deal, Livermore."

Livermore waited until Sullivan was established and then made his move. He went short and cleaned up a net of $4,100 after paying the 20 percent cut and expenses.

Livermore now had a stake of over $10,000, and he decided to stick strictly to the stock market in the future—no more bucket shops. He was banned for good now, and sooner or later, Arnold Rothstein, the Brain, would step into the picture and pay him a visit. If that happened, he would be lucky to keep his life, let alone any money he had made. Besides, he had his stake back, bigger than ever. Now it would be up to him to use it in the stock market.

Besides, he was tired of playing for small points in bucket shops. He liked playing in a bigger game, a legitimate game, through licensed brokers, where there was no limit on the money a trader could make—or lose, as he would find out.

It would become the never-ending challenge of Livermore's life: beating the market. Beating the market was like alchemy—changing lead into gold. The market changed paper into gold and created fortunes beyond anyone's wildest dreams. The market was where $100 became $1,000, $1,000 became $1 million, and $1 million became $100 million. All the trader had to do was call the moves before they occurred—and, as with any great puzzle, the answer was always right there. All the trader had to do was figure it out.

And Livermore remained confident that he could find the answer to the puzzle.

chapter three

The San Francisco Earthquake Rumbles in New York

THE SPECULATOR

Modern usage has made the term speculator a synonym for gambler and plunger. Actually the word comes from the Latin speculari, which means to spy out and observe.

I have defined a speculator as a man who observes the future and acts before it occurs. To be able to do this successfully—and it is an ability of priceless value in all human affairs—three things are necessary:

First, one must get the facts of a situation or problem.

Second, one must form a judgement as to what those facts portend.

Third, one must act in time, before it is too late.

I have heard many men talk intelligently—even brilliantly—about something only to see them proven powerless when it comes to acting on what they believe. If action is delayed until the need is apparent to everyone, it will be too late.

To be evident to all, a danger must be on top of us and out of hand.   My Own Story, Bernard Baruch

LIVERMORE STUDIED HIS MISTAKES OBJECTIVELY. IN LATER years, he often told his sons that "the only way you get a real education in the market is to invest cash, track your trade, and study your mistakes!"

It is emotionally difficult to review your mistakes, since the speculator must wade through his own bad trades and blunders. And these are not simple blunders, these are blunders that cost money. Anyone who has lost money by investing poorly knows how difficult it is to reexamine what occurred.

The examination of a losing trade is torturous but necessary to ensure that it will not happen again. Livermore was brutal in self-analysis. He told his sons his conclusion: "Successful trading is always an emotional battle for the speculator, not an intellectual battle. It is only after a bet has been placed on a stock or a commodity, when the money has changed from cash in hand to stock certificates, that the emotions spring to life."

Livermore equated speculators who traded imaginary stock positions with someone who was a crack shot on the pistol range. How would such a crack shot do in a duel, facing an opponent's loaded pistol? That was when fear raised its ominous head, nerves frayed and split, resolve was challenged, and reason fled.

To speculate, a trader had to be a player, not a theorist, or an economist, or an analyst. A speculator had to be a player with money down on the table. It was not the coach or the team's owner who won the game, it was the players on the field—just as it was not the generals who won the battle, it was the grunts on the ground.

For Livermore, the richest gold mine on the planet was sitting high on the bedrock of Manhattan—the New York Stock Exchange at the corner of Wall and Broad Streets. It looked easy— no exploring necessary, no maps, no staking a claim. It was open at certain hours, and it invited everyone into the mine to try their luck. But very few miners walked out with a pot of gold.

The same facts were available to all the prospectors at the same time. So failures to mine the mountain properly were personal failures, since everyone basically started out even. But the problems were in many ways the same as those in hunting for gold, as well. There were false clues, fool's gold, dry holes, bad climatic conditions, corrupt partners, dance-hall girls, gunfighters, and professional gamblers. And two of the biggest problems were claim jumpers and scallywags who wanted to scam miners out of their gold by trying to buy their claims cheaply or sell them fraudulent maps.

These scallywags, in Livermore's mind, manifested on Wall Street as tipsters. They stood at the entrance to the great gold mine and sold their wares. These hucksters handed out tips to the uninitiated before the uninitiated even got a chance to dig for the gold themselves. An easy road to success is what they promised—hit the mother lode fast, with no work.

Livermore noticed that the novices never asked the simple questions:

- Why have you chosen me to receive this priceless advice?"
- If you have this information, then why aren't you rich?
- What is driving you to give me this advice to buy a stock? Are you secretly selling it to me at higher and higher prices?"
- If capital gains are so easy to make, then why are you only interested in your commissions?

There were many pitfalls on the road to successful speculation, and Livermore knew he was destined to fall into them all. But he was not so much worried about falling into the pits as he was worried about falling into them over and over and over again.

Livermore knew the basic laws of the market, as did everyone:

- When you are wrong there is one thing that cannot be denied—you lose money.
- When you are right, you make money.
- Therefore, you are right only when you make money and wrong only when you lose it. This law cannot be denied, and it is the true law of speculation.

Over his career, Livermore observed that many people jaw-boned about the market, as if talking could reverse their fortunes, or the pain of failing to adhere to the basic laws of speculation would be less if they commiserated with other people. It was one of the reasons Livermore was always silent about his trades. If he won, well, then he had done the right thing. If he lost, he had done the wrong thing. Why complain? Why explain?

His only quest in the analysis of his trades was to find out why he had made money or why he had lost.

For Livermore, life in the market was as the poet Omar Khayyám said in the *Rubaiyat:*

> The moving finger writes
> And having writ moves on
> Nor all your piety nor your wit
> Can cancel out a word of it
> Nor your tears wash away a line

It was 1899, two years before the beginning of the twentieth century. Livermore was 22, he had $10,000 to trade with, and he had seven years of experience to lean on. He knew by now that the stock market was not the same as playing the bucket shops, but he had *beaten* the bucket shops. There was no reason why he could not beat the stock market as well.

He reopened his account at E. F. Hutton as he had promised he would. He traded more cautiously this time, but still followed his old principle of trading for the short term, following the tape on an almost hourly or daily basis. He started to do better. He lived well and made friends.

In October 1900, he married Nettie Jordan, an Indianapolis girl whom he had met in his Midwestern bucket-shop days. He and Nettie lived in the upscale Windsor Hotel on Fifth Avenue. In the summers, Livermore rented them a cottage at Long Branch, New Jersey, on the ocean. He made his first trip to Europe with Nettie during this period, where he purchased more than $12,000 worth of jewelry for her.

Then all hell broke lose in 1901, with a great boom in the market. A bull market developed. America was very prosperous, and the market started to boil—the old record of 250,000 shares traded in a day was broken by a 3-million-share day. Millionaires in steel, finance, and railroads moved to New York to be near the action. Big-shot gamblers ready to put their money where their mouth was came, too. The turn of the century was an exciting time to be alive.

The legends of Wall Street abounded, some of them great characters who would live forever in Wall Street history: John "Bet-a-Million" Gates, John A. Drake, Loyal Smith Page, and the infamous Hetty Green, Wall Street's first female powerhouse.

Hetty Green stood alone. As recorded in Kenneth L. Fisher's book, *100 Minds That Made the Market,* she was as shrewd as they came, turning her $6 million inheritance into more than $100 million. She was also as cheap as they came, wearing foul-smelling, never-cleaned, black, out-of-fashion dresses with stock certificates sewn into the hems. Every day she appeared, a black apparition, drifting from the slum-level flats she owned to the Chemical National Bank vault. She would plop down cross-legged on the floor, then clip coupons and stuff them down into the hem of her dress, all the while eating sandwiches and crackers that she had crammed in her pockets.

Her investment strategy was simple: Make a great many good solid investments that yielded around 6 percent and be as cheap as a person could be. She said, "When I see a good thing going cheap because nobody wants it, I buy a lot of it and tuck it away." She explained further, "If you invest $6 million for 51 years at 6 percent and don't spend a dime of it you wind up with $117 million. What's wrong with that?"

She bought heavily in the financial panics—real estate mortgages, municipal bonds, and railroad bonds. Stocks provided her extra profits. She knew the market well, but she also operated on instinct and common sense. She escaped the Knickerbocker Trust failure in the panic of 1907. How? She went into the bank and came out saying, "Those men who run the bank are too damn prosperous-looking, new suits, new shoes, new ties. I don't like it." She got out only weeks before the collapse.

Hetty Green was the market's only major female player at the time. She said, "I wish women had more rights in business and everywhere else than they do now! Men will take every kind of advantage of women in business that they would not attempt with a man. I have been fighting men in the courts all my life."

Hetty was capable of anything and skilled at getting her way. If nagging and persistence failed to get her what she wanted she would turn on the tears. If the tears failed she initiated lawsuits. Then she always refused to pay the legal fees, often hiring additional lawyers to defend her against her prior lawyers. Once she paid $50 for a gun registration license to carry a revolver. When asked why she said: "Mostly to protect myself against my goddamn lawyers!" She was feared by all who knew her.

Hetty loved only money. She saw her son Ned as her successor. She paid his college tuition on the promise that he would not get married for 20 years. Ned agreed. Ned loved his mother. He had only one leg. When he was 14 years old, Ned had injured his knee in a snow-sledding accident. Hetty had refused to send him to a doctor. She ministered to the cut leg with homemade poultices and put him to bed. When his father got home and heard what had happened he was furious, and took his son immediately to the doctor. The doctor was forced to cut the boy's leg off, because gangrene had set in.

It was an era of great characters.

Livermore was aware of the Hetty Green approach to the market, a combination of thrift and compounding, and he knew it was a sound strategy for some people. It just wasn't for him. He did not believe a return of 6 percent annually was all you could take out of the stock market. And he certainly wasn't interested in living frugally, like Hetty.

The 1901 market was in a frenzy. It was the first frenzied market that Livermore had witnessed as a Wall Street trader. It was to set in his mind the great rule: Nothing ever changes in the market. The only things that change are the players, the pockets, and the memories. The new players have no memory of the previous cycles, because they have not experienced them.

Livermore played the bull side of the 1901 market and made one exceptional long trade on Northern Pacific with his $10,000 stake. He pocketed $50,000. But Livermore looked at this as only a larger stake to play with. He was looking for a big break in the market, a severe correction or a one-day reversal, and then a rally.

In early May, Livermore moved.

"Sell a thousand shares of Steel short at $100," he barked to the clerk just seconds before the market opened. "And sell a thousand shares of Santa Fe at $80."

The clerk disappeared, order slip in hand, to call the trader on the floor. Livermore stood as the market opened and watched the stocks he had shorted fall away, prices dropping like a stone. He felt vindicated; his judgment had been correct. There was chaos as the prices plummeted. But his smile quickly disappeared as he saw the volume. He stood suddenly locked in fear. The volume was huge. The opening activity on the floor was beyond the limits that the traders could handle. It was a fast market. Fills on orders were late—15 minutes, 30 minutes, an hour, two hours—and when they were filled, they were filled at prices far from what the clients had wanted.

Finally, Livermore got a fill on his opening orders. He looked at the fill orders in disbelief. Even though his brokers were as good as any on Wall Street, his fills were awful. The stock he had wanted to sell short at $100 had been filled at $85. The stock he had wanted to sell short at $80 had been filled at $65. These were the prices he had wanted to buy them back at to cover his short positions when the rally came, which he believed would happen later that day. He made an instant decision to buy the stocks back and to cover his shorts immediately.

He yelled at the clerk, "Buy a thousand Steel and a thousand Santa Fe at the market."

The clerk ran off with the ticket to call it down to the floor of the exchange. Livermore's heart sank as he watched his stocks rally. He watched the tape rise. He knew his shorts would be covered at great losses now that the rally was in full swing. He had done the worst thing a speculator could do: He had involuntarily sold at the bottom and bought at the top.

The clerk returned with the tickets. Livermore opened them slowly in the palm of his hand. He had established his short positions at $85 on steel and covered at $110, a loss of $25,000. He lost a second $25,000 on Santa Fe. He had been right, the market had done as he predicted, but he was now broke. He had traded off the ticker instead of off the *real* quotes, which were coming too fast on the floor to be accurately caught by the lagging ticker. In this fast market, the ticker had fallen behind by as much as two hours.

This day provided Livermore with his greatest lesson to that point. He was trading in *real time,* for the short term, as he had done when he was trading in the bucket shops. But the stock market ticker was not reporting in real time—it was stuck in *delayed* time, falling further behind as the day progressed. The tape spit out a long-expired price, not the present price. It was now finally clear to Livermore: Short-term trades were too hard to catch on Wall Street.

Yet he had been right in his basic judgment. The market did exactly what he had predicted; the only flaw had been in his execution. His timing had been off because his orders could not be executed as quickly as he wanted. As a result, he was late in selling and late in buying.

Livermore was busted, once again, in the blink of an eye. The event disillusioned him, left him despondent, depressed, and entirely worn out. Yesterday he had $50,000 and was full of self-confidence. Today he was shaken to the core. His only consolation came from figuring out why he had failed.

He left New York and headed back for Boston and the bucket shops to start over and rebuild his stake. He also had to rethink his lifestyle. He had become used to the high life. It was a lifestyle that took money to fuel, and now he was out of money.

This, of course, had an impact on his married life. Things on the home front had been going well between the newlyweds until Livermore went broke again in May 1901. He asked Nettie to pawn her jewelry—the $12,000 worth he had bought for her in Europe—as a stake so he could go back to playing the bucket shops.

She refused. This caused a permanent rift between him and Nettie, but she did not like the idea of pawning her jewelry. Ultimately, the couple separated. He was now both broke and separated from his young wife.

The market was all he knew. So he took a deep mental breath and decided he had to get a stake and return to Wall Street. He devoted all his energies to this objective: *Get some cash.*

Once again he returned to the bucket shops—but, unfortunately, they still remembered him in Boston. No one would take his orders. He sent people in to do his bidding and place his trades, but they were quickly uncovered. Soon Livermore had no place to trade.

Fortunately for Livermore, a new hybrid bucket shop had been born. This new bucket shop looked even more like a respectable brokerage and advertised its affiliations with a real brokerage firm with a seat on the exchange. And, in fact, on rare occasions, these bucket shops actually did put the customer's orders through to the floor of the exchange, but they were far more likely to *bucket* the order. That is, they kept the order in the house, unfilled, and bet against the customer, just canceling out the transaction with in-house bookkeeping when the customer wanted to close out the trade or, more likely, went broke on the margin swings.

Livermore was not recognized in these establishments, and he quickly hooked up with five of them. They promised him they would stay within one point of the prices that came across the ticker tape. In other words, they would give him basically an *instant fill.*

So Livermore went back to his old method of trading off the tape, taking small gains on many daily trades. He had to build up a stake before he could make his way back to Wall Street. He set up a small office with five direct wires to these new quasi–bucket shops. He traded under an alias as he was still afraid of being recognized. He also had one other wire installed, direct to a legitimate broker in New York, as well as his own stock ticker, once he had made enough profits. He traded for the better part of a year this way and did well enough to buy a car. He started to renew his trading stake. But as his trading and his winnings increased, it became harder and harder to convince these establishments to allow him to trade, particularly since the money was primarily going one way—from their treasuries into Livermore's coffers.

The firms started to play games with Livermore as his trading position size increased. If Livermore went long a stock with a big position on heavy margin, the brokerage firm would go short, catching him for several points when he had to cover. When they were able to play these games successfully, he would lose money.

But normally, he was winning. Finally, when his trading stake was big enough, he reversed the game on them. He found a stock that had been very active at one time but had fallen into disinterest and was trading on hardly any volume, a sleepy stock.

He wired each of the five bucket shops and said, "Buy me one hundred shares of Acme at $81, which was the last recorded trade." When the five brokers confirmed his purchase price to him at $81, he would then wire his real broker in New York, E. F. Hutton.

He now knew what his buy price was: $81. "Buy me 100 shares of Acme at the asking price of $85," he'd tell Hutton. He waited for that sale to cross over the tape and immediately sold his position at the bucket shops against the price of $85, netting 4 points, or $2,000. He would then close out the $85, 100-share position in New York.

Livermore hit the five houses with this several times. Then, unexpectedly, he had a windfall: A stock he played was actually driven up 10 points by his buying. He had 600 shares out, for a profit of $6,000. After this trade, however, the quasi–bucket shops finally figured out Livermore's trick. At one of the firms, he ran into trouble when he went to collect his money.

"Livermore, we're not paying you. You rigged the market! And you been tradin' under an alias."

"Don't accuse me of the things you do," was his reply.

"You pumped up the price by buying in New York. You drove up the price just after we took your position. You drove up the price yourself."

"You give me too much credit. Your crooked mind lays things on me that you are capable of, not me."

"Get outta here. I heard of you—the Boy Plunger, ain't it? Well, that don't work here, and you're headin' for trouble, big trouble. You rigged this market with some of your friends."

"I never trade with partners. I trade only for my own account and you know it! There is no way you can prove your false allegations!" Livermore said.

"It's proven in my mind, that's enough. You cheated us here."

"You have a big firm with many offices. I trade alone. How could I cheat you?"

"I don't know exactly how you did it, but you did it."

"You just said you don't know. You have no proof. You just don't want to give me what I have coming to me." Livermore's voice rose again.

"You bastard!"

"You're not going to scare me away with name-calling. I have a slip in my hand confirming my orders to you to buy and sell for my account. The trade is completed. You owe me the money, two thousand dollars. Are you welching?"

Livermore was yelling now and a crowd had gathered. The one

thing these shops could never allow was to fail to pay off on a completed trade. Because these were shady operations, rumors would fly, and there would be a rush by the customers to redeem their accounts for cash—then chaos, like a run on a bank.

There was silence. The manager finally reached into his cash drawer and yanked out the money. He peeled it out as the customers watched. He whispered to Livermore as he peeled off the last hundred, "Don't come back here. Don't ever come back here, 'Boy Genius.' " Livermore pocketed the money and left.

He had played the exact same trick on them that they had used to wipe out hundreds of customers who traded on skinny margins and were wiped out automatically when the market moved against them.

He got in his car that night and, with a trading friend, headed for New York. On the way, he was up to his usual tricks—which led to a favorite story of his about how close he once came to Yale University.

Livermore and his friend stopped in New Haven and stayed in a hotel. While they were at the hotel, they learned of a bucket-shop operation in town. The temptation was too great, and the next morning they paid it a visit. They received an effusive welcome from the manger of the shop. Livermore was wearing a light tan suit. His friend was wearing a blue blazer and khaki pants. New Haven being a college town, the manager immediately mistook them for Yale students. And the manager was used to fleecing the Joe College types.

The first day Livermore played conservatively, and his trading friend followed his lead. They stayed over a second night and showed up the next morning, just as the New York market opened. They played all day, and Livermore's profits were close to $1,500. On the third day, dressed in their best collegiate outfits, they returned again. Livermore opened the day by selling short 500 shares. The stock collapsed, and Livermore covered the short immediately. The manger slowly paid off the money—$500 margin and $500 profit.

When he was done, the manager glanced over Livermore's blue eyes, his young smiling face, his blond hair. He observed Livermore's polite manner, his quiet demeanor. The manager was no longer the same effusive person, waiting to get wealthy from rich, careless college boys.

Livermore returned with cash in hand and said, "I'd like to sell two hundred Steel short."

The manger looked at the cash in Livermore's fist and did nothing. He just stared before he finally spoke. "You boys aren't college students, are you?"

"We never said we were. You assumed we were," Livermore answered.

"You're ringers, hustlers."

"How can we be ringers and hustlers? If we were, then we would have to rig the market to move in our favor. You've seen that we have been just sitting here, no phone calls, no mysterious behavior, no tricks."

"You got some kind of system for winning, that's what you got."

"You've got a system for your customers to lose. They get wiped out every time they lose their margin. We're playing by those rules. Take this order for two hundred Steel."

"Not on your life, never—you hustled me. You two little bastards hustled me."

"Look . . ." Livermore continued.

"No, I won't look. Just get outta here now, before I lose my temper."

"Looks like you already lost your temper," Livermore said, as he watched the man's face turn from red to purple. "All right, we'll leave."

"And don't ever come back!" Livermore heard the manager yell as the door slammed shut behind him. The manager was not completely wrong in his assessment. Livermore could have been in college, maybe even at Yale. But Livermore was interested in only one college—Wall Street.

He had lost everything twice now, but he knew that was the only way a person learned in the trading profession. You had to lose, because it taught you what not to do, and if you did it again, well, then you were a slow learner and you would lose again. He had been away for the better part of a year now, a lot of time for him to think about the mistakes he had made.

He believed he was now ready to go back to New York, back to Wall Street.

Over his 10 years of trading, Livermore had observed the methods of the technicians, the chartists, and the mathematicians, all the theories and techniques of trading developed by graduates of the superb engineering and technical schools of America. He believed that they all had merit, but his conclusions were developed from actual trading, from hands-on participation in the market and constant analysis. His ultimate method was beginning to form in his mind.

He already believed in some basic guides:

- Always evaluate and appraise general conditions first, and determine the line of least resistance. Is it an upward-trending market or a downward-trending market? Or is it *consolidating*—moving sideways, trying to make up its mind?
- If the overall trend of the market is not in your favor, you are playing at an extreme disadvantage. Go with the flow, bend with the trend, do not sail into a gale.

Livermore was looking for the difference between stock *gambling* and stock *speculation*. And he never used the words *bull market* or *bear market* because these terms tended to make too permanent a psychological mind-set.

He was now playing in a different arena from the bucket shops, and he knew it—that was why he had been wiped out twice. The game was much bigger and therefore it had more risks. Before Livermore could solve a problem, he had to *state* the problem and define the problem to himself in an honest way.

The first thing he analyzed now—something he would analyze for the rest of his life—was the dimension of *time*. He concluded that in his old life in the bucket shops, time for him had been instant; that is, he lived in the moment. He could bet on the swings as they happened, reacting to the moment, the second.

If he was to win on Wall Street, he would have to change his strategy to accommodate a longer outlook, to react to future time. He would have to be patient and anticipate the inevitable advances and declines—make a move and then be patient and wait.

Livermore's final conclusion was clear: *To anticipate the market is to* gamble; *to be patient and react only when the market gives the signal is to* speculate.

And he believed the only way to test this solution, to prove this strategy on Wall Street, was with money. Livermore had been right on the moves, but wrong on the timing. Now he went into the market with a new attitude and methodology.

He did all right—but not as well as he had expected, for two reasons: His trading system was still not what he wanted, and he was listening to the other traders around him. Instead of holding onto a winning position, he sold after a few points profit. He adopted the maxim "you can't go broke taking a profit" as his philosophy. He was also still affected by his old trading methods from the days when he had hit and run, taking his profits before the market turned against him. But primarily it was the barrage of information from other traders that affected his judgment; the never-ending tips, especially from those he thought were savvy, experienced traders.

There was one trader, a major player, whom he particularly admired. This trader gave no tips and offered only one piece of advice to anyone who asked: "It's a bull market," or "It's a bear market," or "It's a sideways market, hasn't made up its mind which way it's going yet." It was this advice that Livermore was later to cherish.

He was now learning that before a play could be made, he first had to decide on the overall direction of the market. Also, once the play was made, it had to be seen through to its conclusion. It was imperative not to sell until he had a good reason to sell—and if the general trend of the market was with him and there were no other extenuating circumstances, well, then he had to play it out.

He also studied losers. He divided these suckers into three classes:

1. Ignorant novices who know nothing, and know that they know nothing, but still want to play the market. Life span 3 to 30 months.

2. Second-grade suckers or, as Livermore called them, semi-suckers, who get their information from suckers of an even higher grade. They have gone through the first phase of being suckers and have now moved into the second phase. They quote market aphorisms and the words of market sages. They are intelligent enough to play the game for a longer time than the basic suckers. Life span up to 42 months.

3. Suckers of the third kind, who look for bargains, buy at the bottom, and wait for the rally. They do okay until they hit a stock that never rallies, or keeps declining.

The one rule that suckers never learn—nor do most market players—is *don't be a sucker!*

Livermore felt that at this point in his career he was still a sucker—but he was also a special class of sucker. He was what he called a *Careful Mike* sucker. Careful suckers listen to others and cuts their profits short. In their rush to avoid risk, they see the biggest part of a stock's move proceed without them. They wait for the dips that never come, or the dips come too fast for them to move, or the stock just simply becomes too expensive, in their minds, to buy again.

Livermore had decided it was the big swings that made the really big money. And if he was correct and patient, and waited through the adversity of negative fluctuations and corrections, he would prevail. This, of course, did not mean he would be stubborn and sit through severe drops in the market. His 10 percent bucket-shop rule stayed with him for the rest of his life: If he lost more than 10 percent against his original purchase price, then he covered his position.

Slowly, through long and deep analysis, constant revision, and actually buying and selling stock, Livermore was evolving, developing, rules—his basic theories on speculating in the stock and commodities markets.

Then he broke all his rules and made a fortune.

He called it his spooky story. He loved to tell it to his sons and close friends.

It was the spring of 1906 and Livermore was 29 years old, vacationing in Atlantic City. He had cleared all his stock market positions and was relaxing on the Jersey shore with a friend, another trader. Of course, he still had his account with E. F. Hutton. There, he had a buying power of between 3,000 and 4,000 shares on margin, at an average price of $100. This meant he had the capacity for a $400,000 position. It was a medium up-trending market climate with stocks steadily advancing.

One morning Livermore and his friend, slightly bored, wandered into the Atlantic City branch of E. F. Hutton to idly check out the market. The market was strong, and Livermore's friend had a good position on the bull side of the market.

"See, strong market, just like I said it would be. Buy something, J.L.," his friend said.

Livermore stood watching the tape in silence as it slid through his fingers.

"You with us, J.L.? Did you hear what I said?"

Livermore was oblivious to his friend. He kept watching the tape in silence. All his trading life Livermore had been struck, on rare occasions, by impulses, premonitions, intuitive urges that he did not understand. In most cases he did not follow them, but he kept track of them, and mostly they worked out. He did not know if it was the unconscious mind making choices based on the accumulated experience of having traded millions of shares or whether it was some kind of a psychic urge. Maybe it was simply the gambler's instinct. He knew it defied all his carefully studied and applied rules. These feelings defied logic or explanation, but they had always made him money. In fact, he did not know what the hell it was, but it was a clear impulse to make a move. So, this spring day in 1906, he moved.

He walked up to the clerk. "Sell a thousand Union Pacific short."

His friend went with him. "J.L., why are you putting out a short line? The market's going up."

Livermore took his order slip and studied his friend before replying. "I don't know why, exactly. I just think it's the right thing to do."

"You know something, don't you?" his friend asked. The clerk was watching now.

Livermore knew if he told his friend he had a tip his friend would rush over and do what he did. "Please, I told you, I don't have a clear reason for doing this."

"I know you never do anything without a reason. In fact, you told me that anyone who trades without a plan, a consistent plan, is a fool. Now you tell me that you have no reason to sell U.P. short," his friend said. "You're breaking your own rules, for crying out loud!"

Livermore said nothing. He turned and walked back to the clerk, "Sell short another thousand Union Pacific."

"You've gone crazy, Livermore. Three days of lying in the sun, taking in the ocean air, and you're having a mental breakdown."

Livermore slipped the order into his pocket.

"We're leaving before you do anything else stupid." His friend took him by the arm.

"Just a second," Livermore said. He went back and sold a third thousand shares short. He pocketed the order form and then followed his friend outside into the sunshine.

Later that afternoon, near the market close, he went back to the brokerage office to check the price of the Union Pacific stock. The stock had risen almost two points above where he had sold short.

"See, J.L., I told you—the market's up, and you lost $6,000 for your foolishness."

Livermore said nothing. He simply smiled and walked back out onto the boardwalk to watch the descending sun.

The next day he went back in the early afternoon. The stock was up slightly along with the market, but near the close the stock started to sell off. Livermore sold 2,000 more shares.

"You are totally crazy, J.L.," his friend said.

"I think you're right, because now I have to go back to New York. I've exceeded my margin and I need to oversee my investment. My vacation is over."

Livermore returned to New York that evening.

That night, April 18, 1906, at 5 A.M., while Livermore was fast asleep in New York, the earth under San Francisco moved, slowly at first, rumbling, then quaking, shaking, shivering, as an underground shock wave began to rock the city. The San Andreas fault was adjusting itself, shrugging its massive shoulders. Most of the city fell, and a few unlucky souls were trapped in the opening and closing maw of what had been solid earth. Tall buildings staggered, collapsed, and fell. The financial district was fiery rubble; the train station was leveled, and the tracks were twisted and bent like soft pretzels. The tremblor was felt as far away as Palo Alto. The Stanford University campus was demolished by the quake. Scores of people were killed.

The next morning Livermore read the newspaper headlines: "Earthquake Disaster in San Francisco." He read on: "The market dropped only a few points on the news."

Livermore knew that bad news in a bull market climate takes a lot longer to sink in with the public than bad news in a bear market, when the climate is already negative. In fact, before the market closed, stocks had rebounded to their former levels. Livermore was short 5,000 shares, but he was flat on the trade. He had made no money.

His friend had also returned to New York. "You were right about bad news coming, but I told you that you can't spit into the wind. And the wind is positive. You should have listened to me, J.L.," he said.

"Winds change," Livermore said, reading the ticker tape, not looking up.

Livermore figured that even if the disaster proved not to be as bad as was originally thought, railroad stocks would not go up.

The next day the news dribbled in from San Francisco and the market drifted down, but not drastically. Livermore was convinced he was right. He went to his broker, got a special line of credit, and sold another 5,000 shares of Union Pacific short.

The next day, the third day after the earthquake, the market tumbled. Union Pacific fell like a stone, and Livermore walked out of the wreckage with $250,000 in profit. He never figured out exactly why he did what he did in listening to his inner voice. It was one subject he did not analyze too deeply. He quietly slipped the cash into his account. Now he could trade with a much bigger line—an additional $250,000—and that was what he thought about the most.

He had cut short his Atlantic City vacation. After the earthquake windfall, he went to the races in Saratoga Springs for a holiday. He loved the entire spectacle of Saratoga: the beauty of the place, the regal setting, the sleek, beautiful horses. Most of the well-dressed, influential people of New York City gathered there every summer for the races.

Once again, Livermore wandered into the Hutton brokerage offices in Saratoga to see what was cooking in New York. He sat quietly studying the tape, looking up at the chalkboard as the prices of the leading stocks were posted. People came by to whisper tips into the ear of the Boy Plunger. Approaching 30, he still looked like a well-dressed college kid. The office manger came over and flashed the order slips in front of him, showing the buy/sell orders from some of the bigger players who were in Saratoga. Livermore just smiled and said nothing.

His attention was focused on Union Pacific, his old friend. Livermore had no feelings with regard to either buying long or selling a stock short. It made no difference, since he had figured that the market went down as often as it went up. He waited patiently in cash, waiting to strike. The Union Pacific volume and price movement Livermore saw on the tape had changed and were now, he believed, in an *accumulation* phase. He did no trading for three days as he watched the stock, ignoring the races. He finally came to the conclusion that it was being accumulated by a professional group of players, based on the tape movement.

The stock was at 160 when, on the third day, he started to buy. He bought in lots of 500 until he had 5,000 shares. He got a frantic call from Ed Hutton, his old, respected friend, a friend who was also well informed and had friends in high places. There was little that happened on Wall Street that Hutton did not know about.

"J.L., you're crazy," Hutton said.

"What are you talking about?"

"They're slipping it to you. The pool that runs the stock is feeding the stock to you as fast as you can take it. Then they are going to walk away from it, and buy it back from you cheap. You're the patsy here. You're the sucker, in a sucker play."

"You sure?"

"Couldn't be surer. Comes from the best source, the top."

"I don't agree," Livermore said. "I think it's being accumulated."

"Yeah, by you! It's going to go down. Listen, I like the commissions, and I want you to be the biggest trader in New York. I'm just trying to save you from disaster."

"All right, Ed," Livermore paused, thinking. He knew that Hutton was a true friend, a friend who had helped him often in the past.

"Thanks, Ed. I'll quit the position."

"Right. You can't expect to win on every play, J.L.," Hutton said, and hung up.

Livermore sat down and looked at the order slips and fills in his hands. After a few minutes, he got up and told the clerk to sell him out. The Union Pacific position was liquidated at $162 a share.

After commissions it was an even trade. The next day Union Pacific announced a 10 percent dividend, and the stock shot up 10 points. Livermore would have pocketed $50,000.

Livermore was in the Hutton office in Saratoga when the dividend was announced. He sat there quietly as the stock shot up. The office manager looked at him and shrugged. He knew what had happened the day before. He knew what Ed Hutton had told him. Livermore smiled and nodded.

Livermore was not angry or upset with Hutton. He looked at the experience as part of his education. How could he get angry when he understood that the market was independent of feelings? The market was pure action, cold, and true only to itself. He believed it always did the right thing, even if he could not see it at the time.

Livermore now resolved to follow only his own method of trading stock. He now knew that tipsters came in all sizes and shapes and wore all kinds of disguises—even close friends with the best intentions. They were to be avoided at all cost.

Livermore had learned some great lessons over the past 15 years. He was one year short of 30. He had a good stake and a good line with his brokers. He had shaken off his bucket-shop methods of trading. Now, after Saratoga, he was going to notch it up a level. Instead of concentrating on stocks, he was going to concentrate on the basic conditions of the market. "Yes," he thought to himself. "Before I pick a stock I will examine the basics of the overall market."

He loved this game, the game of speculation. He loved it for its endless challenge. It was a game that he could never completely win. But he did not have to win all the time to make a lot of money. If he could win on average he could have a great life and a lot of fun.

He was ready.

chapter four

The Crash of 1907

All men naturally desire knowledge.   Aristotle

JESSE LIVERMORE HAD BEEN SEARCHING FOR HIS TRAD-
ing strategy. Slowly, it was starting to form. The first step was to
concentrate on the overall market before making a trade. He
would follow the line of least resistance—up in a bull market, buy
long, down in a bear market, sell short. If the market went sideways, he would wait in cash for a clear direction to be established.

He had no interest in finding a bargain or a cheap stock. He was
not a bottom fisher. He was a trend follower. He was only interested in following the trend, what he called the *line of least resistance.* He was one of the first true momentum players.

Now that he had a basic market strategy, he needed a money-
management strategy to complement it. He was known on the
Street as the Boy Plunger, but plunging had not always served him
well. He had been busted, broke, three times by the age of 30.

He watched the most successful Wall Street traders in action. He
observed that they were all good money managers, each with an
individual approach. He knew he needed his own system.

He now knew it was not *whether* the market or a stock would
turn, but exactly *when* it would turn—timing was everything. But
he also realized that no one could call or predict exactly when the
market would turn or what a stock would do. So, Livermore
developed his *probing,* or testing the market, approach.

The strategy was simple: Do not plunge. Send out a probe
before buying, just as a commanding officer sends out a reconnais-
sance platoon to probe the enemy lines and gather intelligence.
Livermore followed this basic military strategy in stock market
trading, which is, after all, a kind of war.

It is very important to note that Livermore would determine
the number of shares or the size of his investment in dollars before
making the first trade.

If Livermore planned to take a position of 10,000 shares in a
given stock, he would first probe with a purchase of 20 percent of

his planned position—that is, he would buy 2,000 shares. Suppose he paid $100 a share. If the price dropped after he made his first purchase, he would either close out the first position or wait— never taking a loss of more than 10 percent.

He expected the stock price to rise. If it did, he would buy a second position of another 2,000 shares at, say, $101 per share. He would then be in profit.

If the stock continued to rise, he would take a third position of 2,000 shares at, say, $104.

At this point he would own 6,000 shares; he would be 60 percent invested against his objective of a 10,000-share position. But he would have made each purchase at a slightly more expensive level. For Livermore, this was good: It proved to him that the stock was moving in the right direction.

Now he would wait for a further move and a correction. For example, suppose the stock moved from $100 to $112, then had a normal correction down to $104 dollars, the spot where he had made his last purchase.

If the stock moved up from this price of $104, Livermore would make his final purchase of 4,000 shares at, say, $106, giving him an average price of around $105 for the total position of 10,000 shares.

To put it another way: Livermore would establish 20 percent of his planned position on the first purchase, 20 percent on the second position, and 20 percent on the third position. He would wait for a confirmation and then take his final position of 40 percent.

He considered each of these purchases to be a crucial stage in establishing his overall position. If, at any time, the stock went against him, he would be patient and wait, or he would close out all his positions, never sustaining a loss of more than a 10 percent.

The first probe or transaction is crucial; it is the key to this technique. After the first transaction, do not make a second until you have confirmed that your judgment is correct. When the stock has moved in the direction you expected it to move, and you have a profit, your judgment has been confirmed.

Livermore believed that stocks are never too high to begin buying or too low to begin selling short. Livermore believed that there was only one side of the market to avoid. He could be on the bull side or the bear side—it made no difference to Livermore—just so long as he was not on the *wrong* side.

From experience, Livermore knew that one of the hardest things to do as a trader was to sell out a position early if he was wrong on the initial purchase and the stock moved against him.

Trying to explain the market to his boys, he said, "The transaction becomes personal to too many speculators when their judgment is proven wrong and the stock moves against them. It is exactly at this time that the speculator must take action and cut losses. The speculator has been proven wrong, because the stock has moved against him, and must now admit it quickly and close the trade. It is a question of overcoming and control of the ego."

Livermore had come to realize that the big money was in the big swings, in waiting for the basic trend to play out and riding the stock for as long as possible before the inevitable change in the basic trend was seen in the line of least resistance. He would wait for the market to give him the clues. He would not anticipate the market by guessing its direction. Like Sherlock Holmes, he would wait for the clues to appear, the facts to mount up, before making his conclusion.

Livermore now had three important rules to follow in his new trading strategy:

- First, *decide on the overall direction of the market.* Determine the line of least resistance. Be sure of the basic trend.

- Second, *develop a buying strategy.* Probe the market. Test it by trading small positions first. Do not rush in and bet your whole stash on impulse.
- Third, *be patient and wait for all the facts.* Wait for a move to play out. It is the big moves that make the big money.

It was late in 1906 when his new strategy finally paid off. Livermore sensed what he believed was going to be a major change in market direction—a basic change downward. This was not obvious to the major players or the press, who were still calling for the roaring bull market to continue.

He examined all the factors carefully and decided that the market was cresting, even though the line of least resistance still appeared to be upward. He used his new trading approach to confirm this judgment, sending out probes across a variety of the leading stocks. He probed the four leading stock groups, selling at least two stocks short in each of the four groups. His short sales held—that is, the stocks that he had sold short went down, and on the rallies those stocks faltered, unable to make new highs, closing only a few points up, but then sinking, sliding backward off their old highs.

Livermore slowly increased his positions on each failed rally.

The last holdout was Reading, a railroad stock that would not budge. It was supposed to be *cornered,* a stock whose outstanding shares were all controlled by a pool, or a person. Livermore believed no one stock could withstand the basic tidal wave that he saw on the horizon—the change from an upward-trending bull market to a downward-trending bear market. He believed that Reading could not buck the trend. It would collapse along with the others when the time was right.

Livermore decided to help its decline along. He sold short through two brokers simultaneously. He sold 4,000 shares of

Reading at $111. He had the market orders timed to hit the market simultaneously. The orders were filled at diminishing prices. He hit Reading again by selling 2,000 more, establishing his short line of 6,000 shares at a final price of $92. He was well into profit in less than a few hours. Reading then collapsed, as did all the other stocks in which Livermore had established positions.

His first major escapade using his new technique of probing the market had worked. Now he was faced with another problem: when to cover and buy back his shorts.

Livermore had been wiped out and had seen his profits disappear many times before by not closing out his positions and banking his paper profits while he could. This time he did not wait for the market to show a clear sign that it had bottomed out. He wanted his profits. He closed out his positions, put the money in the bank, and left for Palm Beach.

He was weary of trading and wanted to forget about the market for a while. He loved deep-sea fishing, so he went and relaxed. He deserved it. He also wanted to reflect more on his new trading strategy. He had almost a million dollars in his bank account now. It was 1907, he was 30 years old, and he knew he was finally on the right track.

After Palm Beach, he headed for Paris. He liked Europe because there was no talk of the stock market, and he wanted to rest his mind for a while. With plenty of money in his bank account, in a beautiful place with beautiful people, he was content for a while.

But it did not last for long. His passion was the stock market, and soon he was drawn back into it. He read the Paris edition of the *Herald Tribune*. It became clear that the New York market was headed for an even bigger tumble then he had originally thought.

He was sorry now that he had closed out his positions so soon. He really had no basic reason to close out the original positions except that he was fearful of losing his profits. He wanted to put his profits in the bank, which he had done.

He took a fast liner back to New York.

He did not know it, but he was about to witness the panic of 1907.

As soon as he arrived he went short the market again, using probes to make sure he was correct in the basic trend. He established very large short positions in several of the leading stocks. The turn-of-the-century market had been a full runaway bull market to date, with wild gyrations in the prices of the more speculative issues.

The basic financial problem soon became apparent: *call loans.* Call loans were time-restricted demand loans made by banks to brokerage houses. The cash from these loans was, in turn, put up for margin by the brokerage houses for their customers. The loans were the fuel that powered the market—the margin was essential. These loans were made every day at the Money Post between 12:00 and 2:15 P.M., when the bankers appeared on the stock market floor ready to loan money to the brokers. The problem had been developing for months, but it culminated on October 24, 1907.

The problem was simple. The banks did not have enough cash available for the brokers to cover their margin requirements. What money was available was being offered at 100 to 150 percent interest. And the banks, which usually fought to lend this high-yield money, were not interested in extending any further loans to brokerage houses, at any interest rate. It was a credit crunch of the most dire proportions. Stocks plummeted. Livermore kept selling short, pyramiding his position into the weakness.

On October 24, at 12 P.M., chaos ruled on the floor of the exchange. Hundreds of brokers gathered around the Money Post, screaming out their demands for short-term loans, but there was no money available—no money at all. This meant that the brokers had to sell their stock positions on the open market to cover their margins, but there were no buyers for stock. All the buying had dried up. It was the market's worst nightmare—no cash and no buyers—and it had happened quickly. Pure, abject, unadulterated, raw fear swept over the brokers and the bankers.

Wall Street was out of cash.

The brokers ran to R. H. Thomas, president of the stock exchange. He called James Stillman, president of the National City Bank, the richest, most powerful bank in the United States, a bank that boasted of never extending a loan at more than 6 percent interest.

When Stillman had finished listening to Thomas, he simply said "We must go see Mr. Morgan." They left immediately to visit J. P. Morgan, head of the House of Morgan, the world giant of finance.

Morgan listened to Stillman and Thomas as they outlined the disastrous situation, a disaster that could spread right across the nation and cripple its entire industrial base. Morgan wasted no time. When he had heard enough, Morgan rose, and said: "Return to the exchange and tell them that there will be money for them."

They asked, "Where from?"

"From the banks," Morgan answered, staring at the two men. "Where else?"

Thomas sped back to the floor of the exchange and told the crowd that was standing around the Money Post that there would be money for them, "Mr. Morgan has assured us!"

"When?" they yelled in desperation.

"Soon," came the answer.

"How much?" They screamed.

"Enough!" was the answer.

But the clock kept ticking. Finally, at a little after 2 P.M., John T.

Atterbury of Van Emburgh and Atterbury, a close associate of J. P. Morgan, arrived on the floor. The noise disappeared and the crowd stood transfixed, opening a path to the Money Post for Atterbury. When he got to the post, he raised his hand and said "I am authorized to lend ten million dollars."

The crowd went crazy, with brokers yelling out the amounts they needed. Atterbury yelled over the voices. "Quiet, be quiet, one at a time, there will be enough for everyone!"

"Where do we get the money?" one broker yelled.

"You will be told where to go tomorrow! Now take it easy, and let's get this done," Atterbury responded.

This day became a legend on Wall Street—the day J. P. Morgan singlehandedly saved the stock market and perhaps prevented the financial collapse of the nation.

When Thomas and Stillman had left the offices of the House of Morgan, J. P. Morgan had called the presidents of the major banks. He told each of them, "We need to prop up the market with cash, and we need to do it now. We must give them what they need. It is a critical situation."

Each banker replied in the same manner: "We are loaned to the maximum. We have no cash to lend to the brokers to support the market."

"You have reserves!" Morgan exclaimed.

"But we are already below the legal limits!"

"Use the reserves, what the hell do you think they are for?" he told each one of the bankers.

Morgan was a person whom Livermore admired. Morgan was a brilliant person of practical principles, a patriot, a financial giant.

That day, October 24, 1907, was to be branded into Livermore's memory. It was the first time he had ever made more than $1 million in profit, and he had done it in a single day. Furthermore, the day was not yet over. For him it was most important that he had followed his new rules. He had been patient in waiting for the big turn in the market. He had started with small positions, sending out probes into the market to confirm that he was right. And finally, when everything was in his favor, he had done what he loved best: He plunged big time, like a king cobra.

His paper profits and his stock positions were so large near the end of the day, as a result of his pyramiding, that he now had an even bigger decision to make. Morgan's announcement to inject cash had solved only one problem: It reestablished liquidity—solvency among the brokers. But the other major problem was that there was still no demand. Livermore looked over the market near the close, and found there were simply no bids for stocks. Nobody wanted to buy stocks at any price.

Livermore knew that he could perpetrate a monumental raid by starting to sell at the opening the next day. The downward pressure of his hammering the key stocks would cause a further decline. His margin now was ever increasing; his profits had pyramided, risen as the market had fallen. He was in a position to begin the day by selling short 10,000 shares of Union Pacific, the market darling at the time. He could follow by selling half a dozen other stocks that were considered the bluest of the blue chips. He now had the account margin and the trading skills to hammer those issues into oblivion. He was looking at not $1 million profit, but $10 million, $20 million, if he hit the market hard the next morning.

Now it would be his turn to make the big decision. Would he support the market or drive it down and down and down, until the board of governors had to close the exchange, maybe forever?

Before the close of the trading day, while Livermore was studying his next move, a friend of his, Warren Augustus Reed, paid him a visit. During the panic that day Livermore had explained to his friend, who was a banker in a powerful investment banking house, exactly what would happen. Reed had watched Livermore operate in the past and was a believer in his market skill and deadly prowess.

Reed disappeared for a while when he was called away to see his boss, the president of the firm.

Reed returned and explained to Livermore, "J.L., I've been asked to talk to you about the market and request that you refrain from any more short selling. I understand that you are looking at even bigger profits for yourself if you hammer away, but sometimes we have to look at the greater good."

"Auggie, this comes from your boss?" Livermore asked.

"No. It comes from a person more powerful than my boss," he answered.

Livermore knew whom he meant—J. P. Morgan. "You sure?"

"I'm sure. It came from him personally. I was in the office when it happened and heard the conversation."

Livermore thought for a minute. "You know these same men have been selling into this market for months now—feeding stock to the public, knowing that the decline was coming, only inter-ested in looking after themselves, killing the public?"

"Yes, I know, but J.L., isn't that always the way, when prices get too high? The smart, market-savvy people sell to the less-smart people, the public."

"Yes."

"J.L., if we are to get this market under control then we will have to stop the bleeding, the selling, and staunch the supply, or there will be no market left. There will only be chaos."

Livermore pondered his position for a few minutes. "Tell your boss that I am in agreement with what he says. I will not sell any more stock today. I will cover my short positions in the morning by buying in the stock. After that, I will start to aggressively buy additional stocks on the opening. I understand the gravity of the situation."

"Thanks, J.L., I'll report this back to *the man* himself."

Livermore had already analyzed the situation carefully before his friend had shown up. The carnage this day had been horrific, and Livermore felt the exchange was due for a rally on a technical rebound basis, provided it was not raided. Plus, he had some monumental short positions that would have to be covered in a liquid market to preserve his profits.

Finally, he had altruistic reasons for agreeing. Further raiding would severely hurt the country. He was astounded that he had this power in his hands, the raiding power and skill to actually drive the market into oblivion. He was 31 years old.

The next morning Livermore fueled the rally by covering his short positions. As the market continued to rally, he bought another 100,000 shares of various companies, which he fed back into the market that same day as the public jumped in. When the day was over he was worth $3 million—not in paper profits, but in cold, hard cash.

"What a life," he thought. Broke three times before he was 30 years old and, at the age of 31, potentially able to batter the New York Stock Exchange into oblivion. He smiled to himself. He had shared power with J. P. Morgan for one day. Morgan had the power to save the market from oblivion, and Livermore had the power to hammer it into oblivion—even Morgan could not have stopped him. He had gone from being thrown out of bucket shops to being asked by the most powerful banker in America to lay off Wall Street, stop the punishment. His reputation was growing, and he had held the financial welfare of the nation in his hands for one day. What a thrill!

He later told his sons that this had been one of the most important events of his life, when J. P. Morgan asked a favor of him during the crash of 1907. But for Livermore there was no satisfaction in this raw power. The satisfaction, the exhilaration, came from beating the Street. Finally, after thousands of trades and hundreds of hours examining his trading techniques, he knew he was right. The big money was made in the big swings. Clipping points had served him well in establishing a stake, but the big money was in the big swings. He only could catch the big swings if he was patient and waited until they came along, waited until his judgment had been confirmed.

He believed he had advanced over these two days from the gambler class of trader to being a true speculator who looked ahead, evaluated the general conditions, and moved prudently—testing first, and plunging only after he was convinced that all the factors were in his favor.

The Boy Plunger was no longer a plunger at all. At least in his own mind, he was a speculator. From the public's point of view he was still considered a wild plunger, because they saw only the last 10 minutes of a three-act play—they had no interest in Act 1 or Act 2, which were done in secret anyway. It was the results they watched and wanted to emulate.

Livermore now had a plan, an investment strategy that he believed worked, and he knew that one essential secret of success was at its core—the hard work of never-ending analysis.

Now he had to see if this had been a fluke or if he really did have the beginnings of a solid trading approach to the market. But he needed a rest first. He decided to try a vacation again, to enjoy himself. He bought a yacht and was about to head south. He wanted to go fishing, his favorite sport.

But it was not to be, not yet. For Livermore studied and played the commodities market just as he did the equities market.

Livermore was soon as sure that a crash was coming in the commodities market as he had been in the stock market. So before heading out for his vacation and enjoying his new yacht, he set out his probes and finally wound up short 10 million bushels of wheat and 10 million bushels of corn. The wheat did what it was supposed to do—plummeted. But corn was rising in the face of cascading commodity prices. Livermore soon found out why: Arthur Cutten, a brilliant trader, was running a corner on corn.

In the early 1900s, running a corner was common. A pool of people, or sometimes a powerful individual, would determine what the short position was on a commodity or a stock. Then they would launch an assault and buy every single share of stock or, in this case, bushel of corn. This would leave the people who held the short positions with no stock to buy to cover their short positions. These people would then have to accept whatever stock was offered at whatever price it was offered. When a corner happened, it happened fast. Corners had ruined many traders who went in to cover their short positions and simply found that nothing was available or that it was available only at huge losses.

Arthur Cutten was born in Guelph, Ontario, in 1870, seven years before Livermore. Cutten was later to be called the Great Bull as Livermore was to be called the Great Bear. He was built like Livermore—slim and of average height. But unlike Livermore, who dressed in the finest fashions, Cutten dressed in plain clothes of the best value.

It took Cutten five years of hard work as a teenager on the family farm where he was born to save $50. He took the $50 and journeyed to Chicago. There he got a clerical job with A. S. White and Company, at the wage of $4 a week. Cutten was frugal and watched every penny—this remained with him all his life. He was tenacious, diligent, and hard-working. It took him another five years to save up $1,000. He was now 25. But he had more than just $1,000—he also had five years of intensive experience in trading commodities for White.

He and Livermore also had the same code of silence and secrecy. Whenever Cutten could, he hung out in the "Pigeon Roost," a small area above the wild and wooly grain pits of Chicago. He carefully studied the floor traders and the actions of the customers in White's offices. He, like Livermore, worked every night on sheets of long columnar paper looking for trends, patterns, and timing mechanisms.

After five years of hard work for his employer, and for himself in his off-hours, he went to White and said, "I would like to open a trading account here."

"For whom?" White asked.

"For myself," Cutten answered.

"You are a smart young man, Arthur. You must know that a man of modest means cannot trade in the commodities market. It would be sheer lunacy."

"But sir . . ."

"Never mind, you must heed my advice and you will thank me for it later. My advice is to avoid the commodities market, avoid the stock market. It is a fool's game and you know that a fool and his money are soon parted."

Cutten wondered to himself how the fool got the money in the first place, but he was not about to argue with the severe White. "Yes, sir. Thank you, sir."

On his lunch break he went to another firm and opened an account with his $1,000 in cash.

Three months later, he entered White's office. He had his alpaca jacket in his hand. White was on the phone and motioned for young Cutten to sit down. Cutten remained standing and gently placed his alpaca jacket, his trading uniform jacket, on White's desk.

White hung up the phone and looked at the jacket lying on his desk. "What's going on here, Arthur?"

"I've been elected to membership in the Chicago Board of Trade, sir."

"Arthur, we're busy here. Make sense."

"I've purchased a seat on the exchange."

"How?"

"With my trading profits, sir."

White sat dumbstruck. He finally spoke. "So, you are resigning."

"Yes, sir. And I expect I will never work for another man for the rest of my life."

Cutten closed the door on a shocked White. True to his words, Cutten never did work for another person.

Twelve years later, in 1907, Cutten was a legend in the Chicago grain pits. Secretive, tenacious, holding only his own counsel, he was considered a very formidable force. He and Livermore were kindred spirits.

Cutten had found out about Livermore's position. He had Livermore, his only equal, in his clutches. Livermore was short 10 million bushels of corn. For every 10 cents Cutten drove the price of corn upward, it cost Livermore $1 million. He had Livermore cornered.

The thoughts of a nice vacation in Florida were far from a reality now. It was survival mode for Livermore again. On the positive side, he saw the price of wheat decline as he had predicted, so he had a profit in wheat. But it could all be wiped out—*he* could be wiped out—if he did not correct his problem with corn. He needed a strategy to defeat Cutten and extricate himself from this sinkhole. He knew Cutten was aware of his huge short position and would pull out all the stops to annihilate him.

That night, as he lay in bed, an idea came to him based on something he had heard. He moved swiftly. Livermore knew the corner was false; there was plenty of corn available from the farmers, so there was no underlying reason why the price of corn should go up. Cutten was playing with the market. In particular, he was playing with Livermore's financial life.

The first thing Livermore did was to cover the 10 million bushels of wheat he was short at a good profit. This gave him cash in his account to trade with. He had heard that Cutten had begun cornering the oat market along with the corn market. In the oat market, Cutten was up against Chicago's powerful Armour family, trying to catch them in a corner. Livermore confirmed this as soon as he could.

Then Livermore made his major move. He sold 50,000 bushels of oats at the market, then another 50,000, then another, then another—200,000 bushels in all. The price of oats dropped drastically with these sales. He figured the traders would believe what they saw and conclude that the Armours were at work to break Cutten's oat corner. They would also conclude that the Armours would move in to bust up the corn corner next.

The traders did as Livermore had predicted. When they saw the price of oats breaking, the traders jumped into the corn market, selling their positions while the price was high. Livermore was there to buy. He bought all they could shovel his way. He covered the 6 million bushels he was short in 10 minutes and the rest before the market closed that day. He also closed out the 200,000 bushels of oats before the market closed.

His total loss, with his profit in wheat, was $25,000. Within days, Cutten ran the price of corn up another 25 cents. This would have been a loss of at least $2.5 million for Livermore, if he had not been able to cover.

Now he was really ready for his vacation!

He was also ready for a better lifestyle. He moved into a beautiful furnished apartment at 194 Riverside Drive. He had already purchased his first yacht, the *Anita Venetian,* and sent it down to Palm Beach. He was in good company. George Jay Gould, the heir to Jay Gould's fortune, had a similar yacht, the *Atlantic,* a 300-foot, steel-hulled, triple-screw yacht; and J. P. Morgan traveled the globe in his yacht, the *Corsair,* the largest yacht afloat anywhere in the world.

The *Anita Venetian* was a 202-foot steam schooner of first-class construction. She carried the red, white, and blue pennant of the Columbia Yacht Club. Livermore purchased a snappy brass-buttoned blue blazer for wearing on board, along with gray flannel slacks and a handmade captain's hat. He was a dapper captain, ready for fun.

Livermore headed down to Palm Beach to board the waiting *Anita.* He loved Palm Beach and the Palm Beach society. He had a great passion for fishing the waters off South Florida, trolling in the deep, dark blue waters of the Gulf Stream, a current in the ocean that moves up from the coast of South America.

The Gulf Stream comes in closest to the Florida coast off Palm Beach, sometimes getting within three miles of the white sandy beaches of the rich. The pelagic fish, the big wanderers, travel inside the stream, using the 3- to 4-knot current to speed their way north. It was these fish that Livermore was interested in, the big fish, just as he was only interested in the big swings in the market. The giant bluefin tuna; the world-class monster sharks, hammer-heads, tigers, and makos; the run of sailfish; the occasional marlin, wahoo, or king mackerel; and the tarpon down in Key West—these were his prey, the challenging, unpredictable, hard-fighting gypsy fish of the great Atlantic Ocean.

He spent his days on board the *Anita* basking in the warm Florida sun, fishing, and enjoying life. At night he would eat in the great watering holes of Palm Beach, such as the Palm Beach Inn. Located directly on the beach, it contained 425 rooms. He would eat exquisite meals there and adjourn to the ocean-side gallery to have cigars and brandy and chat with his Wall Street friends.

Most nights after dinner he would wander down to the famous Beach Club, or Bradley's, as it was sometimes called after its owner, Edward Bradley, a well-known gambler whose own horses would later go on to win four Kentucky Derbies. Bradley was quiet and secretive like Livermore, but, unlike Livermore, he had a checkered past that stretched all the way out to the Wild West, where he had known Billy the Kid and Wyatt Earp. He had been an army scout during the Apache wars and was credited with aiding in the capture of Geronimo.

"Billy the Kid used to borrow money from me to bet on the Indian pony races," Bradley would tell Livermore, laughing. "Who wouldn't give him money? He'd shoot you dead if you didn't." Livermore used to love to tell this to his sons.

In Palm Beach, Bradley had a secret deal with Henry Flagler, John D. Rockefeller's partner in Standard Oil and a churchgoing Christian. Flagler built the Florida East Coast Railway, which eventually ran the entire length of Florida, all the way down to Key West. Flagler also built four major hotels in Palm Beach. His clientele loved to gamble, so he was willing to strike a deal with Bradley and leave him alone. Bradley's Beach Club ultimately became the longest-running illegal gambling casino in the history of the United States.

Bradley's was simple, but elegant. After 7 P.M. the most informal attire for men was a tuxedo, with no exceptions. White tie and tails were preferred, and there was no smoking in the gaming room. The food was five-star. Bradley paid his chef $25,000 for the season, which was a king's ransom at the turn of the century. His clientele included the elite of the U.S. financial, entertainment, and political worlds. The entrance door was painted white, with a square frosted-glass panel in the center that said "B.C.," for Beach Club.

He and Livermore quickly became fast friends, although they both were reticent and not quick to expose their true feelings. They had a mutual respect and admiration for each other.

Livermore loved to gamble at Bradley's. Bradley was also known as "Bet-on-Anything Bradley." Even so, he rarely lost.

He once told Livermore that luck was a real thing. It went right along hand-in-hand with hard work. He said, "A person either works for a living or gambles for a living. In fact life is a gamble, but if a person chooses to take up gambling for a living it has to be studied intelligently and worked at least twice as hard as any other profession." Livermore repeated this to Dorothy, his wife.

Bradley often walked around with over $100,000 on him. When major players wanted to cash out after winning, he would walk up to them, smile, congratulate them, and peel off $1,000 bills while the croupier collected their chips. The main test for membership was approval by Bradley himself. He would interview prospective members at length and, if he liked them, he would find out the answer to the final, most important question: Could they pay their bills if they lost?"

Armed Pinkerton guards posted everywhere protected Bradley's while remaining inconspicuous. The game room had a trap door installed in case the place was ever raided—the tables could be slid out of view. A guard with a rifle protected the counting room. The guard was positioned at a small window that provided a full view of the gaming room. The guard was a crack shot instructed to shoot anyone who tried to rob the place. The same instructions were given to the Pinkerton agents. Since Bradley's was located on Palm Beach, actually an island, there was no place to run. Thieves gave Bradley's a wide berth and the staff members were very discreet; any talk about the clientele and they were immediately fired. Bradley kept spies on his staff to keep him informed of everything.

Livermore passed many a pleasant evening at the Beach Club playing one of the three games of chance available: hazard, chemin de fer, and roulette. The limits at Bradley's were even higher than those at the casinos in Monte Carlo.

It was on one of these nights at Bradley's that he heard the news of the failure of one of the great cotton players. Ed Hutton was there and told him how Percy Thomas, the Cotton King, had tried to run a corner on cotton and been annihilated. He went broke in March cotton.

Hearing about Thomas triggered an interest in cotton for Livermore. On his return to New York in his private rail car, he studied the trade papers. It became clear that everyone was bearish on July cotton. As July approached, Livermore started to buy cotton. He knew that there was little time left to cover short positions. It was May, and he had no trouble establishing a long position of 120,000 bales. Shortly after he bought, the market turned upward; but the volume was sluggish, and Livermore had a big position, a position hard to sell in this limited time frame.

So Livermore performed one of his famous trading tricks: In the last 10 minutes of trading on Saturday, he stepped in and sent out four separate orders to buy 5,000 bales. This ran the Chicago price up 30 points on the close. Livermore knew this would drive the London market up on Monday to establish parity with the New York market. He knew he was trading on the line of least resistance, but he also knew he was carrying a huge illiquid position.

His strategy worked, and the London cotton market opened strongly—only it was not 30 points higher, it was *50* points higher. Nevertheless, the trading on Monday was strong in Chicago, but not strong enough for Livermore to get rid of his large position. He became worried.

The next morning on his way to work, he met a friend who showed him the front page of the *New York World*. The headline read: "July Cotton Cornered by Jesse Livermore."

Livermore always denied he knew anything about the story, but the market soared on the news. Taking his good luck as it was offered, Livermore sold out his entire position of 140,000 bales.

This became a Livermore trademark: When good luck came his way—an unpredictable windfall—he would take it and run, not wait for more good luck. This, of course, was especially true with big illiquid positions. They could sometimes be hard to sell without driving the market down.

Livermore claimed he had nothing to do with the newspaper article. Whatever the case, he seized the opportunity when it presented itself.

The next day he met a friend, one of the biggest players in the cotton market, who stopped him in the street. "I was waiting for you to try and market that big line of cotton you had. It would have been a hard sell. That was one of the neatest moves I ever saw, J.L. Congratulations."

"I had nothing to do with that story. Nothing at all," Livermore said.

"I don't know how you got the paper to print it. All I can say is I tip my hat to you. I figured that you were manipulating the London market, but compounding it with the newspaper article—now that was a very smart play."

"I told you, I . . ."

"J.L., I would never expect you to admit it. Now, would I?" He winked, "It would be dumb to admit it to me, and you're not dumb, are you?"

He left Livermore standing on the street as he strolled off.

Livermore's reputation continued to grow—some of it true, some of it embellished as it bounced along from lips to ears, to lips, to other ears, all up and down Wall Street. Livermore just shook his head, smiled to himself, and moved on in secrecy and silence.

He felt good, proud of his accomplishments. He had no inkling that disaster lay waiting just around the corner, a disaster of monumental proportions.

★ *chapter five* ★

The Cotton King

The only time I really ever lost money was when I broke my own rules. Jesse Livermore, to his son

JESSE LIVERMORE WAS NOW RICH AND SUCCESSFUL, ABLE to indulge his every passion. And Livermore loved beautiful women. The newspapers went so far as to claim he had fallen for the famous Lillian Russell, girlfriend of "Diamond Jim" Brady.

Russell was known as the "American Beauty." A woman of classic looks, she was born in 1861 in Clinton, Iowa. Her real name was Helen Louise Leonard. She moved with her family to New York after the Civil War. She was taking singing lessons when Tony Pastor heard her and signed her up to appear at his casino. She later appeared with the McCaull Opera Company at Weber and Field's Music Hall, before forming her own company. She was the toast of New York at the turn of the century. She had a great love for jewelry and an outgoing, dazzling personality. It was no surprise when she fell for Diamond Jim.

Diamond Jim was as flamboyant and colorful as Russell. He started as a baggage handler on the railroads, then became a salesman, and finally a supplier of equipment to every railroad in the United States. The first line of equipment he sold, the equipment that made his first fortune, was barbed wire. A man of giant appetites, some people believed he had eaten himself to death when he died in 1917. He adorned his body with diamonds: stick pins, cufflinks, and rings. Diamonds were even sewn into his pants, as buttons to hold up his substantial suspenders. And he loved to give away diamonds, especially to the American Beauty, Russell.

Diamond Jim was a legend as a gourmand as well, reported to have gone to incredible extremes to satisfy his appetites for pleasure. He supposedly sent a spy to the Cafe Marguery in Paris to steal the recipe for its famous sole de Marguery. When his successful spy returned to New York, Brady gave a dinner for Victor Herbert, the composer, and Marshall Field, the department store king, to introduce them to the dish. While they were eating, Diamond

Jim exclaimed, "Put this sauce on a goddamn Turkish towel and you could eat it!"

Livermore was said to have started courting Russell in 1907, just after he made his first million in the panic. He supposedly wined her and dined her all over New York and stole her away from Diamond Jim. The rumors became official when he was reported to have cruised down to Palm Beach with her aboard the *Anita Venetian*.

But it was not Livermore who was courting Russell—it was his good friend Alexander P. Moore, who was married at the time. Moore would later become ambassador to Spain, and he would remain a lifelong friend of Livermore's. Rich and privileged from birth, Moore admired and respected Livermore, the self-made trader.

Livermore smiled to himself when he read about his affair in the *Police Gazette*. The *Gazette* accused him of being the reason behind the breakup of the most famous couple in New York. Livermore loved his little secrets. He, Moore, and Russell knew what was really going on, and that was enough.

Livermore had it all. He was in his 30s and was a legend on Wall Street. J. P. Morgan himself had even once asked him to stop selling short, stop driving the market down. Heady stuff for a young, self-made trader who had had no formal education or bloodline to provide him with social standing or a stake to get established.

He carried on in Palm Beach at the Breakers Hotel in the company of Russell and his elegant friend Moore. He had $3 million in the bank. Life was beautiful. What could go wrong?

The three of them enjoyed a marvelous meal at the Breakers and took two pedicabs, the famous white wicker three-wheeled Palm Beach cabs pedaled by well-dressed black drivers, to Bradley's Beach Club for a little gambling. Russell and Moore headed straight for the roulette wheel, and Livermore sat down for some chemin de fer. After a while he left the table and joined Edward Bradley, the owner, for a drink in the bar.

Percy Thomas, the Cotton King, was also in the bar, sitting by himself at another table. "Shame about the Cotton King," Livermore said.

"Yes. He was one of our best customers." Bradley added, "I like him and we have an understanding that he doesn't gamble until he gets back on his feet. But he's always welcome for dinner and drinks."

The conversation drifted on to other things. Bradley finished his drink of soda water—the only thing he ever drank—and left the table. Thomas came over to Livermore and asked, "May I join you, Mr. Livermore?"

"Sure, call me J.L.," Livermore answered, pointing to an empty chair.

Thomas was smooth, cultured, erudite, and magnetic. He was a powerful force of nature, able to converse on any subject. They talked of music. Livermore loved classical music and light opera. It was one of the reasons he liked Russell so much. He and Moore attended many of her performances.

Thomas finally came out with the reason for the visit. "J.L., I have something on my mind, and I would like to come to the point."

"By all means," Livermore said.

"Let's be partners in the cotton market."

"I'm flattered. If I was going to be partners with anyone it would probably be you. But I'm sure you know I play a lone hand. I always have and I always will. I know you are considered a world expert on the cotton market, and I have admired your plays in the market for a long time. But I play alone. It's one of my rules."

"Listen, young man, I have never seen a trader like you. How you got out of the trap that Cutten set for you in that corn market corner was amazing. Cutten was sure he had you. And how you knew the boys in Chicago would go for that play in oats that looked like the Armours were buyers? A master play, masterful!"

"It was a stroke of luck and good timing, that's all."

"A stroke of inspiration is more like it, and planting that article in the *World*—Livermore corners the cotton market. Sheer brilliance my boy, sheer brilliance."

"I didn't plant that article. I was as surprised as anybody else was. That's why I like to play alone. I don't like explaining my moves to anyone, and I don't take the time to complain if I'm wrong. I simply don't want to have anyone with me to whom I have to explain my actions."

"I understand and respect what you're saying, J.L." He paused. "You know I got wiped out in March cotton, kicked right in the ass, so I'm coming to you at a point of weakness in my life."

"I have been down to rock bottom several times myself and always risen again. You will too." Livermore had brought along his checkbook. He reached in his pocket and took it out, along with a pen. "I would consider it an honor to help you out financially. Just name the amount."

"No sir, I thank you, but that's not my aim. I lost because I don't have your trading savvy, your feel for the market, your timing. And that is what I want, and why I want you to be my partner."

"My position remains steadfast. I trade alone."

There was a long pause as the Cotton King studied the young Jesse Livermore in his black silk tuxedo. He smiled at the young man. "No reason we can't be friends, is there?"

"None at all. In fact, let's have dinner tomorrow at the Breakers. I'll introduce you to my friends."

They had dinner the next night. They enjoyed each other's company at the Breakers bar, on the beach, and in the ballroom listening to the orchestra. Eventually they became inseparable friends. The Cotton King and the Boy Plunger made quite a pair. With the addition of Russell and Moore to the mix, the whispers would cross the room like a soft tropical breeze whenever they entered.

Thomas took special care to tutor Livermore on the cotton markets—the entire history of cotton in America, including the origin of worldwide demand for cotton and where the cotton would come from to fill that ever-increasing demand. He informed Livermore of the newly planted Egyptian cotton fields and considered whether they would work and what effect they would have on the overall world trade. It was a complete and thorough advanced university-level education in cotton, taught by the smartest, most acclaimed expert in the field.

Livermore listened, his brilliant mind absorbing every detail, but there was a problem. He did not always agree with his learned friend because he approached the subject differently. He looked only at market action—the facts of the marketplace—not the fundamentals of the cotton industry. He did not care why things happened in the market, he cared only what happened every day when the market opened. He was interested only in what the tape told him—the current facts, the price.

Livermore also believed that the market did not operate on current information—it already knew the present and was operating on the future, on factors unknown at the time even to the experts. The market was blending the future into the present. And he did not believe the market operated on a fundamentally reasonable basis. He believed it operated most often on an emotional basis; reason did *not* prevail.

Livermore wrestled with a simple thought: The Cotton King went broke. How could he go broke if he knew so much? Livermore also had gone broke; the difference was that he did not think he knew everything. He observed that the market always did what it wanted to do, not what it was expected to do. And the market did it with no immediate explanations. But Livermore still listened attentively, hoping he would learn something.

Livermore had always operated by himself in secrecy and silence. He had developed rules of trading that had cost him dearly, the Livermore laws for market trading. But no person is a robot, always able to control all emotions, innermost drives, and fears and hopes.

Despite his reservations, it was not long before Livermore was under the Cotton King's spell. Thomas believed everything that he said, and he spoke with passion about his favorite subjects. He had convinced Livermore of his honesty and sincerity when he refused Livermore's offer of money to get back on his feet.

The facts he gave about the cotton market were indisputable, and they were logical. Livermore, on the other hand, had little logic to offer on the behavior of the commodity markets. Livermore was a speculator who had been doing his job for 16 years. He did not know cotton any better than he knew steel, coal, corn, oats, wheat, or any other commodity. But he knew how the market acted and reacted.

When Livermore checked some of the facts that Thomas offered against actual market movements, he found that the King often was correct in his predictions. He began to think: "Maybe there's something I'm missing in my trading. Maybe there is a better way to analyze the movements of the markets."

In addition, Thomas had proprietary ways of obtaining information. He had thousands of spies throughout the South who reported to him on crop conditions. These facts were shown to Livermore. The conclusions seemed obvious: It was clear which way to trade the futures market, up or down, based on this secret information associated with expected supply and demand. Every good lawyer, philosopher, salesperson, or liar knows that the way to convince someone is to get them to accept the basic facts, the premises—then they will have no choice but to agree with the undeniable conclusions. Once Livermore accepted the truth of the secret facts Thomas fed him from his secret reports, he had to believe in the same conclusions as Thomas.

This episode became one of the biggest lessons in Livermore's life. It explains why he later would speak to no one, ever, about what he was doing, and why he would ask people to keep their trades and tips to themselves.

During this time he was also very friendly with Bernard Baruch, who had experienced something similar. Baruch commented, "If you know something about the stock I'm trading in, something really, really important, please keep it to yourself. Don't tell me." He added this quote to his boys' market lessons.

When Livermore first met with Thomas, he was bearish on cotton and he had a small short position. After talking to Thomas for about a month, he reversed himself. Of course, Livermore often reversed himself on his stock positions, using deductive reasoning: "If I'm wrong in thinking a stock is going up and long that stock, well then, I must be right if I go short because history has taught me that if it doesn't go up it will most probably go down."

He plunged. He went for a line of 60,000 bales. Since he had broken one of his primary rules about taking tips, playing another person's game, he then proceeded to break a few more.

Cotton moved against him, so, against his own rules, he bought more, dollar averaging down, instead of selling out and perhaps reversing his position. He also had a heavy line of wheat in which he had a profit. He continued to buy cotton until he had accumulated 150,000 bales.

Then he broke yet another rule. He was overextended on his margin, so he sold the profitable wheat position and kept the losing cotton position. Always sell the loser, keep the winner; he knew the rule, but he did not act on it. As soon as he sold the position, wheat went up 20 cents—a potential profit of $8 million and a fact that upset his judgment even more. With his judgment crumbling, his confidence soon followed. His erratic behavior increased.

He bought even more cotton, thinking it was at the bottom, but it was not. He had 440,000 bales in his account when the dawn broke and he saw what a fool he was. He sold out his position. He had lost his millions. He was left with less than $300,000 out of $3 million, a staggering loss of $2.7 million.

He had been seduced by the Cotton King and his logic, and he had paid the price.

Livermore understood that Thomas did not benefit from this personally. His magnetic personality was so persuasive that he had mentally overpowered Livermore when he explained his interpretation of the cotton market. Thomas had been the catalyst for Jesse Livermore's ruin this time.

But Livermore held no animosity for Thomas. He considered it one more lesson learned. He had engaged in another form of taking tips, a lesson apparently not learned well enough the first time. Thomas had presented what Livermore later thought of as slick tips, because they were so well thought out, well presented, and well intentioned; and Thomas did not personally benefit from his information—very, very, seductive. Of course, the price tag was basically $3 million a lesson.

Livermore had been a millionaire for less than a year. He was forced to sell the *Anita Venetian* and the Riverside Drive apartment, along with its beautiful furnishings. Why did he follow the lead of Thomas, whom everyone knew had been busted in March cotton? Was Livermore just a flash in the pan, like so many other Wall Street boy wonders who made a killing and then got killed themselves? People who patrolled the canyons of Wall Street wondered about the Boy Plunger: "What the hell happened to the Great Trader?"

Livermore now needed money to rebuild his former position, and he needed it fast. The emotions he felt over this loss caused him to make another mistake, break another rule. Illogically, he wanted the market to pay him back for his losses. So he went back into the market with a vengeance, but his trading ability was shot. He was an emotional wreck. Instead of returning to the market, he should have gone away to get his emotional balance back. But convinced he was the great trader everybody thought he was, he plunged back into the market, losing the last of his stake. He then operated on credit and went into debt to the people who backed him.

He finally tallied it up, months later. He owed his brokers and creditors well over $1 million. He had lost his $3 million and another million to boot. "Some operator," he thought to himself. "Some bad operator."

It was an emotionally crippled, despondent Livermore who stood on the track waiting for the train to Chicago. He was again down to rock bottom. He planned to go to Chicago in search of bucket shops, or to see if he could perhaps make a living from the grain pits. He was confused and disgusted with himself. The only thing he could be sure of was that he had to get out of New York City, and he did.

In Chicago, Livermore suffered a complete emotional breakdown, a deep depression. He studied his book of trades and fell deeper and deeper into the black hole. His last trades after the cotton fiasco were erratic, almost like those of some other trader. He was trading like a wild gambler, not even as well as he had as a youth. His confidence was gone; he could not recover his equilibrium. Only a year before he could easily trade a line of 100,000 shares or more at his brokerage firm, $10 million of equities. He would be lucky to deal in hundreds of shares now. He had been lured away from his own trading methods, influenced by other traders, and become so upset by his battering losses that his judgment was now just no good. Worst of all, his cocky confidence was gone, the confidence in himself that he needed to survive. He did not have the old attitude: "I made money before, and I shall make it again."

After several months of despair, Livermore finally summoned up the courage to analyze his behavior and try to isolate what he had done wrong. He finally had to confront the human side of his personality, his emotions and his feelings, which he had denied all his life. He knew the technical side of the market, but he did not know his emotions. Why had he thrown his market principles, his trading theories, his hard-earned laws to the wind? His wild behavior had crushed him financially and spiritually. Why had he done it?

He finally realized it was his vanity, his ego. That day when he had held the fate of the market in his hands, when the great J. P. Morgan had asked him to stop shorting the market, had been too much for him. This outstanding success, making more than $1 million in one day, had shaken him to his foundations. It was not that he could not deal with *failure*—he had been dealing with failure all his life—what he could not deal with was *success*.

He had now learned that success is just as hard to deal with as failure. Both can ruin a person. In Chicago he acquired a small stake, borrowed from a friendly broker who knew Livermore's power to generate commissions and wealth.

His troubles were not over.

Years later, Livermore would recount this story to Ed Bradley, late one night in the bar at the Beach Club after Bradley asked him what was the worst experience he had ever had in his early days on Wall Street: he later repeated this to his son Paul.

"A short time after I arrived in Chicago, maybe three months, I got a telegram to come back to New York. It was from a friend of mine who I will call Fred, the office manager of a large brokerage firm. I called Fred and was told, 'J.L., it will be worth your while to come to New York. There is someone here who wants to talk to you.'

"I caught the next train back to New York and had the most incredible experience of my life. One that I would regret all my life. When I arrived in the brokerage office in New York I was immediately taken by Fred to meet the owner, a prosperous and well-known man who I will call Charles.

"After the introductions, Fred excused himself. The owner of the firm got right down to business. 'Livermore, I'm very sorry to hear of the trouble you suffered in cotton. I know you listened to the Cotton King and he got you off your game. Percy means well. He could sell ice cubes to Eskimos. He's convincing. He can't help himself. He would have been a great politician. You are not the first or the only one who has followed the Cotton King down the slide. I know your trading history. I know about the panic of 1907 and how you handled yourself when Morgan sent his message to you. It was all over the Street. Well, to make a long story short I'm willing to back you.' He reached in his pocket and pulled out his checkbook and wrote a check for twenty-five thousand dollars. 'Here, take this. It will get you started.'

"I looked at the check and then back at the man who had handed it to me and asked, 'What's the catch?'

" 'The catch is I want you to do all your trading here, nowhere else,' he said.

" 'What if I lose it?' I asked.

" 'I'll give you more. You will win, and I will back you until you win,' he told me.

" 'I still don't get it,' I said.

" 'Well, I knew you wouldn't. I'm not talking to you and backing you because you are dumb. You are a secretive and silent kind of trader, my kind of trader, so nobody knows how much money you have left, or who your backers are,' he said.

" 'You want a share of the profits for the stake?' I asked.

" 'No, I'll tell you exactly what I want. I have several large investors who really carry the firm's business, and I don't want people to know what they are doing. If you are in the house they will not know who is making the trades. You are famous for trading in large lots, and for trading on the bear side, for your short selling.'

"I was suspicious. 'So I'll be the cover story for any large transactions that come out of this house, particularly on the selling side.'

" 'Yes, exactly,' he said.

" 'It would also be a way for your customers to sell large blocks of stock into the market without it being noticed,' I said.

" 'Yes, but that's not going to interfere with what you are doing, and it's perfectly legal. Let them think what they want,' he countered.

"I was desperate to get back in the action, so I banked the check and started trading. I did well. It was a strong bull market, and in three weeks the twenty-five thousand had grown to a hundred and fifty thousand. Then I made my first big mistake. I went to Charles, the owner of the brokerage house, and said, 'Here's the twenty-five thousand I borrowed from you.'

" 'Keep it Livermore, wait until you have some real money in that account, then you can pay me back,' was his answer.

"This made sense to me. He was getting good commissions. I carried on for a few more weeks. I liked Charles, my benefactor, who was ready to back me when no one else would. I felt a moral obligation to the man, a loyalty. More important, my malaise of the spirit, my depression was lifting. My spirit was returning. I was starting to be my old self again, and I was making money.

"Then I turned bearish on the market and sold ten thousand shares of the Chesapeake and Atlantic railroad short. I was startled the next day to be called into Charles's office, and he told me, 'J.L., I cancelled that ten-thousand-share sell order of yours yesterday, and went long for you.'

" 'But I feel we are entering a downward-trending market,' I said.

" 'No, my boy, the president of that railroad is my brother-in-law, married to my favorite sister. I know things that I can't tell you. The stock's going up,' he said.

"The stock fell, just as I had predicted, and my profits were wiped out. Charles came to me: 'Don't worry, J.L., I'll help you get that back. It may take a little time, but it's bound to make a recovery.'

"And just as he had told me, a little while later he returned with a fistful of credit slips that brought my balance back to a credit. He told me, 'By the way, I've just bought you ten thousand shares of Southern Atlantic, and put them into your account.'

" 'Isn't that another railroad controlled by your brother-in-law?' I asked.

" 'Yes it is, with great prospects for growth,' he answered.

"The Southern Atlantic shares fell, and I was sold out in the next few days, another loss. Again I heard, 'Don't worry, J.L., everything is going to be all right.'

"I made enough to stay alive, but not to pay off my substantial prior indebtedness of over a million dollars.

"I finally figured out what was going on. My benefactor, Charles, the owner of the brokerage house, was liquidating his brother-in-law's estate. His brother-in-law was one of the wealthiest men in America. It was common knowledge that the brother-in-law was sick, incurable, and now after years of sickness, close to death.

"I decided to talk to Fred, the man who had sent me the telegram in Chicago, the office manager of the firm. I had a drink with him one night and told him what I had figured out. I said, 'I believe I've been used as a foil, a red herring, a cover story by Charles to liquidate his brother-in-law's estate. So no one on the Street would know or suspect what was going on while this big estate was liquidated and there would be no deep loss in the price of the estate stocks, particularly railroad stocks.'

"The office manager looked at me and said, 'Yes, I guess that's true, and now that the estate is practically in cash I can tell you about it.'

" 'So the money I received and the losses I incurred in my account were chicken feed compared to what we are dealing with here?' I asked.

" 'Yes,' he said.

" 'So I'm right. I was the firm's decoy, the patsy, that kept everybody on the Street from triggering to what was really going on,' I said.

" 'That was a small part of it,' he said.

" 'What do you mean a small part, what else could it have been?' I asked.

" 'The boss knew we would be entering a bear market, sooner or later. He knew you were a great trader. He saw what you did here, in the first three weeks, before he started trading your account for you. Yes, it was true it was good for him to have you here as a smoke screen for what was really going on. That part is true, but the main reason was he wanted you under the roof here while he was liquidating,' he explained to me.

" 'What do you mean? I still don't understand,' I said.

" 'Listen, J.L., when you were really back on your feet—and you would be, sooner or later—nobody doubted that you would be swinging a line of at least two or three hundred thousand shares. You would have picked up on the fact that there was a huge amount of stock being distributed in those railroad stocks that came from Charles's brother-in-law's estate. You would have triggered to it and raided the hell out of those stocks, driving the stocks down, and down, with one of those classic bear raids you're famous for, and Charles knew it,' he said.

"I was flabbergasted. Because I had lost my confidence, I was not looking for deeper motivations, darker motivations, more intelligent motivations, like I would have normally. I had only seen the surface behavior, not what was behind it. I had never considered the fact that by keeping me chained up in a cage I would not be a factor in upsetting one of the largest stock distributions in history. Charles's sister's estate, when the trading was over, was valued at over two hundred and fifty million dollars.

"I was shaken. I had acted out of gratitude to a man I thought was backing me, helping me, and once again, like with the Cotton King, I had unwittingly done another man's bidding. A smart man, a brilliant man, a man who could find the Achilles' heel of people and could use that weakness to his own benefit.

"What a shock! My benefactor had more confidence in my trading ability than I had in myself!

"But I was not angry with Charles. He had operated for reasons of his own. His sister was the ultimate beneficiary of the estate, and he felt obliged to get the most money for her. I was just a pawn in a more devious man's game. What really disturbed and upset me was that I had missed the action in a good market climate where I could have made up all my losses. Instead, I was still deeply in debt. I had been used, but I had let myself be used by not following one of my own rules—trade alone, and only for my own account.

"I cleared out my desk that night and then walked into Charles's office and said, in my calmest voice, 'I will no longer be trading in this office.'

"Charles looked me in the eye and nodded, no expression on his face. He knew that I had figured out his game. As I turned and headed for the door, Charles said 'We'll miss you around here, J.L.'

" 'I'll bet you will, Charles. I'll bet you will,' I said, closing the door behind me.

"First Percy, the Cotton King, and then Charles, my alleged benefactor. Was I ever going to learn my lesson?"

Livermore finished his old-fashioned and ordered another one. He looked Ed Bradley, one of the most famous gamblers who ever lived, in the eye and smiled. "It's your turn, Ed. You heard my sad story. Tell me one of yours."

Both of these men were famous for their silent and secret lives, but each felt easy with the other.

"All right, J.L., I'll tell you one of mine.

"You know that I love horses, J.L. They are my real passion. I don't know why. I fell in love with horses when I went out west to cure a mild case of tuberculosis. I got involved with those wild and wooly characters that roamed the West in those days and became a scout for the U.S. Army. I used to bet heavily on the Indian pony races whenever I could find them, and later I actually got involved in owning racetracks in New Orleans and Florida. But it was the horses I loved. In fact, I prefer the company of horses to people, present company excluded, J.L. I get my biggest thrill from my farm in Kentucky: watching the colts being born and seeing how they live out their bloodlines.

"One of my early great Kentucky Derby contenders was Blue Larkspur. You know I'm superstitious, J.L., I guess all gamblers are. All my horses' names begin with a B because of my first great horse—Bad News, because bad news travels fast! Anyway, Blue Larkspur had won six of his seven races as a two-year-old and was the even-money favorite for the derby. I bet a hundred and twenty-five thousand on him to win. Then, before the race, the rains came down at Churchill Downs. It poured for hours. I talked to the trainer, and we decided to change Blue Larkspur into mud shoes.

"The race began. The gate slammed open, and Blue Larkspur lost his footing right from the get-go. He slip-slid all over that track, almost fell, coulda broke his leg. He finally got his footing back and finished fourth out of twenty-one in the field.

"After the race, I went down to look at the horse and found that his shoes had not been changed. The blacksmith had something against the trainer, something about a woman they shared. Said he was gonna change 'em to mud shoes when the trainer told him, but instead he skipped right out the back door of Churchill Downs. Could have killed Blue Larkspur.

"You just never know what the hell is going on in people's heads!"

Livermore pondered the story Bradley had told him. He finally asked the old Indian Scout, "Ed, what happened to the black-smith?"

"Now J.L., there's a limit to what I'm willing to tell, and that's a story that nobody's ever gonna hear."

By 1910, Livermore was back in New York with a very small stake. The power had left the long-running bull market, and there was a general apathy on the Street. The action stagnated as the market wandered in a sideways pattern, hard to read.

Livermore went from brokerage house to brokerage house over the next four years. He was able to get lines of credit in various houses, but he continued to trade badly. Still angry and resentful, he was not able to trade with a clear mind, and he suffered badly from his ever-present depression. He simply could not get his emotional balance back.

He also wore the oppressive cloak of a person in debt. He was at heart a New Englander. He had been taught as a boy: "Neither a borrower nor a lender be." He hated being in debt. The guilt lay heavily on his shoulders. He believed people should pay off their debts, and he was in deep debt to his friends—friends he saw every day on the Street. Suicide even began to cross his mind as he sank deeper into a seemingly bottomless depression.

He finally realized that he could give up and end it all, or he could analyze his problem. He chose the latter.

The problem, as far as he could tell, was simply money—or the lack thereof.

Livermore had built up a multimillion-dollar fortune from the few dollars his mother had given him. What was keeping him from doing it again? Charles had thought Livermore could do it—that was why he had corralled Livermore while he disposed of his brother-in-law's fortune. Livermore concluded that he was not the trader he once had been. His mind was not functioning properly, could not function properly with all these constant dark thoughts of debt and failure.

It was not the market's fault. No matter what the market was doing, he knew there were always situations to be found where money could be made. It was the nature of the market never to be still. There were always opportunities.

So what was his real problem? Why was his judgment bad? He was depressed all the time. Why? He was depressed because he owed money, mostly to his friends. He knew he could never trade well again unless he lifted the black oppressive mantle of debt off his shoulders.

He decided to go bankrupt. He had to free his mind of the black thoughts that followed debt. He had to be clear minded to trade and get back in business. He needed a new start.

He paid visits to each of his creditors before he went to see his lawyer to file for bankruptcy. He promised to pay them back.

They smiled and shook his hand. "We know you'll make it square with us, J.L.," they said to him. They, like Charles, had more confidence in him than he had in himself. "We have no doubt you will be back on your feet again. You're not the first, nor will you be the last, to be leveled by Wall Street. You get yourself together. We'll be waiting for you to trade again out of our office."

"I'll pay you back what I owe you, every cent."

"We know you will."

"Yes sir, I will."

"All right, now there is one thing," many of them told him.

"What's that?" Livermore asked.

"We will not be listing our debt in your bankruptcy. No sense, Jesse, in making public what's just between us, is there?"

With the exception of a few brokerage firms, most of his creditors refused to file their debtor claims with the bankruptcy court. It was still a horrific experience for Livermore. It was 1914, and the Great War had just begun in Europe. The stock market was closed from July 31 to December 15, 1914. Livermore was broke and living in a second-rate hotel, the Bretton Hall at Broadway and Eighty-sixth Street.

He visited his lawyer, who filed his bankruptcy petition. Ashamed, he kept to himself and waited. On February 18, 1915, he read a summary of the last five years of his life in the *New York Times:*

> Jesse L. Livermore, whose spectacular rise to fortune during the panic of 1907, and his equally startling losses in cotton a few months later, made him one of the well-known characters in Wall Street. Yesterday he filed a voluntary petition for bankruptcy in the Federal District Court. He gave Bretton Hall, Broadway and Eighty-sixth Street, as his residence, and said he owed $102,474. The value of his assets were unknown.
>
> Mr. Livermore is only 38 years old, and from the age of 16 he has been a speculator. His chance came in 1906, when he came to the conclusion that the market was on the down grade. He began to sell short in Union Pacific, Reading, Copper and Smelters, and in 1907 when the crest came he covered his short contracts and made a comfortable fortune.
>
> In the following August he was attracted by the high price of cotton in Liverpool and scented another slump. He made another big killing and by 1908 was credited with being worth from $2,000,000 to $3,000,000.
>
> In August 1908, however, the luck began to turn against him. He was caught on the long side with 600,000 bales of October cotton, and as the price broke 67 points, he was supposed to have lost his fortune.

Livermore folded the newspaper, laid it on his dresser, rose from his threadbare chair, and entered the small bathroom. He took his time and dressed in his usual dapper manner. He walked down to Wall Street, one of the longest walks of his life. He entered the brokerage offices of Charles, his old benefactor, whom he had not seen or spoken to in four years.

He had removed the cloak of debt; now he had to find out if he could still trade. For Livermore there was only one way to determine if he had lost his touch—he had to lay his money on the line and let the tape tell him if he was right or not. His chances were running out, and he knew it.

chapter six

Back on His Game

There's a fine line between eccentrics and geniuses. If you're a little ahead of your time you're an eccentric, and if you're a little too late, you're a failure, but if you hit it right on the head, you're a genius.   Thomas J. Watson Jr., founder of IBM

LIVERMORE TOOK A FINAL DEEP BREATH AND WALKED into the offices of his former benefactor. He was received immediately and was seated facing Charles. The *New York Times* lay on Charles's desk; neither of them spoke of its contents.

"I need a line," Livermore said, without any preamble.

Charles sat in silence, studying Livermore, keeping his thoughts and emotions to himself. Both of them knew there was no need to talk of the past.

"How much?" Charles asked.

"You decide."

Charles stood and walked to his office window. It was 1915, with a tricky wartime stock market in which a person could make a fortune or lose one in a few minutes of speculation.

"All right, J.L., I'll give you a line of five hundred shares. I'll authorize it today, to be put in your account. We kept your account open, you know."

"You thought I'd be back?"

"Maybe."

"Thank you," Livermore said. The two shook hands, and Livermore walked out of the office. It was a small line for a trader like Livermore, but there was no restriction on the price of the shares. With a $150 stock, he could put out a line of $75,000. It was a start.

Now he had to decide what to do. He had only limited capital. He could afford no losses. He was determined to stick to his old trading rules, but it would be difficult to put out probes and buy small positions to test his judgment. He had no room for mistakes; this might be his last chance. His first trade must be profitable, yet he could not let the pressure of his limited capital force him into bad decisions. He concluded that the market was in a strong upward trend, so he would trade on the upside, buy long. He also knew that stocks tended to react positively when they crossed par at 100, 200, or 300.

His failings, his frailties, were clearer to him; his limitations were known, but they must not upset his confidence. He was anxious to trade in this active wartime market. For this reason, he did not go back to Charles's brokerage firm. Instead, for six long weeks, broke and living on a tiny amount of money, he studied the tape, analyzing every trade as it crossed through the ticker. He knew that if he went to the offices of his benefactor, where he had credit, he might make a play and execute a trade in the heat of the action. He did not want to do this. He wanted everything to be in his favor for this first key trade, so he stayed out of temptation's way, studying the tape. He knew now that his biggest enemy was his own emotions. Every trader had to face this sooner or later.

He needed every factor in his favor.

He finally chose Bethlehem Steel, an obvious choice in wartime years, and a choice known to the trading public. Livermore sat and watched the stock climb to 98, only 2 points from par—100—and he felt that if the stock passed through 100, it would skyrocket. He ran over to the brokerage house and bought 500 shares of Bethlehem Steel at $98. When the stock hit $114, he bought a second 500 shares on margin, giving him 1,000 shares on the long side.

The next day the stock hit $145. Livermore closed out his Bethlehem Steel trade a few days later with over $50,000 of profit. This meant he could exercise a line of $500,000, on 10 percent margin. He was back in the game.

In the aftermath of his bankruptcy, he had no creditors to think about, and now he had a decent line to trade with. His confidence began to return. He could start to trade in his old manner, and he did so with good success for the rest of the year. Putting together a string of profitable trades, he brought his equity up close to $500,000.

His only setback was the sinking of the *Lusitania* on May 7, 1915. Everyone believed the United States would enter the Great War. The market plummeted on the news, and Livermore suffered badly. He covered his positions quickly and finished out 1915 with only $150,000 in equity in his account—not bad, considering. He was definitely back in business, but more important, he had found his trading form. He was now following his own rules and working hard to avoid his emotional flaws.

His ex-wife Nettie appeared in his life again after he started to recover from his bankruptcy. He had seen very little of her since their separation. He gave her a stipend of $1,000 a week to cover her expenses, "To make up for the lean years," he told her. He also set her up with a good-sized home on Long Island and gave her money to fill it with furniture and a car for the garage.

The United States did not enter the war after the sinking of the *Lusitania,* as so many had predicted. The American people were strong isolationists, who wanted nothing to do with a foreign war. It did not take long for the market to recover. Livermore was now trading in a full wartime economy bull market.

The United States was operating at full industrial capacity, shipping out all the products the war-torn world needed, while gold was being shipped to the United States by foreign nations to pay for goods. Things were booming. All through 1916 Livermore remained bullish, actively trading. But like bear markets, bull markets do not last forever, and Livermore started fishing for the top.

He kept his eyes on the market leaders, as he had done in 1906 and 1907, because he knew that when those leaders started to top out and roll over, that would be the first signal to start preparing for a bear market. He also knew that markets did not suddenly

change precipitously in either direction. They gave plenty of signals, clues, if he could read them objectively.

He compared market directions to advancing opposed armies—
the bull army and the bear army. When the leading divisions of the
army, in this case the leading stocks, started to get beaten down
and turned around, that was the time to light the caution lamp.
When they started to roll over and retreat, that was the time to
change the strategy, and start trading in the opposite direction. He
believed that the market leaders of the 1916 bull market gave
strong, if subtle, clues.

The market was like a smooth card player. It did not tip its hand
for everyone to see. Livermore had to be aware, astute, alert, ready
to read the signs, because on an early call for a major market turn
in trend, he would be going against public opinion—public opinion that would still be seduced by the strong momentum of the
existing market. Livermore's experience had taught him to stand
apart from the crowd at these major turning points in the market,
heading in the opposite direction. This had never bothered him,
because it was at these times that he made his greatest money.

He reverted to his time-tested technique of sending out probes,
buying small positions to see if he was correct in his assessment of
the market. Slowly he took positions in 12 stocks, including the
market leaders Steel, Baldwin, American Can, General Motors,
Chrysler, and Anaconda Copper. He sold short a total of 60,000
shares, which was a reasonably modest position for him by this
time. He waited, and the tape dropped about four points across the
board. He knew he was right, doubled his position to 120,000
shares, and waited.

It was at this time that a scandalous leak came out of Washington, claiming that President Woodrow Wilson had issued a peace
offering to Germany and the Allies to end the war. The market

tumbled on the good news, because peace in Europe would kill the healthy wartime economy of supplying foreign nations. Livermore had a steadfast rule that if something serendipitous, an unplanned windfall, should occur, he must capitalize on it and not be greedy—accept his good fortune and close out his position. Livermore also had 120,000 shares of stock to sell, which was a hefty position to liquidate in the 1916 market.

The leak occurred on the morning of December 20, 1916. Livermore was back in Palm Beach; having recouped his fortune, he could afford to vacation in his favorite spot again. He had wandered into the offices of Finlay, Barrel and Company. He had no account with this broker. He was just watching the tape and reading the newspapers when he was shown a private telegram from the home office of Finlay, Barrel.

"Look at this telegram, Mr. Livermore," the office manager said.

"Wilson to offer peace to warring parties, later today," Livermore read out loud. The wire came from a Washington reporter named W. W. Price, whom Livermore had heard about. "You think this is on the level?" Livermore asked the clerk.

"I think so, yes sir," the office manager said.

Livermore thanked the manager, went to one of his own Palm Beach brokers, the E. F. Hutton office, and asked if they had heard anything about the news of a peace offering from President Wilson. They said no. He called Ed Hutton in New York. Hutton said he had not heard anything. Livermore watched the market weaken in front of his eyes. He ordered lunch sent in and set to watching the market.

A little after 1 P.M., E. F. Hutton's telegraph department sent an urgent flash telegram to all of the company's officers. It said the same thing as the wire that Livermore had already read in the Finlay, Barrel offices earlier that morning. Livermore checked the major wire services, but there was no news about President Wilson offering a plan for peace to Germany.

But the *rumor* of peace in Europe had been born, and the market started to sag as people started to unload before the news became known to the public. Then it looked as if the rumor was going to be confirmed, and the market really started to plummet—soon the news of possible peace was on everyone's lips. Bids were pulled, and prices sank.

Bernard Baruch, a friend of Livermore's, was heavily involved in the action. He had been short, like Livermore, and he was pounding away on the short side, selling into any situation that still looked good to him. But Livermore was looking to cover his short position of 120,000 shares, and so at 2 P.M. he became a buyer of stock. He had covered all his shorts by 3 P.M. and the close of business.

Baruch had made a substantial profit recently—over $3 million—with the bulk of it coming during this sudden sell-off following the rumors out of Washington.

A congressional committee was formed to investigate the leak. Baruch admitted to the committee that he had used the leak to trade war stocks, but maintained that he had made a profit of only $465,000.

Livermore, on the other hand, explained to the committee that he was often short the market and that he had established his 120,000-share position seven weeks before the Wilson peace proposal because he felt that the market had topped out.

He was subpoenaed on February 1. The next day the *New York Times* quoted him. "How could I have known that far back that President Wilson was going to make a peace offering to Germany to end the war? I doubt if the president himself knew seven weeks ago that he was going to offer a proposal of peace."

As a result of this famous incident, the New York Stock Exchange changed its rules and banned traders from acting on

news leaks, an idea which, though laudable, was completely unen-
forceable.

It was at this crucial juncture that something strange again happened to Livermore. He told both his sons the story, years later,
one night at dinner:

"I was seeing some friends off at Grand Central Station. I
walked with them to my private railway car, which I was loaning
to them, to take them down to Palm Beach. The porter walked
beside us pushing the trolley with their luggage. When we got to
the car, my friend reached over to pick up his wife's jewelry case
from the trolley, and his hat fell off and rolled under the car. The
porter reached under the car to pick up the Stetson homburg from
the tracks, and he handed it to me to give to my friend. I looked
down at the upturned hat. In the hatband there were initials in
gold, 'W.A.R.,' for Warren Augustus Reed, my friend's initials.

"Well, that was a message to me, boys, a sign, and I raced back
to the office and started selling in earnest. I already was short the
market, but now there was no question in my mind, war was coming to the United States."

Four months later, on April 6, 1917, the United States joined
the Allies in the great European war. The people of the United
States had initially been against entering directly into a European
war, but they had agreed to supply the Allies with war goods and
armaments. However, after a series of incidents involving the German policy of unrestricted submarine warfare and the sinking of
U.S. ships, the United States finally entered the fray and declared
war on Germany.

Near that time in early 1917, Livermore made one of his proudest
walks down Wall Street. He departed from his new offices at 111
Broadway, stopped at each of his creditors, and wrote checks paying off all his bankruptcy debts in full.

"Let me add some interest to the amount I owe you," Livermore offered, but each creditor refused. They simply accepted the checks, smiled, shook his hand, and wished him luck for the future. It was another act that added to his legend on Wall Street.

Livermore was 40 years of age. He decided to make a few changes in his life. He established a $500,000 trust fund for himself, which would spin off an income of $30,000 a year. He would never be poor again.

Livermore was also about to fall in love.

Flo Ziegfeld was a close friend of Livermore's. Ziegfeld was the creator of the *Ziegfeld Follies,* featuring beautiful women, beautiful sets, and beautiful music. The legendary staging of scantily clad women carrying exotic fans, parading around magnificent sets, up and down elaborate staircases, was an extravagant spectacle. It was the hottest show on Broadway.

One day Ziegfeld called Livermore. "J.L., I have someone you just have to meet. A little brunette that lights up any room she's in. You need to meet her, J.L., she'll light up your boring life. It must get boring making all that money. You know, all work and . . ."

"Too much play makes a man poor."

"We only pass through these earthly portals one time, J.L. We are not here for a long time, so it should be a good time."

"I'm not arguing, Flo."

"Well, I'm having a little soiree at my apartment tonight. She'll be there. Will you, J.L.?"

"Yes, Flo, I'll be there."

That night, Livermore walked into Ziegfeld's magnificent penthouse apartment in Manhattan and promptly fell in love with Dorothy Wendt. She was small, a brunette, with the most gorgeous hazel-green eyes he had ever seen—they were piercing and laughing at the same time. She sat with half a dozen people around her, entertaining them all with her lively chatter. Ziegfeld marched through the little crowd and introduced Livermore to her.

Livermore was hooked. He went to all her shows, wined her and dined her all over New York. They fell in love, the dashing financier and the beguiling, beautiful showgirl, a storybook romance.

Livermore had finally found someone whom he was desperate to marry. But he remained married to Nettie, and now he had to get a divorce. He thought that because he had given her a $1,000-a-month stipend and bought her a house and a car, she would accommodate him in his request for a divorce. He was wrong. The divorce quickly became acrimonious. Livermore was in the chips again, and Nettie knew it. She also knew he was in love with another woman. She struck in the courts.

The one thing Livermore did not want to lose in the divorce was his black Rolls-Royce, which he had kept for himself all these years. But he had made the mistake of parking the car in her garage, and she was not giving it up. "It's mine" was her simple explanation when he asked for it.

Livermore went to W. Travers Jerome, the famous former district attorney for New York County. Jerome was a private investigator who cut an impressive figure, solidly built, full of self-confidence, and sporting a slick handlebar moustache. He was famous for his well-chronicled prosecution of one of the most infamous murderers of the twentieth century—Harry K. Thaw—for the murder of the famous New York architect Stanford White.

Thaw, heir to a vast Pittsburgh rail and coal fortune, shot White, an architect and New York society darling, in the Roof Theater of Madison Square Garden—a building White had designed—in plain view of hundreds of people. Thaw's wife, showgirl Evelyn

Nesbit, had told her husband that White, her former lover, had once raped her.

The shooting occurred on the evening of June 25, 1906, during the presentation of the musical *Mamzelle Champagne*. When the cast started singing "I Could Love a Million Girls," which Nesbit described as a "putrid number," Thaw rose and walked over to White's table. He took a pistol from his belt and fired three shots into White's head. He then held the smoking pistol in the air to signal that he was done. He calmly walked back to his own table and sat down. He was immediately arrested and disarmed by a fireman on duty in the Garden.

Lying dead, slumped on his table, head in a pool of blood, face blackened by powder burns, shot into oblivion, was America's most famous architect.

The Thaw trial became the first "trial of the century" involving the rich and decadent, with a courtroom drama that elicited wild, frenzied press coverage. With its exposure of wealth and incredible indulgence, topped off with intimate sexual details, this trial began the practice of mass media coverage of celebrity indiscretions. White's "red velvet swing," on which he liked to have women wearing no undergarments sit and swing in front of him so he could look underneath their dresses, was just one of the sexual details exposed.

Nesbit told the court that White had often beaten her with a whip and had originally met her in his apartment, where he immediately drugged her with champagne and ravished her. She admitted she had sat naked in White's famous red velvet swing while he pushed her so high that her toes touched a Japanese parasol attached to the ceiling. She never properly explained why she returned to White, her former lover, so often after she had become involved with Thaw.

The trial also marked the beginning of great defenses by great lawyers. Delphin Delmas, Thaw's lawyer, offered the "Dementia Americana" defense, which he defined as an affliction of the American male whose wife's purity has been violated.

There were two trials, and Thaw was eventually found innocent by reason of insanity. Thaw spent the rest of his life in and out of insane asylums.

Nesbit lived the rest of her life continually retelling the story of that famous night. She died at the age of 82. Her last words: "Stanny White was killed in 1906, but my fate was worse. I lived."

Livermore visited Jerome, gave him a duplicate set of keys and his power of attorney, and instructed him to go out to Long Island and repossess the Rolls when Nettie was not around.

On September 7, 1917, Nettie Livermore had the famous lawyer Jerome arrested in Oyster Bay, Long Island. The police actually put Jerome in the lockup. His partner Isidore Kresel quickly bailed him out on a $2,000 bond. Putting Jerome in jail was a mistake. He was angry. He called Livermore, and they decided to tail Nettie.

A few weeks later, on September 22, there was a circus atmosphere at the courthouse for the initial hearing on the case. Justice of the Peace Allison Lowndes immediately began the proceedings. "Is Mrs. Livermore in court with us?" she asked.

"I'm afraid Mrs. Livermore is ill, your honor," her attorneys, Frank Acer and Frank Davis, offered. "We would request an adjournment to a later date."

"Your honor, I beg to differ," Jerome said, rising. "I know for a fact that Mrs. Livermore was in New York last night and returned to her home in Long Island at one o'clock this morning. There's nothing really wrong with her."

"I want Mrs. Livermore here, and quick, or I'll throw out this case," the judge said. This was reported in the *New York Times* the next day.

Ten minutes later Nettie Livermore walked into court with an entourage of her sister, her father, and two friends. The judge asked how Jerome had obtained the car, and she was told that Travers had a key to the garage and to the car.

Mrs. Livermore took the stand next.

"What makes you think the car belongs to you, Mrs. Livermore?" the judge asked.

"Mr. Livermore told me when he bought it. He said, 'Chick, this car belongs to you.' "

"How long have you been married to Mr. Livermore?"

"Eighteen years, but we have been separated for a long time."

"Have you paid for any of the upkeep of the car?" the judge asked.

"No."

"Is the bill of sale or the ownership in your name?"

"No."

"Did you know that Mr. Jerome had the power of attorney from your ex-husband to seize the car?"

"Yes."

"Prior to your divorce, how much were you receiving as an allowance for living?"

"A thousand dollars a week, Your Honor."

"Mrs. Livermore, Officer Bowker says he values the car at twenty-five thousand dollars. Are you aware of that, and do you agree?"

"Yes, Your Honor."

"But this bill of sale to Mr. Livermore says ten thousand dollars. Are you aware of that also?"

"Yes, Your Honor."

"It seems you're aware of everything, Mrs. Livermore. I see no merit in your case so I'm dismissing it." The judge's gavel fell and the case was dismissed.

In an article in the *New York Times* on September 23, Jerome said: "The officer must have described the wrong car. Perhaps the twenty-five-thousand-dollar Rolls-Royce he had in mind is the model they make out of solid gold. And I don't think Mr. Livermore would ever say 'Chick, this car belongs to you,' not the Jesse Livermore I know." The press reporters loved Jerome and he loved them, and they were already fascinated by the secretive Wall Street legend, Livermore.

Things were going well for Livermore, and he showed his love for Dorothy Wendt by purchasing a large emerald stone set in a platinum ring on September 24, 1917. The reported price of the ring was $120,000. It was purchased in Palm Beach. This was to be the beginning of a massive collection of jewelry he would buy Dorothy over the years to come.

The next day, Livermore also purchased a very large speedboat, which he called the "sub catcher." The boat was based in Palm Beach and Key West.

Livermore was also receiving wide acclaim. He was grouped together with Bernard Baruch as one of the "new breed" of stock market speculators. The *New York Times* ran an editorial on this subject on May 13, 1917. The headline read: "Exit the Swashbuckling Trader of Wall Street: Present Day Speculator in Stocks Is More of a Student and Economist Than the Sensational Manipulator of Other Years."

They speculate in Wall Street these days in a way different from the methods employed in the free and easy times of John W. Gates, and his coterie of wealthy plungers. "Bet a

Million" Gates was a leader who had a blind following in the stock market, convinced that he would make them all rich. There is no leader anymore. James R. Keene was the last of this class of great operators whose bull-like crushing tactics, supported by much money, swung the market up or down.

No one could charge Bernard M. Baruch with making a display of his stock market efforts. Before the congressional committee which investigated the "leak" of last December, Baruch referred to himself as an investor and speculator in the same manner as any other man would have spoken of his grocery business. He informed the committee, with no more enthusiasm than he might have shown in discussing the weather, that he made $467,000 on the short side of stocks in the month of December.

His reasons for selling stocks when he did, illustrated the new epoch in speculation. He believed merely that prices were too high. Study of the speculative situation persuaded him that the market was about ready for a break.

Jesse Livermore is another operator whose work attracts little attention while he is about it. In a way, Livermore is a relic of the old days, without any of the trimmings. His business is his own affair, and he has never been known to make efforts to influence the market by whispering into the ears of his friends. He harkens back to the past only in the sizes of his purchases and his short selling.

Livermore, the story goes, began selling stocks short last November, a month before prices started to move off. Practically every other trader was buying enthusiastically while he was selling short. He sensed the market tendency to head lower and stood unmoved amid a shower of optimistic references. When the break finally came, he is said to have been short of stocks between 50,000 and 60,000 shares, on which a profit running into the hundreds of thousand dollars accrued.

Baruch and Livermore stand forth as examples of bona fide speculators of the largest caliber. The impression they made on the market of last year however, was only a fraction of the influence which came from a source which is difficult to characterize either as speculative or investment.

A combination of the two might be ascribed to dealings in the war market by the Du Pont group of gun-powder-making-millionaires and W. C. Durant of the General Motors Company. Possessed of great and steadily growing incomes these men put their money to work to great advantage. "Buy and hold stocks for an extraordinary rise."

About the middle of 1915 Wall Street heard that the Du Ponts were putting much of their inflowing wealth into stock of the Baldwin Locomotive Company, the General Motors Company, and the other concerns whose shares, then relatively low, rose to unusual heights in the later frenzy of war speculation. These rumors did not meet with denial, and afterward came reports that great profits had been taken around top levels. Baldwin rose from 26 that year to 154, and General Motors advanced from 82 to 558, going in 1916 to well above 700.

Durant, president of General Motors, has the reputation among his friends of possessing imagination which could make him a leading figure in speculation if he desired to be one. But he has never appeared in the limelight of stock market affairs, although it is known that he has seen tremendous profits accrue on stocks bought at low figures. He buys long before the public sees the speculative merit of the stocks involved. He is said to possess supreme confidence in his own judgment; when he decides to accumulate stocks he buys them and no changes in market conditions of a temporary sort disturb him.

It is said Durant seldom sells what he buys because his judgment tells him that they are good. This is investment buying.

Livermore never commented on what other people said in the newspaper if he could help it, no matter what the press published. He stayed silent on this issue, too. Livermore the mystery man only hopped up the press more.

For the rest of 1917, Livermore did well, except for a lone coffee trade.

Livermore saw the prices of all commodities rising as the United States crept closer and closer to what he believed was inevitable—U.S. involvement in the war roaring in Europe. When the United States finally joined the war, commodities rose 100 to 300 percent in price. The only commodity that did not rise was coffee, so Livermore investigated. The European markets had closed, and now all coffee was being shipped to the United States. The price of coffee was actually below its prewar level. Livermore felt that the efficient German submarine force would continue to sink freighters, which would eventually stop the flow of coffee into the United States. As a result, prices would rise. It seemed simple enough.

Livermore started buying coffee in the winter of 1917. Nine months later, the price was flat, and he closed out his options at a big loss. He went back into the market, where he sent out more probes, buying more futures. He still believed he was right. This time he was proven right—the price rose. He increased his positions as the price rose steadily. He was already counting his extra paper millions when he got a big surprise.

The people who were on the other side of the coffee market, the short sellers, knew they would take a huge hit when they had to settle up because of the high price. They went to Washington, and convinced those in power that the coffee drinkers of America should be protected.

They told the wartime Price Fixing Committee that Livermore had cornered the entire coffee market and was about to take the prices sky-high. The committee immediately fixed on a maximum price and established a limited time to close out all positions in the commodity futures market.

The committee also closed the coffee exchange. Livermore did what he was forced to do. He sold out his positions. His millions in profits drained away like a cup of coffee disappearing down a thirsty gullet. The Livermore lesson was explained in the press: "America needs its cheap caffeine fix and the government agrees!"

But this taught Livermore another valuable lesson: Once again he was right, but he did not profit from it. So now he added the unexpectable to his list of stock market pitfalls. There was nothing he could do under these conditions but lick his wounds and carry on. There were some things that he could not predict, and therefore he could not guard against them. He could only react.

Livermore also was convinced that there was no one powerful enough to control or fix a market for long. If the market was driven to excess in either direction, it would always eventually return to its true value.

If a stock was raided, the stock would go only so low before the insiders, who knew its true value, stepped in to buy, joined by astute investors, who also knew a bargain when they saw one. In a free market, the proper price would always eventually be restored.

Livermore also came up with a method of watching stocks that had broken badly on the downside: He watched for the *rebound*. When the stock reached its ultimate decline—its nadir—it would rebound strongly, swiftly, and head back up to prior levels, if in fact the break had truly just been a raid and there was nothing inherently wrong with the stock. Conversely, if the stock just languished after the break in price, wallowing along in a tight sideways channel, this was a signal that there might be an inherent weakness in the stock. It would probably keep following the line of least resistance and go down some more. Livermore watched for the deciding move in the trend before he made his own move.

Livermore's other stock and commodity trades in 1917 were very successful. Since he was considered the mightiest bear on Wall Street, he often got blamed for price breaks in stocks that looked like bear raids. Because of these price drops, he was also accused of being unpatriotic, regardless of whether he was guilty. Mostly, Livermore concluded, it was an easy way to explain away the erratic movement of a wartime stock market.

In October 1917, Livermore was finally legally divorced from Nettie in Reno, Nevada. How did he do it? He simply gave her what she wanted. He gave her his $500,000 personal trust fund and the house he had purchased in Long Island for her, with all its furnishings. He was not worried. He still had millions in his trading account. He was also clear of over $1 million in debt that he had repaid, even though he had had no legal responsibility to do so. He was finally free and clear of all encumbrances, and free to trade on his own terms. Free to enjoy life again.

Livermore did not care about the money for Nettie. He let it all go with no angry feelings toward her, he was so sure of his ability to make more money again. He kept his railway car, his Rolls, and his yacht. He believed that as long as he had a stake, he would simply eventually make up in the market whatever he had given to her.

On December 2, 1918, Livermore married Dorothy Wendt in the St. Regis Hotel. Magistrate Peter B. Barlow performed the brief ceremony. She was 18, he was 41. She looked beautiful in her wedding dress. He stood tall and straight, his blond hair slicked back, his black tails fashioned perfectly from the finest cloth, a smile on his face, as he slipped the wedding band on her finger.

Later, in the bridal suite, Dorothy read aloud the inscription inside her wedding band: "Dotsie, for ever and ever, J.L." Years later, it still made her blush and tingle with excitement.

This was a major moment for Livermore. He was happy. This time—unlike 1907, when he had everything going for him only to lose it—he would try to deal properly with his success. He vowed that his hubris, conceit, and vanity would be kept under control. He would not lose his head. He had already plunged into those dark chasms of depression and grief. He would strictly follow his hard-earned rules, his laws for trading the market. He would not be careless and lose his fortune this time.

Livermore loved Dorothy. He was ready to settle down and start a family, a family he could be proud of. But he was to find out that, as in his adventure in the coffee market, in life there is the unexpected and then there is the unexpectable. He would come face to face with the unexpectable years later, when Dotsie would shoot their son.

chapter seven

Perfecting His Market Theory

He seldom lives frugally who lives by chance.
Samuel Johnson, *Life of Dryden*

LIVERMORE WANTED TO SUPPLY HIS YOUNG BRIDE Dorothy with everything a woman could desire. The day after they were married, Livermore showed Dorothy their new home, a beautifully furnished townhouse at 8 West Seventy-sixth Street. It was filled with the best of the best: beautiful rugs from Persia, the finest Wedgwood dishes, and glistening crystal glasses. The works of great artists hung on every wall. The bedrooms were sumptuous—Egyptian cotton sheets, pillows filled with pure goose down and covered in silk cases, and feather-filled duvets. The bathrooms all had new fixtures and fittings, including oversized tubs that still looked small in the huge space.

Dorothy was from a well-to-do background, but this overwhelmed her. This was the pure luxury reserved for the very few. She ran from one room to the next, each one better than the last. Livermore stood proudly in the expansive living room, waiting for her to complete her inspection. It was extravagant, but he could easily afford this home.

They celebrated with vintage champagne chilled in a silver Tiffany ice bucket, sipped from Waterford crystal glasses. There was nothing too good for his new love, nothing at all. She looked dazzling in the white gossamer cotton dress she wore, imported from Paris. She stood glowing in the New York morning, sunlight streaming through the clear glass of brand-new windows.

And when he was not with her, he was doing what he loved, what brought all his nerve endings to life—trading the market. Livermore loved the fact that in trading the market there was no end to the learning process. The game was never over, and he could never know enough to beat the market all the time. The puzzle could never be solved. He had learned this lesson the hard way, and that was why he never considered himself a market master. He always considered himself a market *student* who occasionally traded correctly.

Around this time, on January 2, 1920, Livermore purchased a seat on the New York Curb Exchange for $5,000. It was never clear why he did this, since he was never seen trading on the curb. He was also never seen inside the New York Stock Exchange.

Livermore's understanding that he would be a student of the markets all his life was exactly what drew him to the profession. It was never the same; no day was like any other. The market was a fast track where fortunes were made and lost in a heartbeat. Anyone could be a winner if they made the right moves.

Among the most mysterious parts of the puzzle were what other people called Livermore's hunches. But these were not impulsive moves as far as he was concerned; they just looked that way to the uninformed observer. His actions were simply a result of his entire, conscious and unconscious, mind at work—distilling facts; churning information; recalling prior events; reacting to current events; watching his fellow traders; and, most of all, relying on his own judgment, not the judgment of others.

All his life, Livermore spent a lot of time trying to understand his subconscious mind, the mind that never sleeps. He studied Freud and Jung. He knew the power and mystery of the inner mind. It was the wellspring of creative expression. It was the land of mystifying dreams. It was free-ranging, pure random-access thought. Could the subconscious hold deeper answers? Could it be harnessed?

Livermore's swift, seemingly instinctive actions on certain occasions were to become part of his Wall Street legend. People often observed these actions, and many later declared that he acted on a sixth sense—a trader's instinct, or gambler's luck—or that he received subliminal messages from the tape, reserved only for him. Livermore himself did not fully understand some of his actions.

He had been trading from the age of 14. He was now 41—27 years of trading, with millions and millions of dollars passing through his accounts. Livermore read Aristotle. He believed the great philosopher's dictum that "We are the sum total of our experience." It was this pure, real-life experience, distilled through intellect, that fascinated Livermore. Some people called it intuition. Could it ever be understood, captured on a regular basis?

One evening at Bradley's Beach Club in Palm Beach, Livermore was sitting with Ed Bradley for dinner, just the two of them. After dessert Bradley asked him, "J.L., what makes a good stock speculator?"

"Ed, that's a funny question. What makes a good gambler? Maybe similar traits?"

"I think maybe they're a little different, J.L."

"Well, for a stock speculator it's an aptitude for the game, a stomach for the ride, and the ability to see what is happening without emotion. The ability to make observations that others don't and a good memory to remember facts correctly, particularly mathematical facts.

"Finally, Ed, and most important, is experience. To learn from your experiences is paramount. And you need them all. A speculator could have good powers of observation and memory, but not the experience. Or a trader could have experience, but poor memory or poor observational ability, or no mathematical aptitude. A successful trader needs all these characteristics, but the key one—the essential one for sustained success—I believe is experience."

"And the stomach for it," Bradley added.

"Yes, it's not everybody's calling. Not everybody could or should be a speculator."

"Or a gambler, like me. But can you be a little more specific J.L.?"

"I'll make it quick. Only speculate if you can make it a full-time job. Don't take tips of any kind, no matter where they come from. Don't worry about catching the tops or bottoms, that's fool's play. Keep the number of stocks you own to a controllable number. It's hard to herd cats, and it's hard to track a lot of securities. Take your losses quickly and don't brood about them. Try to learn from them, but mistakes are as inevitable as death. And only make a big move, a real big plunge, when the majority of factors are in your favor."

"Kinda like holding a royal flush?" Ed Bradley smiled.

"In the market you very rarely get a sure thing. The market always keeps you on the edge."

"Gambling too, J.L."

"That's why every once in a while you must go into cash, take a break, take a vacation. Don't try to play the market all the time. It can't be done, too tough on the emotions. And finally, and I know you'll like this one Ed, keep some cash in reserve. Like you, Ed—you probably have a hundred grand on you right now."

"Eighty." Bradley smiled.

"I have made some of my biggest moves and biggest profits because I had some cash sitting in reserve." Livermore smiled back. "Now it's your turn Ed. What makes a good gambler?"

"Pretty much what you just said, J.L."

"There must be something else."

"Well, J.L., you know I'm a good Catholic and I never discuss religion, but the fear and love of God was put in me by my mother from when I could talk till I was about twelve or thirteen and I hit the road. So a good gambler always wants God on his side. Second, you live in a nice gentlemanly world up there on Wall Street. At least no one is beating you up or trying to shoot you, which, sad to say, often happens in the life of a gambler. I believe a man must know the manly art of self-defense, not to be a bully but so he doesn't ever have to have any fear of another person."

"The men on Wall Street do all their maiming and killing mentally and financially," Livermore added.

"Yeah and through lying, stealing and cheating, which I will not abide." Bradley sipped his drink and continued, "Finally, like the market, you gotta do and love the math. So while others are talking, and talking, and talking, like they always do, you can be thinking and thinking and thinking, figuring the percentages and the probabilities. This will ensure a fella of financial success—like you, J.L."

"Ed, flattery will get you everywhere with me." Livermore raised his old-fashioned and Bradley raised his glass of soda water. They smiled and clinked glasses, the Great Bear of Wall Street and America's most successful gambler.

Livermore's winters in Palm Beach were more than a vacation. They took him away from New York and the market. Even though he often played the market from E. F. Hutton's Palm Beach office, it was different for him, because it was a different environment.

Plus, the Atlantic Ocean fascinated him. It made him feel small. His life fell into better focus when he got out onto the ocean. Some of his greatest thinking was done fishing, trolling along the 100-fathom bar a few miles off Palm Beach, following the great underwater canyon that ran from Cuba to Nova Scotia, a nautical highway for the great gypsy fish. Or cruising easily on his new *Anita Venetian II,* heading down to Key West for some tarpon fishing, and watching those great Florida Keys sunsets. The ocean was always exciting, ever changing, and it refreshed his soul.

In the 1920s, Livermore made another important discovery that he applied to his trading strategy: *industry group movements.* He deduced from observation that stocks did not move alone when they moved. They moved in industry groups. If U.S. Steel rose, then sooner or later Bethlehem, Republic, and Crucible would follow along. Livermore observed this time and time again, and it became an important trading tool in his arsenal. As Figures 7.1 and 7.2 illustrate, nothing has changed since Livermore's day. The automotive group—here, General Motors and Ford—basically moves in lockstep.

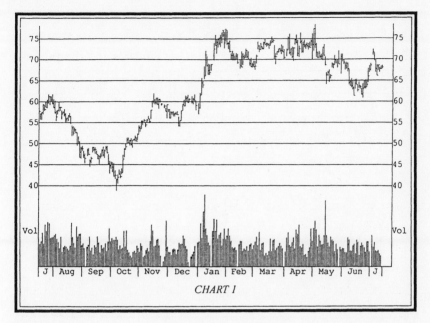

CHART 1

FIGURE 7.1   General Motors Corporation, July 15, 1997 to July 15, 1999. *(Courtesy of Nirvana Systems)*

The group movement premise was quite simple to Livermore. He explained to his son Paul: "If the basic reasons are sound for U.S. Steel's business to come into favor in the stock market, then the rest of the steel group should also follow for the same basic reasons. This, of course also works for the short side of the market. When a group goes out-of-favor for basic, solid reasons it will include all the stocks in that industry group."

For example, Figures 7.3 and 7.4 show companies in the "oil patch" group. As the price of oil plummeted in the late spring of 1998, stock prices of Transocean and Triton Energy, both offshore oil drillers, plummeted because their profit margins were threatened. In fact, all the oil drillers suffered a steep drop in the price of their stocks.

It was also an important clue for Livermore if a particular stock

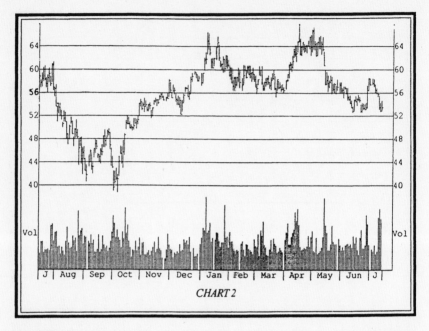

FIGURE 7.2   Ford Motors Company, July 15, 1997 to July 15, 1999.
(Courtesy of Nirvana Systems)

in the favored group did not move up and prosper with the others. This could indicate that the stock was weak or sick, and therefore might be a good short sale. At the very least, a trader should be cautious in buying any stock that does not follow the overall group action.

This works in reverse, as well—if the group is going down, and one stock is bucking the trend and going up, then the speculator should beware.

The only exception to group movement is when a single stock makes up 50 percent or more of the total sales of the group—sooner or later, the rest of the group must follow this stock. For example, Figures 7.5 and 7.6 show charts for Lucent, a leading telecommunications company, and for the overall telecommunications equipment and service group. It is clear how important the

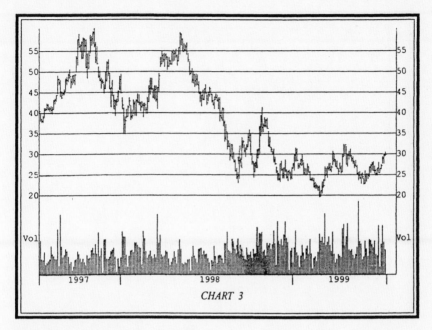

CHART 3

FIGURE 7.3   Transocean Offshore, Inc., July 15, 1997 to July 15, 1999. *(Courtesy of Nirvana Systems)*

dominant stock is to this group—in fact, in such cases, the leading stock *is* the group.

Livermore believed in trading the market leader, trading the most powerful stock in the group. He didn't look for the bargain, the weak sister; he went with the leader, the anchor of the group. He also noted that this was not always the conventional leader of the group. Occasionally, a smaller, well-managed stock in the group would assume leadership, perhaps with a new product, and knock out the old leader.

Livermore observed that entire groups went in and out of favor with each new major bull market. The leading stock groups of one market most likely would not be the leading groups of the next major market. And Livermore followed only the leading groups, because he believed that if he could not make money with the

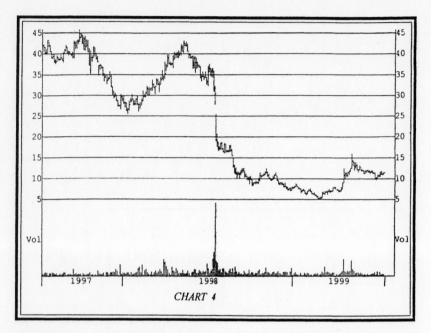

FIGURE 7.4   Triton Energy, Ltd., July 15, 1997 to July 15, 1999.
(Courtesy of Nirvana Systems)

leading active issues and groups, then he would not make money speculating in the market as a whole.

It was Livermore's experience that stock group behavior was an important key to overall market direction, a key ignored by most traders, big or small. He believed that groups often provided the key to predicting changes in trends. As favored groups got weaker and collapsed, it usually meant a correction in the market as a whole. This was how he called the market turns in 1907 and 1929—the leaders always rolled over first.

Livermore also used this same group-action technique in trading commodities.

Personally, things were going well for Livermore. In 1919, Dorothy gave birth to a son, Jesse Jr. He and Dorothy talked things

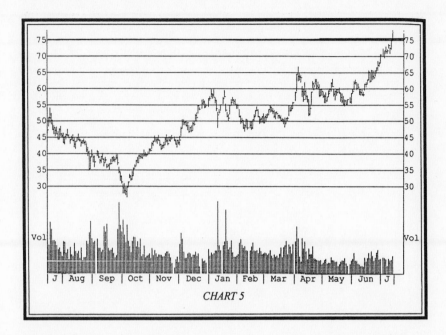

CHART 5

FIGURE 7.5   Lucent Technologies, Inc., July 15, 1997 to July 15, 1999. *(Courtesy of Nirvana Systems)*

over and decided it would be best to bring up their family outside New York City. They went house hunting and eventually settled on King's Point in Great Neck, on Long Island.

The estate they bought, Locust Lawn, sat on 13 acres of beautifully landscaped grounds and was bordered on one side by Long Island Sound. It was more than a century old and had once been a farmhouse. Dorothy enthusiastically took on the project of renovating her new home.

Dorothy's mother became her constant companion; she actually had a suite of rooms designed for her mother in the renovated mansion. Dorothy did nothing without first consulting her mother. When they were finished with the designers, they simply went to J.L., and he wrote them a check for whatever they wanted. The estate was renovated and soon filled up with antique furniture,

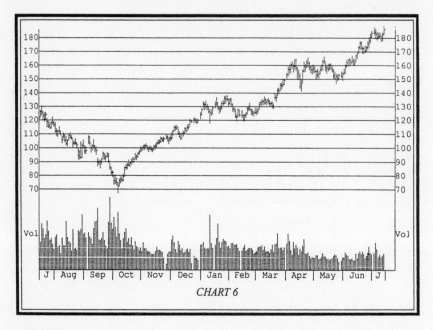

FIGURE 7.6   Telecommunications equipment and service group, July 15, 1997 to July 15, 1999. *(Courtesy of Nirvana Systems)*

beautiful art, exquisite silver, and tapestries. One tapestry, worth over $25,000, was 60 feet long, and depicted Greek soldiers and gods in full battle.

When Dorothy and her mother were finally finished some two years later, the house contained 29 rooms and 12 bathrooms. In the basement was a bar, a playroom, and a full barbershop. There was a full-time live-in barber to shave Livermore and clip his hair every day. J.L. and Dorothy each had massive walk-in closets and huge bathrooms.

Livermore had more than 50 custom-made suits, along with hundreds of ties and custom-made shirts. Livermore stood 5 foot 10½, but he had always wanted to be 6 feet tall, so he had 20 pairs of custom-made elevator shoes that raised his height 1½ inches.

When Dorothy, or "Mousie," as Livermore now called her, was done with her remodeling, she placed a large brass plaque in one of the front columns and renamed Locust Lawn "Evermore."

The dining room table was shiny black walnut and sat 48 for dinner. The kitchen would have been a proud fixture in most hotels. The permanent staff of four worked at giant hooded stoves, preparing food retrieved from the massive refrigeration units. Dorothy loved dinner parties where she could shine and be admired, and Livermore loved to participate in his quiet, powerful way.

She had as many parties as she could; any excuse, and she threw a party. Even the powder room became a legend, with its huge, perfect magnified mirrors circled by glowing stage-lamps, fronted with tufted satin seats and damask-covered chaise lounges where the women could relax and reapply their makeup while spreading delicious gossip.

Livermore loved it all, and he loved the fact that he did not have to do any of the planning or arrange any party details. That was Dorothy's job, and she loved it. Thanks to Dorothy, he made the acquaintance of many people, including many beautiful women and show-business people. Unfortunately for Mousie, he had a passion for women in show business.

Livermore tried to limit the parties to the weekends when the market was closed. During the week, when the market was open, he followed a strict discipline, like an athlete in training. He went to bed at 10 and was up in the morning no later than 6 for his quiet time, his solitary strategy time. He ate breakfast alone in the nook off the kitchen, where he could see the sprawling lawn that ran down to Long Island Sound and his 300-foot yacht, with its crew of 14, glimmering in the rising sun. He could also see the yachts belonging to his neighbors, Alfred Sloan of General Motors and

Walter P. Chrysler, both equal in size to his own. He went to work by himself in his chauffeured Rolls; or, in the summer, he took the Chris-Craft from his pier to the yacht. Then he would take the yacht into the city. It was about an hour's cruise.

After they moved in, Dorothy learned that one of the servants knew how to make beer, and she had a brewery built in the basement. Prohibition was in full bloom. Eventually, Dorothy would go around to the neighboring estates and deliver beer. She would take the orders on Friday night and Saturday morning and deliver the beer in her chauffeur-driven Rolls-Royce convertible on Saturday afternoon. Sometimes she would have Livermore's Rolls trail hers, also stacked with cases of beer for their friends. She had the time of her life, laughing and gossiping with her friends, fielding calls from people like Walter Chrysler, Alfred Sloan, and Charlie Chaplin, as they placed their beer orders and chatted her up.

Chaplin would often drop by, play a game of billiards on the imported English billiard table, and pick up his beer. Chaplin played a good game of billiards, and so did Livermore. Chaplin loved Dorothy's humor, and would listen to her for hours trying to figure out how she could be so naturally funny.

In the living room stood a Steinway grand piano. Livermore loved opera and classical music, and he would often have famous opera singers like Madam Shumann-Heink, renowned pianists and composers, Broadway stars, and popular singers of the day sing and play at parties.

Their existence was romantic and exciting. In 1923, just before the house was completed, Dorothy delivered a second boy, Paul.

Livermore had been actively trading for 32 years by 1923. He was 46 years old, but he still had an unquenchable thirst for knowledge about his chosen profession, and he was a constant student of the technical side of the market as well as its psychology. He

PERFECTING HIS MARKET THEORY

concluded that there might be millions of minds at work in the market, but there was basically only one psychological pattern that had to be studied and understood. Human nature is fundamentally the same.

Later in life, Livermore was asked an important question by his sons, Paul and Jesse: "Dad, why are you good in the market and other people lose all their money?"

"Boys, the stock market must be studied, not casually either, but deeply, thoroughly. It's my conclusion that most people pay more care and attention to the purchase of an appliance for their house, or when buying a car, than they do to the purchase of stocks. The stock market, with its allure of easy money and fast action, induces people into foolishness and the careless handling of their hard-earned money, like no other entity.

"See, the purchase of a stock is simple, easily done by placing your purchase order with a broker, and later a phone call to sell completes the trade. If you profit from this transaction it appears to be easy money with seemingly no work. You didn't have to get to work by nine and labor for eight hours a day. It was simply a paper transaction, requiring no labor. It appears to be an easy way to get rich. Simply buy the stock at ten dollars and sell it later for more than ten dollars. The more you trade, the more you make, that's how it appears. That's ignorance, and ignorance is dangerous.

"There's also fear to deal with, which you will find out when you grow up. Fear and violence lie buried just beneath the surface of all normal human life. Fear, like violence, can appear in a single heartbeat, a fast breath and the blink of an eye, the grab of a hand, the noise of a gun. When it appears, natural survival tactics come alive, normal reasoning is distorted. Reasonable people act unreasonably when they are afraid. And people become afraid when they start to lose money, their judgment becomes impaired. This is our human nature in this stage of our evolution. It cannot be denied. It must be understood, particularly in trading the market.

"The unsuccessful investor is best friends with hope, and hope skips along life's path hand in hand with greed when it comes to the stock market. Once a stock trade is entered, hope springs to life. It is human nature to be positive, to hope for the best. Hope is an important survival technique. But hope, like its stock market cousins ignorance, greed, and fear, distorts reason. See, boys, the stock market only deals in facts, in reality, in reason, and the stock market is never wrong. Traders are wrong. Like the spinning of a roulette wheel, the little black ball tells the final outcome, not greed, fear, or hope. The result is objective and final, with no appeal."

Both boys wondered if the stock market was for them. Was it too dangerous? Should they just leave it to their father?

Livermore asked to be given no tips, and he, in turn, gave no tips. He realized that, in many cases, tips were offered on a good-faith basis by people who really did have the other person's best interest at heart. Tips could come from a relative, a loved one, or a friend who had just made a serious investment and wanted to pass on their good fortune. His motto was simple: All tips are dangerous. They take all different forms. Take none of them.

There were tips that were purposely spread to provide false and misleading information. These tips usually concealed an agenda that might never be disclosed. Tips, Livermore knew after years of trading, could come from any source. They could be disguised as real and irrefutable information. A respected banker or an influential person interviewed by the press who had performed well in the past might provide the tip. A well-known insider who had fully disclosed a large position in the stock, or an executive with the company, might provide the tip.

And the tip very often made logical sense. An example: "Our industry has taken a severe beating over the last two years and the public reaction has been overdone. Our current prospects never looked better. I have to say, based on objective valuation, we are the biggest bargain in the stock market right now."

There were tips spread by rumors about pending buyouts or mergers. They were easily spread and passed along by the press, often as scoops or exclusives.

There were also those who managed vast amounts of money and honestly believed what they were saying and had put their money where their mouths were. They had put up good hard cash to back up their opinions, and they wanted the public to follow suit. Like the old bucket-shop saying went, "The only way a stock goes up is if some sucker buys it."

Said Livermore to his son Paul: "I believe that the public wants to be lead, to be instructed, to be told what to do. They want reassurance. They will always move *en masse,* a mob, a herd, a group, because people want the safety of human company. They are afraid to stand alone because they want to be safely included within the herd, not to be the lone calf standing on the desolate, dangerous, wolf-patrolled prairie of contrary opinion.

"This is where it gets slightly complicated because I always wanted to trade along the line of least resistance, so I was generally moving along with the crowd, the herd, most of the time. It was when the change in trend started to appear, the change in market direction, that was the most difficult change to catch and act upon. So I was always hunting for the clues to the change. So I was always ready to separate myself from the popular thinking, the group thinking, and go the opposite way.

"It is the most difficult time in a speculator's trading life. These major changes in trends were hard to catch, but I did not want to ride the sled downhill with the crowd, unless I had sold stocks short.

"With this in mind, I developed two rules that I followed all the time.

"First, do not be invested in the market all the time. There are many times when I have been completely in cash, especially when I was unsure of the direction of the market and waiting for a confirmation of the next move. Whenever I deduced that a change was coming, and I wasn't sure exactly when, or how severe the change might be, I cashed in my positions and waited.

"Second, it is the change in the major trend that hurts most speculators. They simply get caught invested in the wrong direction, on the wrong side of the market. To determine if I was right in my appraisal, that a change in market trend was coming, I used small position probes, placing small orders, either buy or sell, depending on the direction of the trend change. I did this to test the correctness of my judgment.

"There were other factors as well to mark the end of a major market move. There was usually heavy volume, but the prices stalled, they did not go up and make new highs on the leading stocks. There was no strong continuation of the current move. This was a clue, a warning. At the end of a market move it is usually pure distribution, as stocks go from strong hands to weak hands, from the professionals to the public. It is deceptive to the public who view this heavy volume as the mark of a vibrant, healthy market going through a normal correction, not a top or a bottom.

"I was always alert to look toward volume indications as a key signal at the end of a major move, either in the entire market or an individual stock. Also I observed that at the end of a long move, it was not uncommon for stocks to suddenly spike up in a straight shot with heavy volume and then stop, roll at the top, exhausted,

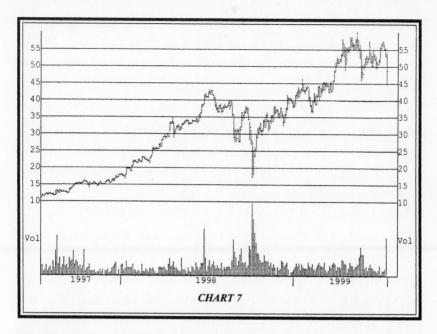

CHART 7

FIGURE 7.7   Capital One Financial Corporation, July 15, 1997 to July 15, 1999. *(Courtesy of Nirvana Systems)*

and then retreat, never to make a "new high" before the onslaught of a major correction.★

"This last gasp of heavy volume also provides a great opportunity to sell out any illiquid large holdings. I knew it was foolish to ever try to catch the tops or the bottoms of the moves. It is always better to sell large holdings into an advancing market when there is plenty of volume. The same is true on the short side; you are best to cover the short position after a steep fast decline.

"Remember the most important thing to successful speculation is to determine the direction of the line of least resistance. Put the

★Figure 7.7 provides an example. Capital One Financial's terrific volume and downward spike in early October 1998 shows a clear high-volume climax bottom that indicates the downward trend has changed. *Volume* is often a key confirming signal to indicate a change in direction.

wind at your back and sail forward easily. Keep the wind out of your face, and when the market hits the doldrums getting nowhere, moving sideways, then get out, take a break, have some fun, go fishing.

"Come back into the market when the wind has picked up again, and the sailing is clear and good. Staying out of the action is always difficult for an active trader, but I grew to know it was essential at times to be out of the market. There is nothing more important than your emotional balance."

On October 5, 1923, in order to practice his new techniques and theories, Livermore moved his offices uptown, from 111 Broadway to 730 Fifth Avenue, the Heckscher Building. He designed the offices very carefully. He wanted to be away from the Wall Street atmosphere, out of earshot of any tips. He also wanted to gain more secrecy in his operations and more security, so that no one would know his trades.

He hired Harry Edgar Dache as his assistant, a hulking bruiser whose sheer size belied his intelligence. Dache had been in the merchant marines and had traveled the globe many times. He spoke six languages, including Latin. He was a voracious reader, knowledgeable in many areas, and a terrific administrator. He ran the office with secrecy and perfection. He was completely loyal to Livermore and very protective. The boys loved Dache; Jesse Jr. and Paul were enthralled with his magical stories of traveling the seven seas. He was their unofficial tutor, chauffeur, companion and bodyguard, especially when they went to Palm Beach.

There were no windows in the anteroom of Livermore's new offices, only a few chairs and Dache's desk. Behind Dache was the solid floor-to-ceiling door to Livermore's private offices. There were no signs or identification on any of the doors. When letting someone in to see Livermore, Dache would always first confirm

Jesse Livermore, the legendary Boy Plunger and Great Bear of Wall Street, in his office in 1929 just after the Great Crash, when he went short the market and made over $100 million. His skills were at their peak. His life slid downhill from this point; 10 years later he would kill himself. (*Photo copyright © Bettmann/Corbis. Used with permission.*)

This painted portrait of Dorothy Livermore, Ziegfeld showgirl, was commissioned by her husband, Jesse, before she was 20 years old. The pearls, valued at $80,000, were stolen during the Boston Billy gang's robbery of their mansion. (*Photo courtesy of Patricia Livermore*)

Jesse Livermore and friend, Ed Kelley, president of United Fruit, on Livermore's yach after a day's fishing. Livermore had a passion for fishing and the water. He often cam up with great market ideas on the ocean. (*Photo courtesy of Paul Livermore*)

The original *Anita Venetian* with a 40-foot launch tied alongside. In all, there wer three *Anita Venetians;* the last one was 300 feet long. (*Photo courtesy of Paul Livermore*)

sse Livermore and his wife, Dorothy, on March 3, 1926, dressed for a costume ball
Evermore. Dorothy loved throwing lavish parties for 100 people or more. (*Photo
urtesy of* New York Daily News)

March 18, 1925—The Breakers Hotel in Palm Beach on fire. Dorothy sent the bel hops back into the Livermore's suite to save their 24 pieces of Louis Vuitton luggag (*Photo courtesy of Historical Society of Palm Beach County*)

Ed Bradley's Palm Beach Beach Club was the longest-running illegal gambling casin in American history. Bradley, the greatest gambler in America, was a fast friend of Jess Livermore, the greatest stock speculator. (*Photo courtesy of Historical Society of Palr Beach County*)

vermore's mansion, Evermore, at King's Point, Long Island. The dining room table commodated 46 for dinner, and the basement housed a live-in barber. Livermore's 0-foot yacht was anchored out back. Evermore was the scene of many grand par-s until it was finally auctioned off on June 27, 1933. (*Photo courtesy of* New York aily News)

The dashing Livermore clan: Paul, Dorothy, and Jesse Jr., pose in front of Evermore. (*Photo copyright © Bettmann/Corbis. Used with permission.*)

Jesse Livermore on the porch of the Breakers Hotel, where he took a large apartment every winter. He traveled to the hotel in his private railway car and had his yacht sent down to Palm Beach ahead of him. (*Photo copyright © Bettmann/Corbis. Used with permission.*)

esse and Dorothy Livermore and friends at the Livermore's vacation home in Lake Placid, New York. Livermore hunted and played golf there. (*Photo courtesy of Paul Livermore*)

Dorothy Livermore and friend in a white vicker pedicab on the grounds of the Breakers Hotel. This was a common means of transportation at the hotel in the 1920s and 1930s. (*Photo courtesy of Paul Livermore*)

Patricia and Jesse Livermore Jr. during some happy times on the way to Hawaii. (*Photo courtesy of Patricia Livermore*)

Jesse Livermore and his third wife, Harriet, during a party for 80 people in their 10-room apartment on Park Avenue in New York City. Livermore loved beautiful women, to the detriment of his marriages. (*Photo copyright* © *Bettmann/Corbis. Used with permission.*)

Publicity photo of Paul Livermore, Jesse's youngest son. He appeared in movies and television series before moving to Hawaii. (*Photo courtesy of Paul Livermore*)

Ann Livermore, Paul's wife, a singer who appeared with the big bands and such singers as Tony Bennett and Frank Sinatra. (*Photo courtesy of Ann Livermore*)

Jesse Livermore, his wife, Harriet, and Paul arrive in New York on December 8, 1935 after leaving the bedside of Jesse Jr., who had just been shot by his mother. (*Photo cou# tesy of* New York Daily News)

After shooting her son Jesse, Dorothy Livermore stands in a Santa Barbara, Californi; courtroom before Judge Ernest Wagner on a complaint of assault with a deadl weapon with intent to kill. (*Photo copyright © Bettmann/Corbis. Used with permission.*)

Undersheriff Jack Ross, District Attorney Percy Heckendorf, and Sheriff James Ross look at the spot where they believe Dorothy Livermore shot her son Jesse, at her home in Montecito, California. She actually shot him on the staircase. (*Photo copyright* © *Bettmann/Corbis. Used with permission.*)

Jesse Livermore sits before the bankruptcy referee on May 15, 1934. Livermore always paid his bankruptcy creditors back when he got back on his feet, even though he was not legally responsible. (*Photo courtesy of* New York Daily News)

Jesse Livermore, the former Boy Plunger of Wall Street, and his wife, Harriet, set sail to Europe on the *S.S. Rex* after his 1934 bankruptcy. Before boarding, Livermore said "I hope to relieve my mind of some of my troubles." (*Photo courtesy of* New York Daily News)

Jesse Livermore and his wife, Harriet, on November 27, 1940, at the Stork Club, his favorite nightclub. Looking distant and wan, he would commit suicide the next day (*Photo courtesy of* New York Daily News)

esse Livermore Jr. on November 28, 1940, as he arrives at the Sherry Netherland
Iotel in New York City to identify the body of his father. (*Photo courtesy of* New York
)aily News)

Jesse Livermore was subject to deep, black depressions all his adult life, during succes
or failure. This photo was taken on November 26, 1940, two days before the Grea
Bear of Wall Street took his own life. (*Photo copyright © Bettmann/Corbis. Used with per
mission.*)

se Livermore was a powerful individual who cherished secrecy and protected his
ivate life. (*Photo courtesy of Paul Livermore*)

Jesse Livermore Jr. on March 23, 1975, as he is led from his home to a police car after shooting his dog, attempting to kill his wife Patricia, and sticking his gun in the chest of a New York police

the appointment by intercom. Then he would rise from his desk and use his key to open the door for the visitor. It was a theatrical ritual that Dache performed to show the visitor the difficulty in gaining entrance to the inner sanctum of the great trader's offices.

Behind the door was the massive open room with the green chalkboard that ran the entire length of the room. At least four markers would be working in silence, each covering a section of the board and responsible for specific active stocks or commodities that Livermore was trading or observing closely. Each marker wore headphones that connected to callers on the floor of the exchange, who would call up the quotes on each individual stock transaction—the bid, asked, and sold price. This gave Livermore an edge on the ticker tape, which was usually delayed at least 15 minutes. Livermore wanted the most current information he could get. He had learned as a young man how important fresh quotes were.

If Livermore was active in several stocks or commodities, he would often increase his staff on the chalkboard from four to six. These markers would work all day on the catwalk in silence, only taking a break for lunch, when they would usually be replaced by Dache, so no quotes were lost. These board markers would always track two or more stocks in the same group. If Livermore was trading General Motors, he would track Chrysler as well, to observe the group action.

In the middle of the office was a massive conference table of shiny mahogany with eight comfortable leather office armchairs. On the rare occasions when Livermore had guests to his office, he would always sit facing the chalkboard so he could watch the quotes as he listened. Often he would break off the meeting to enter his office and place trades in private.

Livermore's private office was very large, with heavy paneling of oak and mahogany. His desk was large, made out of highly polished mahogany. On his desk were in- and out-baskets, a pad and pencil, and nothing else. The entire wall across from the great mahogany desk was clear plate glass, so he could see the market action on the board as it happened.

There were also three black telephones on his desk. One was a direct wire to London, the second to Paris, and the third to the floor of the Chicago grain pits. Livermore wanted first-hand, fresh information, and he was willing to pay for it. He knew that wars were won on information—intelligence—and that the general with the best intelligence was the general most likely to win. He wanted no "rumors of war"—he wanted specific, accurate information.

Paul Livermore, his son, would often come to this office as he grew up, especially on his summer breaks. He would sometimes be allowed to work the board. The board markers were trained to work with a code. If a stock suddenly had a deep price fluctuation, they would use a secret code to note this on the board. Only the board crew and Livermore knew these codes. This was what Livermore later disclosed as his market key. On occasion, guests in the office would ask, "J.L. what are those weird columns on the chalkboard, some kind of hieroglyphics?"

"They make perfect sense to me," Livermore would respond.

"You wanna explain them to me?"

"No," he would smile. "If I did, then you would be as smart as I am."

"Just tell me what to buy and sell and when. Keep it simple for me."

"You know I never recommend a stock, but I would be glad to tell you whether I believe the market is going up or down."

"It always goes up or down, J.L."

"You're right, of course, but the trick is *when* it is going to go up or down."

"And *what's* going to go up or down, J.L. Don't forget, it's *what* stocks are going to go up or down—that's what we all want to know. What stock will rise, and when."

"Anyone who knows the general trend of the market should be able to do well."

"Whatever you say, J.L. Whatever you say."

One day Livermore was sitting in his office talking to his son Paul. "Turn around Paul, and look at the stock board," Livermore ordered. Paul turned and studied the markers as they moved on the catwalk like well-choreographed dancers.

Livermore continued, "You see, son, those markings on that board are as clear to me as a musical score is to a great conductor. I see these symbols as alive, a rhythm, a pulse that makes beautiful music. It all makes perfect sense to me.

"You see, son, for me the board is alive, like music. We are able to communicate. It's something that has come to me only after years of hard work and practice, not unlike a great conductor of a great orchestra. What I feel when I look at that board can't be shared, any more than a conductor could articulate what he feels when he plays Mozart just the way it should be played. The board and those men are playing a symphony to me, a symphony of money that sings to me, that makes love to me, that envelops me in its song."

Paul studied his father and he believed every word. It was a rare moment for Paul, to get so intimate with his father, who was so private, stingy with his emotions, frugal with his love.

chapter eight

Stock Pools and Scandals

The principles of successful stock speculation are based on the supposition that people will continue in the future to make the same mistakes that they have made in the past.

Thomas F. Woodlock

LIVERMORE LOVED TO PLAY CARDS, ESPECIALLY BRIDGE.
He played a high-stakes game of bridge every Monday night at his
home in Great Neck. He would invite his neighbors, Walter
Chrysler and Alfred Sloan, and usually his good friend Harry
Aronhson, a silk merchant who lived in New York. Aronhson was
extremely rich, and he loved to watch Livermore and his raids.
Once in a great while he would participate in a raid, as well. He
would go to Livermore's offices and sit in silence, just watching
the great trader at work.

One day Livermore got a call at his office from Ely Culbertson,
the world champion bridge player.

"Mr. Livermore, I understand you are quite a bridge player,"
Culbertson said.

"We play a friendly game once in a while. We're not in your
class, Mr. Culbertson."

"Please call me Ely."

"Well then, call me J.L."

"I had a favor to ask you. I have been told you are very skilled
with numbers, and I wondered if you could figure out some probabilities for me. You know, the probabilities for certain finesses to
work and certain point counts, the probabilities of making a game
with certain card point counts, things like that."

"Well, Ely, give me the problems, and I'll see what I can do."

Culbertson spent the next 30 minutes outlining his questions to
Livermore, who took specific notes. One week later, he called
Culbertson back and read off his answers. Culbertson was
impressed. Livermore invited him to join their game on Monday
nights.

"I'm afraid your games are too rich for me, J.L."

There was a silence. "Look, don't worry about the money,
whoever has you for a partner will cover the bet for your team,
you can keep the money if your team wins. We just would all

enjoy playing with you. I called the boys, and they agree it would be good for us to play with the world's best bridge player. Don't worry about the money. Are you in?"

"How can I lose?"

"Okay. I'll switch you over to Harry Edgar Dache, my office manager. He will get the necessary information from you so we can send a car to pick you up. You're welcome to stay overnight; we have plenty of bedrooms. The game never goes much beyond ten o'clock during the week. We start at six and have sandwiches at eight."

"All right then, I'll see you on Monday night."

They incorporated Culbertson into their game by setting up a handicap; whoever had Culbertson as a partner got penalized 1,000 points. But they were all such good players that they soon eliminated the handicap and played even. It was more of a challenge. Livermore and his friends could not have been more excited to sit and play with, and sometimes against, the world's best bridge player.

It was because Livermore and his friends all loved to play cards— poker, gin, and bridge—that Dorothy got her "yacht pool" idea. One Monday night, she walked in early with the butler, who was carrying the sandwiches, and interrupted the game. "Fellas, I have an idea for you to think about. You know your wives and I, we love to play cards too. So I thought maybe you would consider a *yacht pool*. You know, you each have your yachts parked in the back of your houses, like we do. So why not just take one yacht at a time down to Wall Street, instead of each of you taking your own? Then you could play cards on the way down and also on the way back, especially during the summer when the weather is so nice."

"And what's in it for you, Mousie?" Livermore asked.

"Well, then we girls could go play on the other boats, or even go for a cruise."

The men broke out laughing, and the next morning the only yacht pool in America was formed.

By the mid-1920s, it was well known on Wall Street that Livermore was one of the most skillful market traders. The press often exaggerated his reputation, and it was enhanced by the mysterious and secretive way that Livermore traded. He sometimes used up to 50 brokers to hide his trading activities; no one could easily get to him. To the press, he was the mystery man of Wall Street, silent and secretive.

At this time in history, from the turn of the century to the late 1920s, it was common to form pools on various stocks. These pools were made up of investors and insiders who would pool their stock in a particular issue. This was done to control the wild fluctuations that might occur if big blocks were suddenly offered for sale in a stock with thin volume. At least, that was the theory offered by the promoters: Pooling created an orderly market. In fact, most of the time they were just interested in distributing stock to the public as expeditiously and at the best price as possible.

When individuals inside the pool wanted to get rid of their equity holdings, they often went to a trading pro, like Livermore, to sell their stock. This was usually done by the trading pro for a fee. Livermore preferred to get a series of *calls* on the stock, so that he could buy the stock at preset prices. As the stock price rose on the exchange, he had a chance to buy down the stock, exercise the calls, and cash in. He often used his own money to set the market up for the distribution of the pool stock. That way he did not have to explain his actions to anyone.

Market manipulation was commonplace in the stock market at the turn of the century, and there were no strong regulations to prohibit this kind of trading. It was not considered illegal as long as no false or misleading statements were issued. But it was illegal to have *wash sales,* in which stock would be bought and sold only by the insiders in the pool. This would churn the stock into life, and simply drive the stock price up as it passed back and forth through the same pairs of hands.

Livermore had seen a lot of manipulation and just about every trick in the book when it came to rigging a stock's action. Livermore was therefore always an obvious choice to run a pool. He was approached on a regular basis. If he believed that it was a good situation, he would become the pool trader.

He would first evaluate the company to make sure that it had promise and could legitimately support a rise in the stock price. Second, he had to be sure there was no possibility of bankruptcy or sustained losses in earnings. He would then apply his basic trading rules, pretesting the stock's action, before he said yes. The overall stock market's line of least resistance would also have to be basically positive. Livermore believed that no degree of manipulation could take a stock higher in a bear market climate.

Livermore was always very wary of his partners in any pool operation. They would often try to manipulate the manipulator. He used the ticker tape to broadcast his activities on any pool operation that he ran. He knew that there were thousands of tape-readers like him who would pick up, almost immediately, when a stock started to operate outside of its normal pattern, with increased volume and a sharp spike upward in price. He knew this would spark the interest of other traders and immediately bring in new players with buying power. This was commonly called *painting the tape.*

Livermore also knew that this increase in action would inevitably bring in short sellers, players who bet on the negative side of the market, figuring it was only a pool play. These short-sellers could later be squeezed by driving the price higher. They would then have to buy in and cover their short positions. This would also drive the price higher.

Livermore's strategy was to build a strong base for the stock on the way up, setting the stage to unload a huge amount of pool stock onto the market. He had studied other great pool operators such as James R. Keene, Jay Gould, and Commodore Vanderbilt. Their strategy was simple: Manipulate the stock to the highest point possible, and then sell the pool's stock at the top and on the way down, while the market was churning.

Livermore knew the psychology: When the stock came alive, so would the greed of other speculators and investors. He particularly liked sleepy stocks that he could wake up, but he never violated his basic trading rule of first determining the line of least resistance. Otherwise it was impossible, Livermore believed, to drive a stock up, no matter how strong the pool was.

"The tape is the best means of getting tips spread," Livermore told his friends. It worked well for him. Often his partners were more worrisome to him than was the stock manipulation.

Unlike his regular trading techniques for his own account, when he would sell into a *rising* market, when Livermore ran a pool, he sold out the bulk of the pool's stock *at the top* and into a *falling* market.

If the stock plummeted in price too fast, he would stop selling, and perhaps even buy a little stock for support until the public came back in. He knew the psychology of average traders, who often *wished* they had sold at the top, and as a result he would wait and not sell four or five points off the crested high. He would hold his stock position, and wait for the powerful rally that he believed was inevitable. He would sit and wait for a rally that might drive the stock back up to the old high.

Also, Livermore knew that people like a bargain. It is their nature to try to buy stock when it is cheap and sell it when it is expensive. People often think a stock is cheap because the price is lower than it was a few days before, when in fact it may decline even further. Livermore knew that the wise trader waited until a bottom had been firmly established and tested before going in and buying stock.

The public was more inclined to believe that whatever had been happening would continue to happen, and the pools depended on this. A stock that had suddenly come alive and started to rise in price would continue to rise in price. This was usually backed up by carefully manufactured rumors that were released on a planned basis by the insiders.

Livermore knew that selling on the way down was a time-honored way of achieving distribution. Wake up a sleepy stock, let the tape tell speculators and investors that the stock was now alive, let the tape provide the tips. Most of all, sell on the way down, not on the way up. This was the key to manipulating a stock and achieving distribution of large quantities by the big pool operators—and it has remained the key ever since, because human nature never changes.

This is one of the reasons why both experienced and inexperienced stock speculators are subject to manipulation and often get fooled. They believe the insiders are feeding out their stock on the meteoric upward rise of a stock. They are often wrong. The public is usually being fed the majority of the insider or pooled stock after the stock has crested by reaching new highs and is rolling over, starting its decline. This is often the reason why a stock cannot make a new high—there is simply too much supply hanging over the market. It is often insider or informed distribution that makes it impossible for a stock to rise in price.

Livermore was well aware of this in his personal trading. It was one of the reasons that new highs were so important to him. A true new high meant that the stock had broken through the overhead supply of stock—now it was being accumulated again, and, most important, the line of least resistance was strongly upward.

He was basically alone in this thinking in the 1920s. When the majority of people saw that a stock had made a new high, they sold it immediately and looked for a cheaper stock.

Livermore had long ago realized that the stock market was never obvious. It was designed to fool most of the people most of the time.

His rules were based on thinking against the grain: cut your losses quick; let your profits ride unless there's a good reason to close out the position; the action is with the leading stocks, which change with every new market; new highs are to be bought on breakouts; cheap stocks are often not bargains, because they have little potential to rise in price. The stock market is a study in cycles. It never goes up forever, nor does it go down forever, but when it changes direction it remains in that new trend until it is stopped. Livermore didn't buck the trend.

In June 1922, the New York Stock Exchange listed the Piggly Wiggly grocery stores for trading. The builder and owner of this chain of retail stores was Clarence Saunders, a corpulent 40-year-old from Memphis, Tennessee. The shares were issued and the stock promptly tanked, falling drastically in price.

Saunders, upset with the stock price, rounded up $10 million in cash and came to Wall Street to get the price of his stock up. He went directly to Livermore. Their partnership created the last corner in the history of Wall Street.

"Mr. Livermore, I want to get the price of my stock up. I have a war chest of ten million for you to use to do it. Will you?"

"It's selling at $35 right now. Is it worth more?"

"Yes. It came out at $50, and that was an undervalued price."

"How many shares are there in the market?" Livermore asked.

"Two hundred thousand float. I got the rest!"

"When do you want to start?"

"What's wrong with tomorrow?"

"Give me a few days, Mr. Saunders, to check things out."

"Okay. You haven't told me what it will cost me for your services."

"Normally, I don't take a fee; I just take a schedule of calls on the stock. But this is a unique situation, so we can decide on a fair fee for my services later."

Livermore checked out the market and they met a few days later.

"Okay, Mr. Saunders, I think we can work out a deal. I want twenty percent of the increase in value of the stock."

"That's fair enough. Can you start right away?"

"I'll start tomorrow."

The next day, using Saunders' $10-million war chest, Livermore quietly started to buy the stock in the open market. By the end of the first week, he had bought 105,000 shares out of the total float of 200,000. He went back to Saunders.

"Mr. Saunders, I have been able to buy over half the float, and the price hasn't budged. It's still $35."

"What in tarnation does that mean?"

"It means that there is not a lot of interest in your stock."

"Blast it! There will be! Use that money I gave you. That's what it's for. That stock is worth a whole lot more than $35. So stick it to 'em!"

Livermore went back into the market, and by March 1923 he had pumped the price up to $70. He was now faced with what would be one of the most important decisions of his entire career. The Street had triggered to the fact that Piggly Wiggly was being cornered. But most traders thought it was a pool at work, headed by the inexperienced owner, Saunders, trying to get rid of his stock. As a result, these seasoned traders started to short the stock, borrowing the stock now to be replaced when they actually bought the stock back later.

Livermore saw the problem by the time he had accumulated 198,000 shares for Saunders out of a float of 200,000 shares. The problem was that his friends on the Street were in a terribly vulnerable position. They could be ruined. He was called to see Saunders.

"Livermore, you did a heck of a job. You got the price of the stock to over $70, and there is no stock left for anyone to buy. I want you to call for delivery of all the stock that has been borrowed to cover the stock that has been sold short."

"That will drive the price of the stock up to . . ."

"Whatever we want it to be!" Saunders laughed. "Until I decide to sell those smug bastards back a little of my stock."

"I won't do it. It is not a wise thing to do."

"What are you talking about? You won't do it? We made a deal!"

"Too many of my friends will be ruined. I didn't make a deal to destroy my friends."

"Are you crazy, Livermore? How could they be your friends if they went short a stock you were running?"

"It's part of the game, Mr. Saunders. It all balances out."

"Maybe it's part of *your* game. But it ain't part of *my* game. They ignored my stock and now they're gonna pay for it." He studied Livermore, who remained impassive. "And Livermore—what do you mean by it isn't a wise thing to do, drive the price up?"

"It will drive the stock up in a sudden spike. The other traders will know it's a short squeeze, and there isn't any real demand for your stock, so they will lay off the issue, and ultimately it will fall like a stone."

"Bunkum! You're just talking for your friends now, because I got 'em by the balls and I intend to squeeze. They didn't show me no mercy, and this is my only play on Wall Street. I'm not some big-shot trader like you who has hundreds of plays to choose from. Besides, you're getting twenty percent of the value of the stock over $35. We can drive the stock up to over $100. That's another fortune for you."

"Keep it! I'm out, if you demand delivery of the stock certificates."

"You never heard of what old Daniel Drew said about people who sell short? 'He that sells what isn't his'n, must buy it back or go to pris'n.' "

"Yes, I've heard that before Mr. Saunders, and I've also heard 'Don't do unto others what you would not like them to do to you.' I'm going to be making my living here for a long, long time to come."

"Well, if that's your last word, then good luck to you. Thanks for the help, sorry you didn't make any money for your trouble."

"There will be other deals. Goodbye, Mr. Saunders." Livermore walked out.

The next day, Saunders did exactly what he said he was going to do. He demanded delivery of all stock that was on loan to cover the short positions. In hours, the stock spiked from $70 to $124.

But a mysterious rumor had started on the Street, from an unknown source, that Saunders had cornered the stock. This was against the new stock exchange rules. The rumor reached the board of governors, which stepped in that afternoon and suspended trading in Piggly Wiggly. The stock fell like a stone to 82 as the rumor was proven true. Livermore's friends were home free and safe.

Saunders later went bust. But he never stopped talking about how he had held stock market victory in his hands, only to be screwed royally by that swindler Livermore and his bastard friends.

Livermore was always a mystery to the press. He would never confirm or specifically deny the rumors that followed his trades. He was supposed to have lost $8.5 million in Mexican Petroleum ("Mexican Pete") by being on the short side of a runaway bull market in the stock. The stock advanced a nonstop 75 points and reportedly caught a lot of investors on the wrong side of the market. Livermore was rumored to be included.

"Gentlemen, gentlemen, I will neither confirm nor deny the things you have asked me about Mexican Pete," he said to the *New York Times* on June 29, 1922.

"Why is that sir?" one reporter asked.

"Because I don't want to spoil a good joke."

"Go ahead and spoil it, Mr. Livermore, tell us what happened. We heard you lost eight and a half million dollars for yourself and your friends and you made a private settlement to get out of the trap you found yourself in."

"No, I'm having too much fun to spoil this joke. I'm enjoying myself too much to bother you with the facts." Livermore smiled. "Look fellas, you printed that the stock got away from me on the upside on the day that I was attending Lillian Russell's memorial services at the Hippodrome. I did not attend those services, and on that day I left the office at five o'clock. I have witnesses to prove it, which I had already told you yesterday, but you printed what you wanted anyway."

"Just tell us about Mexican Pete and the beating you took, Mr. Livermore," the *Times* reporter said.

"You printed that I made a settlement with the Mexican Pete group to cover my shorts at $225 a share. You were told this by a certain stock exchange house. At that very time, four in the afternoon, when I was supposed to be making that settlement with my lawyer, with my friend Mr. E. L. Doheny present, I was actually up in Poughkeepsie watching the boat races. I have witnesses to confirm that also."

"So you're denying this then?" a reporter yelled.

"What I have told you is enough to give anyone sane an opportunity to draw their own conclusions as to whether I was the one caught short of Mexican Petroleum. But I have to say this, in addition, if I did happen to be the one caught short of Mexican Petroleum, I would have taken my licking in the market and bought back the stock to cover my position, no matter what the price was. Gentlemen, I have never made a private settlement in my life, nor will I."

"What about the story published yesterday that you got caught short with one hundred thousand shares, Mr. Livermore?"

"The reporter who wrote that story must have been inexperienced in the ways of Wall Street. At least he should have given me the sense not to go short almost the entire floating supply of Mexican Petroleum shares. If that reporter had really known how much stock of Mexican Pete I purchased on the afternoon I was supposed to be at the Hippodrome, such ridiculous stories would not gain circulation."

All through the 1920s, stories like this appeared in the press. Livermore helped sell a lot of newspapers, even though he tried to avoid publicity. It only made the press more insatiable to know about him.

One story that was never disclosed by the press shocked his son Paul. He had asked his father to tell him a story that no one else knew.

"All right, son. After the Great War ended in 1918, before you were born, I felt that cotton would fall in price on a short-term basis because the military demand would cease to exist. But I also thought the demand would pick up again later as the nation got back on its feet.

"So in 1919—quietly, in secret, using hundreds of brokers—I started buying cotton. The price fell as I had expected, and over about an eighteen-month period I realized that I had almost secured a full corner on cotton. I had bought almost every single bale of cotton. This fact did not escape the eyes of the U.S. government.

"As soon as I had my full position I got a call from the secretary of agriculture to immediately come to Washington and meet with President Wilson. I took the train to Washington and went straight to the White House, where the secretary and the president were waiting. I was ushered in directly to see the president.

"After greetings were exchanged, President Wilson began. 'Mr. Livermore, it has come to our attention that you have cornered the Chicago cotton futures market. Is that true?'

" 'Yes, Mr. President,' I said.

" 'Now we know what a smart fellow you are, and the price of cotton is nice and low now, and you have properly figured out that the projections for cotton demand in the next little while is high as the nation comes back from war and prosperity begins in earnest.'

" 'Yes, Mr. President,' I said.

" 'We know you understand about inflation, Mr. Livermore, and with you having a corner on cotton you can pretty much name your price as the demand grows,' the secretary of agriculture said.

" 'And we don't want inflation Mr. Livermore. Higher prices in something as important as the cotton market will be very bad while the nation is trying to get on its feet, don't you think?' the president added.

" 'Yes sir,' I said.

" 'Let me ask you a question, Mr. Livermore, a question that has my full interest.'

" 'Yes sir,' I said, and waited.

" 'Why? Why did you corner the cotton market?'

" 'To see if I could, Mr. President.'

" 'You cornered the entire United States cotton market, to see if you could, Mr. Livermore?' the secretary of agriculture blurted.

" 'Yes sir. It got out of hand a little at first, and then I wanted to see if I could do it, that's all.'

" 'Well, Mr. Livermore, what would it take for you to undo it, before the other traders really find out what's happened here and start to drive up the price?' the president asked.

" 'Nothing sir, just you asking me here today, that will do it.'

" 'How, how will you do it?' the secretary asked.

" 'I'll sell it just like I bought it, in an orderly way, and I will sell only for what I basically paid for it. I'm not interested in anything that will hurt the country.'

"We shook hands and I lived up to my promise. But I always have to smile when I think of this story. Nobody except the secretary of agriculture and the president and myself ever knew about what had happened.

"And now you too, son."

It was in the 1920s that Livermore acquired his gun collection. Firearms had always fascinated him. He built a shooting range at Evermore after the house had been finished. The shooting range was down on the beach level. He excavated a long corridor, beginning at the ledge where the beach ended and the rolling lawns began. About 6 feet high, it ran 100 feet and divided into a Y. The sides were supported with timbers, and at the end of the shooting alley was a wall of heavy wood, then sand, then a 1-inch-thick steel sheet to stop the bullets.

He had a large collection of handguns, shotguns, and rifles, and he spent lots of time with Dorothy and the boys, teaching them about firearms. Paul, an expert marksman, could fieldstrip a .45 automatic and reassemble it in minutes when he was 11 years old. Jesse Jr. and Mousie were also crack shots.

Livermore kept his handguns locked up in the library, along with his extensive collection of high-powered rifles and shotguns.

Livermore often hunted in the woods surrounding his home in Lake Placid. He also had a large collection of classic Purdy shotguns, made for him in England, for bird shooting.

Livermore also built a skeet range that fired clay pigeons off into Long Island Sound. He often shot skeet for $5 a bird, sometimes shooting from the hip, blasting the clay pigeons into smithereens.

Dorothy was also a great shot, especially with a rifle. She could give anyone a run for their money on the shooting range. She had no fear of guns.

One day the boys went into the library and the downstairs gunroom and counted the guns: There were 405 guns of one kind or another in the house. Livermore told his boys the shooting range helped him relax.

Livermore had constant stress to deal with in the markets.

Livermore had direct wires from his offices to more than 50 brokerage firms. In 1923, he ran a pool that he later regretted—Mammoth Oil, which was involved in the Teapot Dome scandal. Two close associates, E. L. Doheny and Harry F. Sinclair, came to Livermore in October 1922. They wanted to distribute 151,000 shares of stock to the public at $40 a share. They wanted Livermore to engineer the distribution and at the same time try to run an orderly market in the stock.

Mammoth was a Sinclair Oil subsidiary that had received profitable oil leases from the U.S. Navy—through, as it was later disclosed, the direct help of Albert Fall, the secretary of the interior.

The Mammoth issue was immediately oversubscribed once the public heard that Livermore was running the stock. The first day, sales opened with 8,000 shares at $43 a share; the day ended with total sales of 40,000 shares, with a closing price of $40.75. The sale of stock went well, and the 151,000 shares were sold to the public within three days.

But on February 16, 1924, the Teapot Dome scandal broke. The scandal rocked the market. The price of Mammoth Oil fell like a stone. Livermore was in Palm Beach at the Breakers when the news hit. He had been there since December 28, 1923. Traveling with him was his private telegraph operator.

He had traveled to Palm Beach in his own private railway car. The car was opulent, with three bedrooms, a galley, and a large living and dining area. The boys each had their own nannies, who traveled in the train's regular sleeper cars, as did the chef and the butler. Livermore always kept the car at the ready in the New York train yards. When he was in Palm Beach, the railway car was kept in the Miami train yards. He also used it when he traveled to his home in Lake Placid, or when he went to Chicago to visit the grain pits during heavy speculation.

The Teapot Dome scandal involved two cabinet members: Secretary Fall of the Interior Department and Secretary Denby of the Navy. It was an elaborate scam. Naval oil properties had been transferred to the Interior Department; naval coal lands in Alaska were to be transferred in the same way. After a suitable passage of time, the Interior Department, headed by Secretary Fall, would then lease them under very favorable conditions to private enterprises, including Mammoth Oil.

President Coolidge's entire administration was placed in jeopardy. Correspondence and other documentation clearly proved the fraud charges. Mammoth plunged on the news, and then the entire market followed.

Livermore had already sold out his Mammoth Oil and was a bear at the time of the scandal. He had shorted a number of other stocks. But he was named as a fringe player in the scandal and was placed under federal court subpoena.

On February 16, 1924, the *New York Times* eagerly covered the story:

Every day that passes brings out some new sensational development in regard to the oil hearing; this has undermined the
confidence of a lot of people in the stock market. If this
investigation fever of Senators and Congressmen keeps up
and branches out into investigation of other matters, it is
going to disturb confidence in a great deal more. I think it is
very foolish trying to be an optimist on the stock market at
the present time.

The *Times* went on the next day to report:

The speculatively inclined accepted the message of Jesse Livermore's as gospel yesterday and at once turned into bears.
The decline was under full-speed at noon and every class of
shares was affected.

The scandal had erupted. Livermore remained in Palm Beach
and eluded the subpoena for a while, but was eventually called
before a congressional committee. He gave his testimony and was
not bothered again. It was not as easy for Doheney and Sinclair,
who were both indicted for bribery. Sinclair was ultimately sentenced to nine months in prison, while Doheny was acquitted of
all charges. Fall was convicted of bribery. He was the first U.S. cabinet member ever to go to jail.

Livermore's final comment to the press on the matter was:

In the future, men of higher caliber should be sent to Washington. This country is a business nation, and it should have
at the head of its various governmental branches the most
successful businessmen in the country.

Livermore was later accused of trying to manipulate the press in
order to affect the steep downward decline of the market during

the scandal. His response was published in the March 8, 1924, edition of the *New York Times:*

> Mr. Jesse Livermore has offered a reward of $25,000 for proof that he had sent or contemplated any of the messages referred to in the various rumors about him trying to affect the market.

More rumors started flying, and Livermore sent a wire to the press from the Breakers in Palm Beach:

> I emphatically deny the rumor which was so industriously spread throughout the country that I was to issue a statement of some kind this afternoon. I have sent no messages or wires nor have I made any private statement to anyone; therefore the rumor that was started yesterday, was started by some unscrupulous person or persons. Three weeks ago, on February 14, I received requests from two brokers and one prominent capitalist asking me my personal opinion on the immediate future of the stock market. I sent them a short and concise statement of my views and stated at that time it was a confidential message meant only for them personally.
>
> Someone, without my permission, gave the message out, and it was sent broadcast over a number of private wires, and later carried by the newspapers. Having had the confidence of a personal and private message betrayed, there will be no more personal messages sent or given by me to anyone.

Livermore was becoming an expert in handling the press and using it to his benefit. His mysterious and secretive ways on Wall Street only increased allure, mystery, and fascination, fueling the fires of public curiosity and selling more newspapers.

The last issue he ran was the initial public offering of the

De Forest Radio Company. The issue, 75,000 shares, was offered on November 8, 1924, at $21 a share. The offering was tremendously oversubscribed and later was listed on the New York Curb Market.

In 1924, Wall Street was on fire with the introduction of commercial radio, and the De Forest issue was timed perfectly to coincide with the overheated demand for any high-technology radio stock.

The issue later went bankrupt.

In the meantime, Livermore was enjoying himself at his beloved Palm Beach. His yacht was moored there, and he was ready for some big game fishing.

In January 1925, he took his boat and six guests down to the Florida Keys. In the Keys, Livermore hooked into a big shark. He fought the fish, strapped in the fighting chair, for 55 minutes. The rod suddenly went wild as he released his grip and fainted in the chair. The captain and crew carried him to his stateroom.

He was confined to his stateroom for three days, recovering. But it did not upset the fishing. The total catch was reported as 256 fish, along with a giant stingray, which was harpooned in the Gulf Stream. The stingray towed the boat for five miles before it was brought alongside. It weighed 590 pounds and had a spread of 22 feet. It measured 30 feet from the head to the end of the stinger.

But life wasn't all fun. There was always a threat in the air for those who were famous for their enormous wealth. On March 15, 1925, Mrs. Louis Goldstein, wife of an assistant district attorney for Kings County, was sitting on the porch of the Breakers Hotel dozing. It was raining heavily. She was awakened by the raised voices of two men in a heated discussion.

"What would a million dollars be to him?" one of the men asked. "Why, he makes that much in a single speculation on the stock market."

"We could take the older boy, Jesse Junior, for instance. He's a high-spirited youngster and runs around all the time by himself. It would be the easiest thing in the world to grab ahold of him."

Mrs. Goldstein, now fully awake, got up from her seat. She knew Livermore, and she knew these men were referring to him and his son. She walked over to the two men on the porch so she could have a good look at their faces. The two men looked up at her and then looked away, pulling up their collars and pulling down their hats. They rose from their chairs and hurriedly walked off the porch into the pouring rain.

Mrs. Goldstein immediately reported the conversation to Livermore and he, at once, sent a wire to New York to have a detective sent to Palm Beach to stay with the boys for the rest of the season.

But the detective never got to Palm Beach.

On March 18, Dache and the boys were returning from a car trip to the Everglades in the Rolls. Dache was driving, and the boys were sitting up front with him. He saw the smoke first as they approached the Breakers. Huge dark clouds of smoke were enveloping the far end of the hotel. Dache parked the car and walked to the expansive front lawn to watch the fire with the boys.

Dorothy was in the crowd and ran to the boys. "Oh, thank God you were out in the car with Harry."

"But our end of the hotel isn't even burning yet," Jesse Jr. said.

"It will," Dache said.

Just then Livermore arrived. He had been down on the yacht with the crew getting ready for a cruise to the Florida Keys. "What happened?" he asked.

"This place was a firetrap at best, J.L., old dried-out wood baking in the tropics. An accident waiting to happen."

"J.L., I hope our luggage will be all right. I had it packed for the cruise."

"We can always buy more luggage, Mousie," he said.

"But our initials are on all the pieces, and they all match so nice." They each had 12 pieces of Luis Vuitton hand-crafted monogrammed luggage. "I asked the bell captain to try!" Dorothy continued.

"Try what?" Livermore asked.

"To go back and try to save them," Dorothy answered.

"J.L., look at that." Dache pointed to the corner where they had their suite of rooms. "Look up at those windows, I can't believe it."

Luggage was showering out through the fourth-floor window. When it landed on the lawn, it was picked up by a crew of bell-hops who carried it away from the fire toward the beach.

"Mousie, I think that's our luggage. I'm dumbfounded," Livermore said. "Mousie, you stay with the boys while Harry and I go see if we can help." The two men ran toward that corner of the building. They got there as the bellhops were stacking up the last of the 24 pieces on the beach.

Dache got there first and inspected the luggage. "This is incredible, this luggage falls four stories, bounces on the grass, gets kicked and piled up in the sand, and there isn't a mark on it."

Livermore examined the luggage. "You're right, Harry. It's amazing that Mousie would ask them to go back into the fire, and that they would actually do it, and it's amazing that the luggage survived."

"Without a scratch or a dent. You ought to buy this Louis Vuitton stock."

Livermore smiled. "I think I might buy it, Harry, but there's one problem."

"What's that, J.L.?"

"The stuff never wears out. Or breaks. No repeat sales!"

They laughed and gave Dorothy the high sign that everything was fine.

The Breakers was rebuilt in record time, just one year. Schultz and Weaver, the same firm that had designed the Waldorf Astoria in New York and the Biltmore Hotel in Coral Gables, designed the new and improved Breakers Hotel. By 1927, many people considered this new Breakers to be the finest resort in the United States. The Livermores agreed, and rented a suite of rooms well in advance of the new hotel's opening.

It was an active spring for Livermore. On April 9, 1925, he was injured at his mansion in King's Point. He was inspecting a newly constructed wing of the mansion when he walked into a dimly lit staircase and fell 20 feet. He was placed in his limousine and sped to his house at 8 West Seventy-sixth Street in Manhattan.

Physicians were summoned to the house, where they diagnosed him as having a broken right arm and some broken ribs. This diagnosis was confirmed by X ray, and he was confined to his home.

Livermore did not trade in stocks again until August 25, 1925. He conducted business from his Lake Placid home. Rumors circulated that he was long 50,000 shares of U.S. Steel and held an important position in White Motors. Livermore refused to confirm these rumors.

On October 27, 1927, Livermore bought a new apartment in New York at 825 Fifth Avenue, between Sixty-third and Sixty-fourth Streets. This would become his New York residence. Dorothy was thrilled with the new apartment, and along with her mother, as always, she spent great time, effort, and money in decorating their new home.

chapter nine

Boston Billy

I find all this money is a considerable burden.

John Paul Getty Jr.

ON SUNDAY, MAY 29, 1927, ARTHUR BARRY; JAMES F.
Monaghan, known as "Boston Billy"; Eddie Kane, former chauffeur for Livermore; and Anna Blake, an attractive young woman
with bobbed blonde hair who was Barry's girlfriend, sat around a
midnight campfire at Evermore, the Livermore estate. The full details of the dramatic events that followed during the next several
hours were subsequently covered by both the New York Times and
the Daily News from May 31, 1927, until December 27, 1929.

The men were settled on their haunches in a patch of open land
under a big oak tree. Blake sat on the grass. They could see the shim-
mering, moonlit water in front of them and the long pier where the
Chris-Craft was tied up. The Livermore yacht sat anchored in deep
water, about 100 yards off the pier. To their left, they could see the
massive house through the forest. They were waiting for the lights to
go out. They knew there was a dinner party going on. They even
knew who the guests were: millionaire silk merchant Harry
Aronhson and his wife, close friends of the Livermores, who had
come from New York on the yacht for the weekend. Kane, Livermore's former chauffeur, had informed Monaghan about the small
dinner party and the layout of the Livermore mansion.

Barry and Monaghan were dressed in dark gray business suits,
shirts, ties, and fedora hats. They were clean-shaven and about 25
years old. Livermore was later to comment that they looked more
like Wall Street clerks than burglars. Barry was muscular and
brawny; Monaghan was of average size and weight, about 5 foot 10
and 160 pounds, but he was the fiercer of the two.

They sat around the campfire roasting hot dogs. They had even
brought a little picnic bag with buns and drinks in it. They chatted
calmly as they waited for the clock to reach 3:30 A.M.

"So, the safe may have up to a million in jewelry?" Barry asked.

"Yeah, that's right. This guy Livermore is crazy about his wife
and has given her millions in jewels," Kane said. "They're all from

Harry Winston and Van Cleef and Arpels, first quality, easy to take outta the settings."

"Easy to fence," Monaghan said, biting into his hot dog, sipping from a bottle of beer.

Kane continued, "Word is that Livermore has such a fear of going broke, because he's been broke before, that he gave his old lady the jewelry so's if he busted out again he could take the jewel stash back and hock it for at least a cool million. The jewels are his stake to start over. Rumor is that he has actually done it, hocked 'em, on occasion with that big-shot jeweler Harry Winston who made 'em in the first place."

"High-class hock shop. Buy the jewels for your wife, then hock 'em back to the jeweler. Pretty nifty, these rich folks, but they're just like everybody else when they get in trouble. They take back their gifts and hock 'em," Blake said.

"You know from experience, huh, Anna?" Monaghan said.

"Shut your face, Billy," Barry said. "How do you know all this, Eddie?"

"Hey, the house slaves get to know everything about their masters. Don't you know that?"

"Yeah, I heard of that," Monaghan said. "This ain't my first job."

The gang had stolen an expensive canary-yellow Chrysler roadster from the garage of Walter Roesler, one of Livermore's neighbors. Roesler himself had borrowed the car for the day from his friend George Owens. It was a high-profile, well-known car in Great Neck. They had hidden it off the road near the entrance to the Livermore estate.

They watched over their campfire as all the lights went out in the mansion. Hours later, at 3:45 in the dark morning, they watched the embers of their campfire sizzle and die as they poured the last of the beer on it. Barry and Monaghan stood, straightened their ties, adjusted their fedoras, and headed for the mansion. Kane and Blake also stood.

Monaghan picked up his ladder, which was leaning against a tree. It was about 4 feet long and 2 feet wide. It was a metal ladder that could be broken down into five 4-foot sections and easily reassembled to its full length of 20 feet. The ladder had been designed by Monaghan and custom built for him. He had used the ladder on other second-story jobs. Boston Billy always left the ladder behind him after a job, as his signature.

They walked to the solarium, which they knew was just under the master bedroom. Monaghan opened the metal ladder and locked each section in place. Quietly they placed the ladder against the building and made their ascent. Later, one of Blake's footprints would be discovered in the soft earth around the flowerbed.

Barry and Monaghan made the ascent onto the balcony. Monaghan took out a butcher knife and quietly popped the brass clasp, and they entered the hallway that led to the anteroom of the Livermores' master bedroom. The butcher knife would later be found discarded among the shrubbery. Kane and Blake returned to the hidden getaway car to wait for the pickup signal.

Dorothy Livermore lay in bed awake. She had heard a noise. She poked her husband in the ribs. "J.L., did you hear something?"

"No, Mousie, now go back to sleep."

"I'm sure I heard something. Listen." They both listened and both heard a noise.

"I'm getting up to see what's happening," she said.

"I'll get the gun."

Dorothy left the bed and slipped on her robe. She entered the hall that led to their massive closets and to their individual bathrooms. A dark figure wearing a hat and carrying a gun stood in black silhouette in the hallway.

"Can I help you?" she calmly asked Barry.

"Probably. Probably you can help me. Go back into your room and tell your husband to stay in bed."

Dorothy did as she was told.

Livermore sat on the edge of the bed. He gently lifted the telephone receiver from the hook and placed the open phone on the table, hoping the operator would hear what was going on.

"I think you should just take what you want and leave," Dorothy said to the stickup men. "I have my two little sons asleep in this house, and I don't want them hurt."

"They won't be hurt, just sit yourselves down and remain calm," Barry said.

"Where are your guests sleeping?" Monaghan asked.

"Down the hall, fourth door on the left," Dorothy said.

"I'm going down there. You keep these two here," Monaghan said.

He walked down the hall, entered the room, and woke the Aronhsons. He placed the muzzle of his gun against Mrs. Aronhson's temple. "Now sir, give me that platinum wristwatch you're wearing, that star sapphire ring, and get up and go over to the dresser and give me the pearl stickpin and the cash that's laying on the dresser." Aronhson did as he was told. Monaghan counted the money. There was $200. He stripped out two $1 bills. "Here, use this to take a cab home," he said, handing the cash to Aronhson. "Now, if you value your life and Mr. and Mrs. Livermore's life, you will lie here until they come to get you."

Monaghan walked back to the master bedroom and joined Barry.

"I hope you didn't hurt our guests," Dorothy said.

"No. Your guests are fine, just fine. I even left them two dollars for a cab ride home."

"Two dollars? They live in the city," Dorothy said.

The men laughed, even Livermore. "Well they can take a cab to the train station, can't they?" Monaghan said, smiling. "Let's see your hand."

Barry held the barrel of his pistol against her arm while Monaghan slipped a beautiful blue sapphire ring off her finger. Monaghan then went to Livermore, took a similar ring off his finger, and said, "Hey, almost a matching pair, how sweet."

"Oh, please, don't take those, they were Christmas presents!"

Monaghan looked at the rings and sighed, then looked back at Dorothy, who was crying. "I beg your pardon then, ma'am," he said, and handed back the two rings, worth more than $15,000.

Monaghan continued, "We're more interested in what's in the safe. Open it, Mr. Livermore."

"There's nothing in it," he said.

"We'll just take a look anyway," Barry added, still holding the gun on Dorothy.

"I can't see the combination without my glasses," Livermore said.

"Where are your glasses?" Monaghan said.

"In the dressing room."

"Take me there," Monaghan said, putting his gun against Livermore's shoulder. He escorted Livermore into the dressing room, and they emerged with the glasses.

The thief walked Livermore directly over to the portrait that was hung in front of the hidden safe. He swung the portrait clear. "Open it!"

Livermore slipped on his spectacles and attempted to open it, but his hands trembled so badly that he was unable to work the combination. "I can't seem to work it," he said.

"Step aside, sir," Monaghan commanded. "I'll fix it. Wait a minute." He left and vanished down the ladder for a bag of burglary tools. In seconds he was back. With a hammer and chisel, he popped the safe like it was a child's toy. He took out a few papers and cast them aside in disgust. "That's it? Just these worthless papers?"

"That's all there is!" Dorothy cried, "Now take what you have and leave, please."

The thieves quickly went through the bedroom and the dressing rooms. There were jewels scattered everywhere. They gathered up a pearl necklace worth $80,000 and a sapphire and diamond ring of Dorothy's worth $15,000. They already had the $200 in cash taken from Aronhson, a pearl stickpin valued at $2,000, and a square diamond ring worth $1,000. The Livermore jewels were properly appraised and insured for 80 percent of their value.

The thieves left behind over $20,000 in sapphires that were lying on the dressing table. They also ignored Livermore's gold cuff links and diamond studs. They discussed the jewels as they gathered them, describing them and estimating their value as they dropped them into a bag.

In all, they were in the house for almost an hour, taking their time chatting and examining the rooms. The police were later to comment that in most such robberies, the thieves would be in and out in less than 10 minutes.

The thieves exited down the steel ladder and trotted to the end of the driveway, where Blake and Kane were waiting in the Chrysler roadster. They jumped into the car and raced toward the Manhasset railway station.

Mrs. John Gernan, who lived near the railway stop, observed the men and the woman between 5:30 and 5:45 A.M. on Sunday. She watched the group from her window. She told the *New York Daily News* on May 31, 1927: "I was unable to sleep and was awake early Sunday, and I heard an automobile and looked out. I saw a canary colored Chrysler automobile with three men and a blonde girl. Her hair was short. She wore a sport coat and no hat. She appeared young, about 18. Because of the early hour I wondered what the girl was doing out with three men. I watched them drive toward the railroad station, stop the car, and get out. They walked in the direction of the station, disappearing from my view."

Mrs. Gernan had good powers of observation: "I didn't hear a train come through, but then I wasn't listening particularly. In fact, I went back to bed and to sleep. I knew it was the car that was taken from Walter Roesler's garage, the car that belonged to George Owens, because later in the day, after the police found the car, I saw the owner come and drive it away."

What Mrs. Gernan could not see was the gang stealing a taxicab and driving it into New York City, where they abandoned it.

On Monday, nerves shattered by the robbery, the Aronhsons beat a hasty retreat to New York. They had planned to remain over Memorial Day but changed their minds. Livermore provided his Rolls to take them into the city.

Dorothy was not inclined to have her holiday spoiled. She called some friends in New York, and by noon, six guests, plus the Livermore children and their nannies, boarded the Livermore's palatial yacht. The yacht was fully provisioned. They left from the private pier behind the estate, without leaving word when they would return.

Meanwhile, Percy G. Rockefeller, who had been robbed of $19,000 at dinner during a previous Boston Billy burglary, had engaged the Burns detective agency to investigate independently of the police. On the news of the Livermore robbery, Burns immediately sent down a detective, Michael Rincones, who was joined by Detectives Paul Crowley and Jesse Mayforth of the Nassau County Police Department. All three men were heavily armed and on patrol at the Livermore estate.

Captain of Detectives Harold R. King of the Nassau County

Police Department was named the lead investigator in charge of the case. There had been a string of other such robberies on Long Island and in New York. The police suspected the Boston Billy gang of having stolen over $1 million in jewels and cash over the prior three years. The gang was suspected in the robberies of Percy G. Rockefeller of Greenwich, Connecticut; William Durant of Deal, New Jersey, the largest shareholder of General Motors; Joshua E. Cosden of Port Washington, Long Island, who was robbed during the Prince of Wales's visit; and several other wealthy and powerful people.

Livermore found out from the police why removing the telephone from the cradle did no good. The switch on the telephone was set on intercom, so it would only connect to the other phones in the house, and all the servants were asleep.

On Wednesday, June 1, Livermore read his mail. The postmark was Brooklyn: "We are coming to see you again tonight, and we are coming to see you on business." Signed: The Gentlemen Robbers. The letter was written in pencil.

That evening, a servant answered the phone; a man's voice was on the other end.

"Is Mr. Livermore in?" the man asked.

"No," the servant replied.

"Tell Mr. Livermore that it would be a serious matter if he didn't heed the warning we gave him."

After reviewing the letter, Captain King sent four plainclothes officers to the Livermore estate for security. Livermore also had his own private detectives on the job.

On June 5, six days after the Livermore robbery, the police got a break. The Nassau County Police Department got a phone tip that a suspect in the Livermore robbery was on an eastbound train due at Ronkonkoma at 7:13 P.M. Ronkonkoma was 50 miles from Pennsylvania Station on the main line of the Long Island Railroad, at the end of the Long Island Motor Parkway.

The train pulled into the station at Ronkonkoma on time. Waiting were three Nassau County detectives, led by Captain King, and one Suffolk County detective. They were waiting on the platform for the passengers.

Arthur Barry and Anna Blake exited the train. The detectives moved in, walking quickly up to the couple. When Barry spotted the four detectives he reached for his hip, as if to draw his gun. He then bolted and ran back on the train. Blake stayed on the platform. One of the detectives moved in on her. The three other detectives drew their guns and followed after Barry, racing down the aisles of the train, from car to car in a wild chase. They finally boxed him into a corner. Guns drawn and pointed, Captain King shouted, "Give up now, or you're dead."

Barry surrendered.

Meanwhile, on the platform, the detective moved in on Blake as she tried to dispose of a small pasteboard box. The detective ripped the box out of her hands and cuffed her. Inside the box was stolen jewelry worth $15,000.

The detectives hurried the captured suspects into the car they had driven from Mineola, Long Island, and sped off, headed for Blake's home.

The wild chase and gunplay had caused the passengers and the station agent to believe that the detectives, who were in plain clothes, were really robbers who had attacked and kidnapped a couple of innocent passengers. The passengers alerted the station agent, who immediately called the Suffolk and Nassau County police and informed them that a robbery and kidnapping had taken place on the train station platform at Ronkonkoma. He described it as an old-time, wild-West-style train robbery and kidnapping. Believing the report, the Suffolk and Nassau County police put out a general alarm for a Ford or a Chevy with New York license plates 2Z33. The alarm was called off when the license plate checked out to be issued to the Nassau County District Attorney's Office.

Meanwhile, the detectives were quickly taken to Blake's home, where they also arrested Barry's brother.

The next day, June 6, in a room on the top floor of the Nassau County Courthouse at Mineola, Arthur Barry signed a confession that he and his associate, whom he knew as Bill or Earl "Boston Billy" Williams, committed the $100,000 robbery on the Livermore estate the previous week. Barry had cut a deal with Nassau County District Attorney Elvin Edwards. Edwards had promised that in return for making a clean breast of the whole story, he would free Barry's companion, Blake, and his brother William Barry. And he would drop all charges against them, since Barry insisted they had nothing to do with any crimes he was involved in.

After Barry signed his confession, a group of detectives headed for New York. They raided a rooming house on the West Side of Manhattan, near Central Park, just missing Boston Billy Monaghan by minutes. Barry had provided the address as part of his plea agreement.

Jesse and Dorothy Livermore were brought into the district attorney's office in Mineola soon after the confession was signed. They were unable to recognize Barry as one of the burglars since it was dark at the time of the robbery. But the incidents that surrounded the robbery and the circumstances of Barry's arrest convinced them that he was one of the robbers.

For instance, Barry reminded Dorothy that when she had asked him for a cigarette, he gave her one and lit it for her; and that he had returned her sapphire pinky ring when she asked him not to steal it and had said "I hope it brings you luck."

The police were also able to identify an $800 wristwatch that had been stolen from a residence in Rumson, New Jersey. This was the first tie-in with a string of reported burglaries.

In his confession, Barry said that he had met Monaghan at the Pennsylvania Station and that Monaghan had shown him a newspaper article reporting that the Livermores would have guests at a party that night. They rode to the Great Neck station and walked to the Livermore estate. Barry explained, "I went into this scheme with Billy to rob this place, and I knew it was contrary to law. I was sincerely sorry after I found out that Mr. and Mrs. Livermore were such good sports under the stress of the circumstances. But I still went through with the job."

Barry went on to explain that they had found the Chrysler roadster at a neighbor's house and stolen it. He explained that they drove to the Great Neck train station and just missed the train, so they commandeered an Overland taxicab that was standing empty at the station and drove to the outskirts of New York City, where they abandoned it.

The police checked Barry's prints and came up with warrants for his arrest in Massachusetts and Connecticut. They also discovered that he was charged in Scarsdale, New York, with the 1923 murder of Patrol Sergeant John Harrison, but Barry insisted that a companion had done the actual shooting, and the charges were dropped to assault. He was sentenced to three months, but couldn't stand it in jail. He escaped with only 15 days left to serve in his sentence. A friend had smuggled a saw into the jail.

The press described Blake as an attractive blond about 35 years old, a little over 5 feet tall, and dressed in a black silk coat over an unusually long black dress, topped off by a close-fitting black hat with gold embroidery. She and William Barry were not charged, as agreed in the plea bargain.

The police got deep into the information given to them by Barry and were astounded as the number of robberies he disclosed kept increasing—from 8 to 15 to 22 homes. The list of people robbed read like the social register: Percy G. Rockefeller; William

Durant of General Motors; F. W. Wheeler, head of the American Can Company; Alfred Berolzheimer, head of the Eagle Pencil Company; and Colonel John C. Stillwell (retired).

It also surfaced that the only one who could have provided inside information about the Livermore estate was the former chauffeur, Eddie Kane. A warrant was drawn for his arrest.

At this point, the police finally revealed how they had tracked down Barry and Blake. They had received two anonymous telephone calls, which they traced to a pay phone in the Bronx, one on Tuesday night and one on Wednesday night before the arrest on Sunday. The caller did not identify himself. He told the Nassau County police of a split in the gang over the division of the spoils in the Livermore robbery, including the information that one of the gang members had been hit over the head with an iron rod during a fight. The caller gave Barry's name and revealed the time and destination of their train. He also provided descriptions of Barry and Blake.

Barry was questioned further on the murder of Sergeant Harrison. He claimed it was Monaghan who had committed the murder. This enraged Monaghan when he read about it in the papers, and he actually sent a handwritten letter to the *New York Times*. He described Barry as "a lying rat who would send his own brother to the chair." Monaghan also claimed that he had proof that Barry had killed Sergeant Harrison.

The number of robberies continued to climb. Barry took the police on a tour of 22 houses in Westchester County alone, where he and Monaghan had looted over $500,000, mostly in jewelry. In one of the houses in Rye, Mr. Murray, the victim, said to Barry, "I want to thank you for the gentlemanly way in which you robbed me. Do you remember what you did with the college pins that were in the loot?"

Barry pointed to a place in the grass by some bushes, and said "We threw them there. They were worthless to us."

When the police left, Murray was on his hands and knees looking for the pins in the grass.

The cops took Barry up to Scarsdale, where he reenacted the
details of the murder of Officer Harrison. Monaghan was described
as a gunman, a hard drinker, and a great ladies' man.

The final tally for all the burglaries grew to $2 million over a
three-year period. On July 6, Barry was sentenced to 25 years in
prison at hard labor. He looked down at his smooth, white hands
and smiled a grim, resolute smile when he was sentenced.

Blake ran up to him, threw her arms around him, and kissed
him hard on the mouth, slipping a roll of bills into his hands for his
prison expenses. As he was hauled off, she collapsed in tears. Barry
blamed Monaghan for ratting him out. He said he was just about
to sail to Europe and a new life with Blake when he was arrested.

On July 7, Detective Gordon Hurley of the Nassau County
police waited at the back door of a bungalow in Sound View, Connecticut. Detective Charles Sheraton of the Burns agency stood by
the front door. Sheraton had been retained by Percy G. Rockefeller after he had been robbed at gunpoint. Sheraton had been on
Monaghan's trail for seven months now. He had just missed Monaghan on several occasions. He was not going to miss him again.

On a prearranged signal, they broke the front door open. Monaghan was inside. He sprang for his gun and ran through the house
for the back door. Detective Hurley stood in the rear doorway and
calmly shot Monaghan through the leg as he dodged from side to
side in the hallway. Monaghan collapsed in a heap and screamed in
pain. He was taken to Memorial Associated Hospital, where he
received treatment.

In the hospital, Monaghan admitted to several robberies, but
not the Livermore robbery. He also denied killing Scarsdale Patrol
Sergeant Harrison, as his former partner Barry had claimed. After
his arrest, Monaghan told the police that he was an avid reader of

the society news. This gave him his leads. He would find out what families were giving dinners, when they were giving them, and who the guests were going to be.

Eyewitnesses later confirmed that it was Monaghan who had robbed their houses.

His mother, Mary Monaghan, came to visit him in jail. She broke down and wept when they met. She said, "I hope you will come out of it all right, my son."

He replied, "Well, ma, we'll wait and see. I've got a good lawyer."

Later she told reporters, "He may be a criminal, but I still love him." She cried, "I trust in God to bring him through. I will stand by him, and he can have my last dollar if he needs it."

The next day, they brought Barry in from Sing Sing prison to testify against Monaghan before a grand jury. Barry persisted in his accusation that Monaghan had killed the Scarsdale police sergeant. But Monaghan accused Barry of the killing, saying "Barry is only trying to blame me so he can get himself into the clear."

Nassau County District Attorney Edwards decided to ask the Nassau County Grand Jury to indict James Monaghan, alias Boston Billy, as a fourth offender under the Baumes laws, which would mean life imprisonment without parole for Monaghan, if convicted. Monaghan had three prior felony convictions in Massachusetts and was wanted on a fugitive warrant for escaping from prison.

On July 21, a check of the spoons used by prisoners revealed that one was missing. Monaghan's cell was searched, and the guards found a spoon filed down into a device that could be used to pick a lock. The Nassau County sheriff immediately ordered that Monaghan be placed in solitary confinement. Monaghan resisted violently. He was finally subdued. He screamed, "I'll go crazy in solitary. Let me out of this dump."

"If he gets any worse," Sheriff Stronson said, "I'll put him in a straitjacket."

The next day, while locked in solitary, Monaghan set fire to his mattress. The sheriff then placed a guard outside his cell.

The day his trial was to begin, July 29, Monaghan pleaded guilty to the charges of burglary. The charge of killing Scarsdale Patrol Sergeant Harrison was dropped. Monaghan received a 50-year sentence. As he entered the courtroom for sentencing he was heard saying, "Well, here I am. I'll get life, I suppose, but I'll be out soon."

His escape threat was taken seriously. He was taken to Sing Sing prison under heavy guard, right up until the prison ferry picked him up at College Point. On the way there, Monaghan again vowed to Sheriff Stronson that he would escape from prison.

On January 6, 1929, Nassau County detectives brought in Eddie Kane, the former chauffeur involved in the Livermore robbery, from Kenosha, Wisconsin, after a two-year search. On January 7, Kane pleaded guilty. On May 22, Kane was sentenced to three and a half to five years in a state penitentiary.

Both Dorothy and Jesse Livermore were shocked to find out that Kane had aided the robbers. They refused to believe he was involved until he finally confessed to the crime.

The report of the possible plot to kidnap his children in Palm Beach in March 1925 and the 1927 robbery by the Boston Billy gang, as well as the gang's subsequent threats and the long pursuit of the robbers, left Livermore badly depressed and very protective of his family.

But it did not stop the irrepressible Dorothy from throwing grand parties whenever the spirit moved her.

★ *chapter ten* ★

The Crash of 1929

*There is nothing unique about the crash of '29. It is something
that happens about every 20 to 30 years, because that is the
length of the financial memory. It is about the length of time
needed for a new set of suckers to come in and imagine that they
have a new and wonderful fix on the future."*
John Kenneth Galbraith, *The Great Crash of 1929*

LIVERMORE'S CONCENTRATION ON THE TURBULENT, boiling bull market of early 1929 was briefly distracted by a surprise lawsuit.

On April 4, 1929, 93 investors sued the Mizner Development Corporation, which included Livermore and T. Coleman Du Pont as directors, for $1.45 million. These investors claimed that they had suffered in the crash of the Boca Raton land boom. Maximilian Morgenthau, the son of former ambassador to Turkey Henry Morgenthau, led this group of disgruntled investors.

Morgenthau filed an 870-page complaint. It was the longest complaint ever filed up to that time. The complaint stated that the Mizner Development Corporation had committed fraud. It stated that the Boca Raton, Florida, lots had been misrepresented and that the Mizner Development Corporation, the promoter of the development, had operated without any prior knowledge of real estate sales and management.

The complaint further stated that the criminal operation was initiated on April 12, 1925, when the promoters had appointed as president Addison Mizner, an architect with no experience in real estate development. Mizner had then appointed his brother, Wilson Mizner, a playwright with no qualifications in real estate, as secretary of the company.

The press had a field day with the suit. The corporation's directors quickly and privately settled it. The details of the settlement were never disclosed. The entire matter quietly drifted off the newspaper pages.

The problem had begun in 1925, when Addison Mizner, a famous Palm Beach architect, had the brilliant idea to develop Boca Raton, an undeveloped area just south of Palm Beach. Mizner wanted to build the world's most architecturally beautiful playground. He wanted to construct a magnificent 1,000-room hotel, a polo field, and a casino in the first year and expand from there into a massive land development scheme that would include three more major hotels.

A syndicate, the Mizner Development Corporation, was formed to oversee and finance the ambitious development. The group was made up of leading financial, entertainment, and social luminaries, including Harold Vanderbilt, Paris Singer, Jesse Livermore, Irving Berlin, W. K. Vanderbilt II, Addison and Wilson Mizner, Elizabeth Arden, T. Coleman Du Pont, and Rodman Wanamaker, to name a few.

The syndicate purchased two miles of beachfront around the Boca Raton inlet and 1,600 acres of land. An offering of $500,000 of the new syndicate's original $5 million capital investment was offered for sale to the public. It was sold out in less than a week. Land prices in the area surrounding the proposed development skyrocketed.

This ad appeared in the *Palm Beach Post* on May 15, 1925:

The owners and controllers of the Mizner Development Corporation are a group of very rich men and women of unlimited means who propose to build from the creative genius of Addison Mizner what will most likely be the most wonderful resort city in the world. The combined wealth of the stockholders probably represents over one-third of the entire wealth of the United States. It is reasonable to suppose that every lot buyer should make quick and large profits.

The prominent backers' names were used in all the ads and marketing efforts to promote the corporation. On August 6, the directors were elected. Du Pont, recently elected senator from Delaware, was made chairman of the board, and Livermore was made head of the finance committee. It did not take Livermore and the finance committee long to find out what was going on and to object to the use of their names in promoting the development project. They strenuously denounced this bandying about of their names as if they were personally guaranteeing the financial success of the project.

They also objected to promising the new purchasers of land that three more hotels would be built, including a Ritz-Carlton, as well as three golf courses, polo fields, and miles of excellent paved streets throughout the development.

Finally, before the year was out, on November 24, Du Pont resigned, saying to the press that proper business methods were not being used, although the project had great possibilities. Livermore and several other directors resigned, as well.

These resignations and problems in the press brought about the immediate demise of the Boca Raton land boom. In its first six months of operation, the marketing company had achieved sales of over $25 million. But with the board of directors breaking up and Du Pont's negative comments appearing in the *New York Times,* sales ended abruptly, and the project shut down.

This left Livermore with another good lesson: Stick to what you know, which in his case was the stock market. He set back to work to recoup the money he had lost in the Florida land deal, a deal his prominent Palm Beach friends had told him just could not fail.

From the winter of 1928 until the early spring of 1929, Livermore was a full-fledged bull in a runaway bull market, but he was looking for the market to signal the turn, the inevitable turn, and he was waiting to sell out his long positions. Experience had taught him that it was always best to sell *early* into a strong market, especially when he had substantial line of stocks to sell off.

In the early summer of 1929, still in the heat of a bull market, Livermore finally sold out all his long positions. He made a list of the leading stocks that he believed were overextended.

The line of least resistance had changed from bullish to sideways movement. He asked himself whether this sideways movement was merely a correction from the upward spike of the bull market, or the beginning of a major change in the direction of the overall market. Had the market trend changed? Was it changing in front of everyone's eyes, and was the greed factor too strong for people to see the top?

All of Livermore's experience and instincts screamed at him, telling him this was a top. But he knew timing was everything. It was not *whether* the top was coming; it was *when* the top was coming. He had been wrong before by going in early only to find out that he had been correct but had made his move too soon. He decided to follow his developed method of sending out probes to establish small positions on the short side of the market.

Operating out of his war room, his suite of offices in the Heckscher Building at 730 Fifth Avenue, he began his operation secretly. Constantly changing brokers, using as many as 100 brokers to disguise his moves over the next six months, telling no one of his strategy, using his secret symbols on the chalkboard, and keeping away from the press until all his positions were established, he tested the market.

He sent out his probes by selling several stocks short, small positions. The market continued upward, and he had to cover them, losing well over $250,000, a small part of his capital. He had his full crew of six chalkboard markers working everyday on the long catwalk. He was active on his direct phone lines to the London and Paris markets. The direct line to the grain pits in Chicago showed him that the prices of all major commodities were dropping to all-time lows, across the board. Because of his constant and never-ending queries into economics, both in the United States and abroad, he felt that the world was looking at a serious deflation.

He set out a second line of probes, testing his strong feelings again, but they did not hold, and he had to cover them when the market moved against him. But then in the late summer, for the third time, he set out his probes. They held.

They were suddenly profitable—not big profits, but at least they were profitable. Now he fully believed he was right.

His patience had paid off. It was one of the reasons he liked fishing, if you did the right thing, were persistent and patient, eventually you would catch fish. Now that he had a fish on the hook, he had to reel it in. This time he knew he was right. And he was prepared to back his play with sizable positions.

He was famous as the Boy Plunger, the Great Bear of Wall Street, and the Lone Wolf of Wall Street. He was ready to truly live up to his reputation.

In the summer of 1929, Livermore set out his short line while the market was still strong enough to accept his trades. It was also easy for him to borrow the necessary stock against his short positions, because practically everyone was bullish and thought it madness to be selling short. Things could not be better: The economy was great, liquidity was great, there was plenty of money around for businesses to borrow, and there was no sign of inflation—in fact, consumer prices were falling. His friends asked him why he would want to sell.

Livermore watched all this, and his famous instinct took over—his gut instinct, which he believed was not instinct at all. Rather, it was the sum total of all his experience and all his knowledge that was keeping his dreams fitful at night, stealing sleep—subconscious rumblings.

There were plenty of signals as the market finally topped. It did not just shoot up in a spike in one grand climax and fall to earth. No, like all markets before, it moved inexorably, slowly, like a giant ship at sea, but the market gave signals, signals that Livermore had seen before: The leaders were struggling, unable to make new

highs; the smart money was selling into the strong, driving greed
of the public.

The public had arrived in the market in full force. The mechan-
ics, the barbers, the shoe clerks, the paper carriers, the housewives,
and the farmers were all trading on 10 percent margin. It was
apparent to them that winning in the stock market was an easy
game; invest your money and prosper. It was a new time in history,
a time like never before, a time of endless prosperity, with a simple
formula: Buy stocks and get rich. Stocks went one way—up, up,
and up. This was a new era of perpetual prosperity—and, most
important, the little guy could participate.

Livermore watched stocks rise with wild capitalization, good
stocks selling at 30, 40, 50, 60 times their annual earnings. These
were stocks that had normally traded at 8 to 12 times earnings.
Plus, the wild speculative stocks, like the new high-technology
radio companies, took off. They were the trendy, favored stocks.

He also observed the leaders, the stocks that had led the market
upward. He watched as they stalled and corrected, failing to make
new highs, drifting back when they met a wave of distribution as
the smart money hit the road.

In the fall of 1929, Livermore sat in his office and watched
through the big glass window as his crew of six markers, wearing
headphones, marked the movement of stocks on the green chalkboard. The symbols made music for him, but it was now a wild
crescendo, the climax to the end of a great symphony, years and
years of sweet music. Now the end was near; the tempo was up,
out of control, on the verge of wildness; the chords were often dis-
cordant to his ears. He moved out of his office and sat for hours at
his long, shiny, mahogany conference table. He sat in silence,
watching the markers moving on the catwalk. As he watched, his
resolve grew. This was the end. Every once in a while he would go
into his private office and make a trade. He would then tell Harry

Edgar Dache, his trusted assistant, who would enter it into the book.

Often, at the end of the day, as a game, he would race Dache for a tally of where he stood, his exact equity balance, to the penny. Livermore would do the calculations in his head and, just as Dache was about to shout the answer given by the machine, he would hold up his hand and utter a number quietly, the number he had calculated mentally. Dache would just nod. Livermore was always correct.

Then it struck—the storm broke.

The cataclysm struck in full fury as soon as trading began. In the first 30 minutes of business, immense blocks of stocks— 50,000 shares at a time of Chrysler, General Electric, International Telephone and Telegraph, and Standard Oil—were dumped on the market by wealthy individuals and institutions at prices that stunned onlookers. AT&T, which had reached a peak of $310 per share in the heady summer days of the bull market, smashed all the way down to $204 in a sickening slide. U.S. Steel skated past 190, 180, 170, and kept going down. RCA, a former favorite at 110, went begging at 26. Some brokers lost their nerve and sold out their customers needlessly, lending further momentum to the downward spiral. Others lost their minds. Spectators watched in mute horror as one trader ran screaming like a lunatic from the floor of the exchange. Those who remained among the shouting, frantic mob took on the furtive, frightened look of hunted things.

By noon, more than 8 million shares of stock had been sold, a furious pace enveloped the trading floor as all previous trading records were shattered. Shortly thereafter, the members of the governing committee of the exchange held a secret meeting in a cramped, smoke-filled room beneath the floor of the market and anxiously debated whether to suspend trading completely until the panic subsided.

Across the news tickers that morning came a sequence of terse urgent messages: "Federal Reserve Board is in session in Washington with Secretary Mellon. Cabinet is meeting. President Hoover conferring with Secretary of Commerce Lamont. Leading bankers gathering at the office of J. P. Morgan Jr., to discuss the deteriorating situation." As the extent of the financial debacle became clear—15 billion worth of stock values had vanished into thin air, wiping out the life savings of investors across the nation—the human toll began to mount.

Businessmen whose companies went bankrupt suffered heart attacks. Ruined speculators leaped from hotel windows, or shut all windows and turned on the gas, or swallowed poison, or simply shot themselves. Behind them, in the wreckage of lifetimes of hard work, dreams and fatal illusions, they left notes that read: "Everything lost. Tell the boys I can't pay what I owe them."

The great crash, when securities on the nation's stock exchanges lost more than a third of their value in a heartbreaking avalanche that haunted the memories of an entire generation. When the dreams of hundreds of thousands of American investors—mostly members of the middle-class including secretaries, clerks, elderly spinsters, and small-business men—vanished in the smash-up along with hard earned savings. The great crash that battered the country, inflicting severe psychological trauma whose effects were still plainly visible more than a decade later.

William Klingaman, *1929: The Year of the Great Crash*

The next day, Black Tuesday, was worse: The market fell 11.7 percent in one day.

Livermore was personally blamed for the crash. Even the *New York Times* ran an article attributing the crash to his strong and constant short-selling attack on the market. Once again he was the center of a major drama, and his life was threatened.

The calls seemed never-ending. He personally answered the phone. He told Dache to put the angry calls through to him. The threats came in letters and telegrams, as well. After a while he stopped answering the phone. But the calls worried him for his safety and the safety of his family.

For Livermore, there was no joy in the misery of others. He wondered how his life had come to this sad point. It was his greatest single day in the market, his greatest victory. Why did he feel so hollow and empty?

In the early part of the twentieth century, depression was considered a mental condition caused by emotional instability or weakness of character. Clinical depression had not yet been discovered. Chemical imbalance as the cause of aberrant behavior was a theory not yet born. For serious cases of depression through most of the century, patients were often subjected to electroshock treatment. Electrodes were attached to the skull, and a terrific blast of electricity was applied to the cranium, searing into the brain. There is no proof that this therapy did anything but cause brain damage to the patient.

In 1930, besides his depression, Livermore had other personal problems. His wife Dorothy, his beloved Mousie, was drinking heavily, and her mother had become her complete alter ego. They shopped together and traveled together. Her mother's residence occupied one entire wing of the mansion at Evermore, and Dorothy sought her advice on every household and personal matter. Their main preoccupation was spending Livermore's money, primarily in decorating the various Livermore homes.

Dorothy's mother also loved to gamble. She was well off and used her own money. She was a good gambler. She won more than she lost.

On a European trip in 1930, they traveled to Spain to visit the American ambassador, Jesse's good friend Alexander P. Moore. Livermore had covered for Moore in his torrid affair with Lillian Russell. While they were in Spain, Moore introduced Dorothy's mother to the king of Spain, whom she promptly engaged in a torrid affair. The affair lasted for several months. She stayed on in Spain, gambling at the casino almost every night and having her fling with the king.

Dorothy thought it was charming, since her mother had been a widow for years. Livermore and Moore were bewildered by the whole affair and just shook their heads in silence.

Livermore often resented his mother-in-law. He felt isolated from his wife, and he believed that her mother's presence was a barrier between them. He was never an outgoing, gregarious type of person, and he kept his feelings to himself, so he never mentioned these feelings to Dorothy. He was, in fact, like his straitlaced New England parents, emotionally constipated. Reticence to display his feelings was ingrained in his personality. He considered it necessary to act like a poker player in his business, to never tip his hand or to react emotionally. Because of this inability and unwillingness to express his emotions, the stress on him was permanent. The only relief came when he sold out his market positions and took a vacation, or went out on his yacht, something he did more and more as he grew older.

He had another recreation, a secret recreation. Livermore had a weakness for beautiful women. And some women had a weakness

for a powerful man with unlimited money and the seductive aura
of a secretive life spent stalking the dark corridors of Wall Street
and the dimly lit halls of high finance.

He cut a mysterious, elegant figure, always dressed perfectly in
his Saville Row suits and perfectly groomed. He was shaved every
morning by his personal barber and had his hair perfectly trimmed
daily. Livermore always had access to beautiful women through Flo
Ziegfield and others like him. He also met many women at the
endless parties thrown by Mousie and his neighbors on Long Island.

Livermore started spending more and more nights in secret
liaisons in New York during the week. Rumors were born and
started to subtly circulate in the high societies of Long Island's
Great Neck community and the caverns of Wall Street. These
rumors eventually found their way to Dorothy's ears. She confronted her beloved J.L.

"J.L., I'm hearing terrible things about you."

"Like what?"

"Other women, beautiful women, showgirls like I used to be,
who are associated with you."

"Look Mousie . . ."

"No. I won't have it, and I refuse to discuss it."

"But you brought this up for discussion."

"Don't try to get off the subject and distract me. I simply don't
want to discuss it. Tell me it's not true, J.L."

"It's not true."

"That's the last of it then, and if it were true, I want it to be
untrue, and stop."

"Don't worry, Mousie."

She smiled and took his hand. She did not believe him, but she
hoped he would stop. She drank more, and threw more parties at
Evermore, on the yacht, at the Breakers in Palm Beach, and at
their home in Lake Placid.

Livermore did not stop. His affairs continued, but his private life never interfered with his business life, because his business life was his *real* life, the life he truly loved and the game he could never get enough of. The mental challenge of speculation was the high of his life, the vital force that coursed through his veins. It was an endless thrill for him, just as the ticker tape itself endlessly unraveled its secrets. Each secret he found on trading the market was a revelation to him, made him feel like an explorer opening the door to King Tut's tomb and viewing the secrets within for the first time.

chapter eleven

When to Hold and When to Fold

There is a tide in the affairs of men
which taken at the flood leads on to fortune.
Omitted, all the voyage of their life
is bound in shallows and in miseries.

Shakespeare, *Julius Caesar*

LIVERMORE SPENT A GREAT DEAL OF TIME AT THE BEACH Club in Palm Beach during 1930. He and Ed Bradley, the owner, had become fast friends. Gambling was illegal in Florida when Bradley set up the club, but he had the tacit approval of Henry Flagler, the railroad baron and partner in Standard Oil. This was the only real approval necessary.

Bradley's articles of incorporation said that the Beach Club was incorporated for social purposes, including any games or amusements that the management and its members might from time to time agree upon.

The rules included an age restriction of 25, a prohibition on smoking in the gambling area, a requirement that all debts be settled in 24 hours, and a strict dress code that required full evening dress after 7 P.M., without exceptions. White tie and tails were standard attire; a tuxedo was the minimum dress allowed.

An unwritten rule of the Beach Club was that no Florida residents were to be admitted. This rule was copied from Monte Carlo, where the locals were not allowed entry to the casino. But this was just a convenient rule for Bradley to apply at his discretion. He did not want any of the locals hurt too badly financially, because they might raise a ruckus with the law. He used his own personal judgment, and he admitted only those locals whom he considered suitable for admission. These, of course were the rich and powerful citizens who helped guarantee he would remain open. Bradley's Beach Club operated in Palm Beach under these and other rules for more than 45 years.

One January evening in 1930, close to 7 P.M., Livermore walked into the casino dressed in white tie and tails. Livermore enjoyed clothes. They hung very well on his slim body. The tails had been custom made for him in England. He had had four sets made several years before, and they remained unaltered. Livermore's weight never varied.

He went into the gaming room and found his close friend Walter P. Chrysler, still in his golfing outfit, sitting at the roulette wheel, fully engrossed in the spinning wheel and the little black bouncing ball. He sat down next to him. Chrysler looked up and saw that Livermore was dressed for the evening.

"Hello, Walter."

"Hi, J.L., you're dressed. Is it that late?"

"It's ten to seven," Livermore answered.

"Time flies when you're losing money."

"Bad?"

"About five grand on the wrong side of things."

As the clock moved minutes away from 7, Bradley walked up to the roulette wheel. The croupier looked at him. Bradley reached out for the little black ball. The croupier handed it to him.

"Walter, it's almost seven. You need to change clothes."

"I need to change my luck. Ed, I'm down about five grand here. I want to play it out."

"When you change and come back. We'll keep your seat for you. We're open until four in the morning," Bradley said.

"Ed look . . ."

"Walter," Bradley stared at him for a second. He was not used to being questioned. Neither was Chrysler. Bradley reached into his pocket and took out his lucky silver dollar. "Suppose we flip for whatever you're down."

"All right."

"You call it, Walter."

"Heads."

Bradley flipped the coin and as it arched over and headed downward he snatched the coin out of the air.

"You win, Walter," Bradley said, not looking at the coin. He nodded at the croupier to replace the chips that Chrysler had lost.

After Chrysler left, Livermore and Bradley settled down at a small cocktail table in the dining room. The dining crowd did not hit the club until at least 8. It was quiet. Bradley ordered his soda water, Livermore his old-fashioned. They sat in silence for a moment.

Livermore broke the silence. "You always get your own way, Ed?"

"Not always, but I don't like to see my rules broken. You must have rules, don't you J.L.?"

"Yes, and I'm sorry to say I break them once in a while."

"I hear you didn't break them in the Crash."

"No, not this time. This time I played by my rules and I did okay."

"A gambler and a stock speculator have to play by their rules, don't they, J.L.?"

"Yes, it takes long enough to figure them out, doesn't it?"

"A lifetime, because you never entirely figure them out, like you never really figure a person out."

"Ed, how can you figure a person out when you can't figure yourself out?"

Bradley laughed. "You're right there. We live with ourselves twenty-four hours a day and there's nothin' more important to us than ourselves, and most of us still don't know about ourselves."

"And let's not even bring up the subject of women."

"No, I'm perplexed enough as it is." Fresh drinks came and Bradley held up his glass. They clinked in a toast. "Here's to never understanding women. The mystery is too much fun. And here's to some good luck in that department once in a while."

"Cheers," Livermore responded.

They sat in a comfortable silence for a few moments. Livermore broke it. "Ed, I can say with no flattery that you are one of the greatest gamblers in the world. You have played all over the country, and you consistently win. I have a question for you."

"Shoot."

"What do you think it takes to win in the stock market?"

"I asked you that same question a while back, J.L. Besides, what would I know about the stock market?"

"Please, Ed." Livermore took a sip of his drink. "I know you won in a big way in the commodities market in Chicago, years ago."

"All right, I'll try to answer you, J.L." Bradley paused for a moment, then answered. "I think it takes three things. Timing. When to get in the market and when to get out, or when to hold and when to fold. It takes money management. You can't ever lose your stake, or the entire game is over. And it takes emotional stability. Yes; maybe most important, it takes the ability to control your emotions when you're in the play. That's it."

"Sounds like the principles of a good gambler."

"Life's a gamble, J.L."

Livermore smiled, and this time he held up his glass. "How about a toast to people who live by their wits?"

"Who live by their wits and know when to call it quits." They clinked glasses. "I like that, J.L. Yes sir, I like that."

Timing was everything to a speculator. It was never *if* a stock was going to move; it was *when* a stock was going to move up or down.

The crash of 1929 solidified Livermore's belief in what he called *pivotal points*. Black Tuesday was the biggest pivotal point in the history of the stock market—the market fell 11.7 percent in one day. Livermore formed the core of his timing strategy based on pivotal points.

He attempted to explain the concept to his sons when they were older. "Boys, *pivotal points* became one of my true trading keys, a trading technique that was basically unknown in a formal way in stock speculation in the 1920s and early 1930s. Pivotal points are a timing device I use to get in and out of the market.

"I divide pivotal points into two categories: The first I call a *reversal* pivotal points and the second I call the *continuation* pivotal points.

"The reversal pivotal point is not easily defined. In my mind, it is a change in basic market direction, the perfect psychological time at the beginning of a new move, a change in the basic trend. For my style of trading, it did not matter if it was at the bottom or the top of a long-term trending move. The essential thing to understand about this technique is that the reversal pivotal point marks a definite change in direction. The continuation pivotal point only confirms the move.

"The reversal pivotal point flags for me the optimum trading time. Reversal pivotal points are almost always accompanied by a heavy increase in volume, a climax of buying, which is met with a barrage of selling, or vice versa. This battle, this war between buyers and sellers, causes the stock to reverse its direction, to top out, or to bottom out in a decline. It is the start of a new direction in trend for the stock. These confirming volume spurts often end the day with a 100 to 500 percent increase in the average daily volume.

"I have noticed that these reversal pivotal points usually come after long-term trending moves. This is one of the reasons why I always felt that patience was so necessary for success in catching the big moves.

"You definitely need patience to be sure that you have identified the reversal pivotal point of a stock. I developed tests. First of all, I would send out a probe—I would buy a small percentage of the position I would eventually establish if I were correct with the first trade. I also checked the entire industry group, or at least one other stock in the group, to see if it had the same pattern. This was all the confirmation I needed.

"The second very important type of pivotal point, the *continuation* pivotal point, usually occurs during a trending move as a natural reaction for a stock in a definite trend. This is a potential

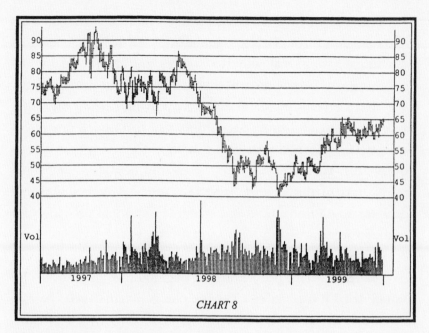

CHART 8

FIGURE 11.1   Schlumberger, Ltd., July 15, 1997 to July 15, 1999.
(Courtesy of Nirvana Systems)

additional entry point in an ongoing move, or a chance to increase your position, providing the stock emerges from the continuation pivot point headed in the same direction as it was before the correction.★

"For me, a stock's price is never too high to buy, or too low to sell short. By waiting for continuation pivotal point signals, I gained the opportunity to either open a new position or add to a current position, if I had already established one. I don't chase a stock if it gets

---

★Figure 11.1 shows two clear reversal pivotal points made by Schlumberger, an oil drilling and service company. The first, in late 1997, led to a decline in price, and the second, at the end of 1998, led to an increase in price. The company also formed a continuation pivotal point in mid-1998 when it hit $86, confirming the descent—in this case, to $40 near the end of 1998.

away from me. I would rather wait and pay more after the stock has regrouped and formed a new continuation pivotal point, because this continuation pivotal point is a confirmation and provides insurance that the stock will most likely continue with its move.

"I also used this pivotal point theory to find many successful short-selling plays. I looked for stocks that had traded down to a new low for the past year or so. If they formed a *false* pivotal point—that is, if they rallied from this new low and then dropped down through the new low—they would most likely continue down from there and establish additional new lows for the move.

"By correctly catching the pivotal points, I could make my initial purchase at the right price from the beginning of the move. This insured that I was never in a loss position and could therefore ride out the normal stock fluctuations without risking my own capital. Once the stock had moved off the pivotal point and I was in profit, I was risking only my paper profits, not my precious capital.

"My early years of getting crushed because I had bought the stock at the wrong time in its move gave me the clues to develop this new theory of pivotal points. If you buy before the pivotal point is established then you may be too early. This is dangerous, because the stock may never form a proper pivotal point to clearly establish its direction. If you buy more than 5 or 10 percent above the initial pivotal point then you are too late. You may have lost your edge, because the move is already under way.

"The pivotal point gives the only tip-off you need to trade and win. A speculator has to be patient, because it takes time for a stock to run out its logical and natural course.

"The key to my later theory of trading is to trade only on the pivotal points. I have always made money when I was patient and traded on the pivotal points.

"I also believe that the largest part of a stock movement often occurs in the last two weeks or so of the play, and that the same applies for commodities. So, once again, a speculator has to be patient, get into position and wait, but at the same time must be completely alert for the clues when they come, good or bad."

A danger signal, often a signal to exit a trade, a signal that made Livermore sit up and take notice, was the one-day reversal. This is a stock movement that often happens at the end of a long-term move. A one-day reversal occurs when the high of the day is higher than the high of the previous day, but the close of the day is below the close of the previous day and the volume of the current day is higher than the volume of the previous day.

Figure 11.2 shows an example. All during Schwab's rise, following the trend, the line of least resistance, it had only normal reactions. Then it suddenly had an aberrant reaction—a dramatic rise of over 15 points in three days that developed into a spike. During the last day of the ascent, the rally broke near the end of the day, and the price of the stock fell, closing near the low of the day. The next morning, it opened and fell further. These one-day reversals are often accompanied by increased volume. This scenario was a screaming danger signal to Livermore.

Livermore believed that if a trader had the patience to sit with the stock all during its rise, after the one-day reversal the trader must have the courage to do the right thing, acknowledge this danger signal, and consider selling the stock. Livermore firmly believed in patience and courage.

The pivotal point theory allowed Livermore the chance to buy at the exact *right time*. He never wanted to buy at the lowest price or sell at the top. He wanted to buy at the right time and sell at the right time.

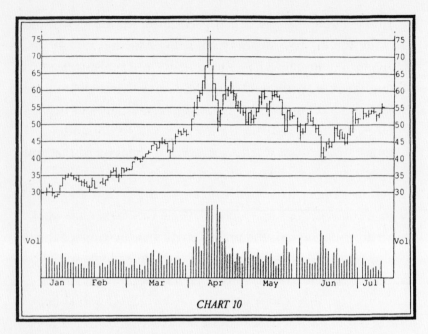

CHART 10

FIGURE 11.2   Charles Schwab Corporation, July 15, 1997 to July 15, 1999. *(Courtesy of Nirvana Systems)*

This required patience to wait for the perfect trading moment to form. He did not care if the right formation did not occur on a particular stock he was following, because the pattern would appear on another stock sooner or later. Patience, patience, patience—that was his key to timing success.

Livermore always considered time as a real and essential trading element. He often would say it's not the thinking that makes the money—it's the sitting and waiting that makes the money.

This has been incorrectly interpreted by many people to mean that Livermore would buy a stock and then sit and wait for it to move. This is not so. There were many occasions where Livermore sat and waited in cash, holding little or no stock, until the right situation appeared. He was able to sit and wait patiently in cash until the perfect situation presented itself to him. When these

conditions came together, when as many of the odds as possible
were in his favor, then and only then would he strike.

Buying on the pivotal point assured him the best chance of
coming into the situation, just as the action was about to begin.
And once he was sure of his play, he was not afraid to make his
commitment. He was not called the Boy Plunger for nothing.

His decision was always clear, as he wrote in his own book, published in 1940, *How to Trade in Stocks:*

> When a speculator can determine the Pivotal Point of a stock
> and interpret the action at that point, he may make a commit-
> ment with the positive assurance of being right from the start.
>
> But bear in mind when using Pivotal Points in anticipating
> movements, that if the stock does not perform as it should,
> after crossing the Pivotal Point, this is an important danger
> signal which must be heeded.
>
> I have found the study of Pivotal Points fascinating almost
> beyond belief. You will find a golden field for personal
> research. You will derive a singular pleasure and satisfaction
> from successful trades based on your own judgment. You will
> discover that profits made in this way are immensely more
> gratifying than any which could possibly come from tips, or
> the guidance of someone else. If you make your own discov-
> ery, trade your own way, exercise patience, and watch for the
> danger signals, you will develop a proper trend of thinking.
>
> Every time I lost patience and failed to await the Pivotal
> Points and fiddled around for some easy profits, I would lose
> money.

Livermore knew that this pivotal point theory applied to trading in
commodities, as well. While he did not consider this method fool-
proof, it was a core part of his trading strategy.

He also stated that there was probably a lot more to perfecting the use of pivotal points in the future. He was sure people would develop better trading methods from his basic premise. He promised that he would not be jealous of their success.

Livermore said that it was okay to anticipate the action of the market or a stock, but that traders should not take action until the market has confirmed that their judgment is correct by its action. Then, and only then, should they move with their money.

Pivotal points were an essential confirming signal for Livermore. He explained further to his sons that the market will often go contrary to what speculators have predicted. At these times, successful speculators must abandon their predictions and follow the action of the market. Prudent speculators never argue with the tape. Markets are never wrong, but opinions often are.

New highs were always good news for Livermore. To him, they meant that the stock had pushed through the overhead resistance and was very likely to advance. Livermore was not a chartist. He calculated everything from a numerical base.

Figures 11.3 and 11.4 show several new-high breakout formations like those that appeared to Livermore on a regular basis. Livermore worked with them in numerical form, but charts have been used here for expediency. Figure 11.3 shows that Best Buy, a consumer retailer of electronics, appliances, and entertainment software, broke out of a long consolidation at $30 in December 1998 and kept right on climbing to new highs. Figure 11.4 shows that Nortel Networks, a manufacturer of telecommunication equipment, formed a strong reversal pivotal point at $30 in September 1998 and powered through to a new all-time high of $65 in April 1999.

Why these formations repeat themselves is basically unknown. Livermore explained it as human nature in his own book, *How to*

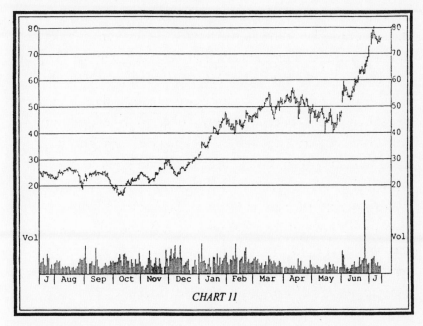

FIGURE 11.3 Best Buy, Inc., July 15, 1997 to July 15, 1999.
(Courtesy of Nirvana Systems)

Trade in Stocks: "All through time, people have basically acted the same way in the market as a result of greed, fear, ignorance, and hope. That is why the numerical formations and patterns recur on a constant basis."

For his overall market and industry-group timing cues, Livermore was always very sensitive to the *market leaders*. He tracked them carefully, watching them like a hawk through the glass panels of his office as they were posted on the green chalkboard.

Tracking the leaders provided strong timing clues for the general overall direction of the market. Trading several stocks in each of the major leading groups also helped confirm when a specific industry group was falling out of favor and reversing—or, vice versa, coming into favor.

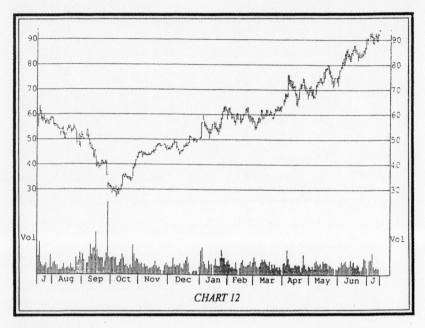

CHART 12

FIGURE 11.4   Northern Telecom, Ltd., July 15, 1997 to July 15, 1999. *(Courtesy of Nirvana Systems)*

The leaders, in Livermore's mind, were also surrogates for the Dow Jones averages. When these leading groups faltered, it was a warning signal, and his attention to the overall direction of the market was heightened. The signal occurred when the leaders stopped making new highs and stalled, often reversing direction before the overall market turned.

This was one of the essential timing clues for Livermore in the 1907 and 1929 crashes. The leaders faltered and began to turn as the craze for secondary stocks in the overall market broadened. Of course, the wild speculation in these ancillary issues spoke volumes to Livermore, because he had been through crashes before.

Livermore developed a sophisticated system of following the current leaders. His interest in them was twofold. First, they were the only stocks he would speculate in. He wrote in *How to Trade in Stocks:*

> Confine your studies of stock market movements to the prominent issues of the day, the leaders. It is where the action is. If you cannot make money out of the leading active issues, you are not going to make money out of the stock market.
>
> Second, this will also keep your trading universe small and controllable, so you can focus and trade the stocks with the greatest potential. Don't let greed drive your moves by trying to catch the exact top and the exact bottom.

Livermore also believed that timing should never be dictated by high prices. High prices were never a timing signal to sell a stock. He often said that just because a stock was selling at a high price did not mean it would not go higher.

Livermore was also just as comfortable on the short side, if that was the direction of the trend—just because a stock had fallen in price did not mean that it would not go lower. He never bought stocks on declines, and he never shorted stocks on rallies.

Buying stocks as they made new highs and selling short as they made new lows was a contrarian point of view, and this has remained a contrarian point of view with many investors through history.

Livermore let the market tell him what to do, he got his clues and his cues from what the market told him. He did not anticipate, he followed the message he received from the tape. Some stocks keep making new highs and can be held for a very long time, as shown in Figure 11.5. Cisco Systems, a leader in networking solutions for the Internet, had basically gone up for five straight years.

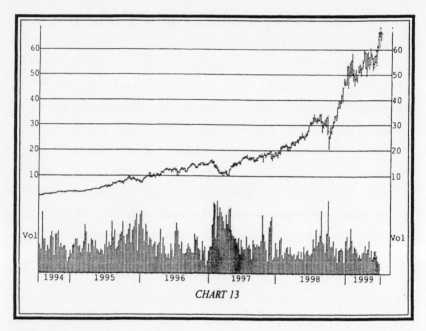

CHART 13

FIGURE 11.5   Cisco Systems, Inc., July 15, 1997 to July 15, 1999.
(Courtesy of Nirvana Systems)

1,000 shares in 1994 would have cost $2,000; five years later, in 1999, that investment would be worth $70,000.

Livermore told his son Paul, "Every stock is like a human being: it has a personality, a distinctive personality. Aggressive, reserved, hyper, high-strung, volatile, boring, direct, logical, predictable, unpredictable. I often studied stocks like I would study people; after a while their reactions to certain circumstances become more predictable.

"I am not the first to observe this. I know people who have made a lot of money in the stock market by analyzing the personality of a stock, and following that personality, reacting to it by buying and selling it according to its personality traits. But beware, not often, but sometimes, personalities change.

"I firmly believe that as long as a stock is acting properly, progressing with normal reactions such as consolidations and corrections, and proceeding in the direction of the trend, there is nothing to fear, no reason for a speculator to be concerned. And the fact that a stock is selling in new high territory should only encourage the speculator.

"On the other hand, a speculator must never become so complacent or relaxed as to miss the clues that the stock has 'topped out' and is creating a *pivotal point* that will set it off in a new direction, perhaps a reversal in trend. My motto son, is: 'Be ever vigilant for the danger signs.' "

Livermore traded to beat the game, and a big part was having the right timing. His quest was never-ending. His theories of pivotal points, his approach to new highs, his industry leaders and industry-group theories, were all new at the time, and they remain controversial. But it was the mental challenge they presented that was his passion.

But like anyone else, Livermore also liked what the money could do. Having money was *fun*.

It was 1931, and Paul Livermore was about to turn 8 years old. As a surprise, his parents decided to bring the Barnum and Bailey Circus to the 13-acre grounds at Evermore.

Tents were built during the night, and bleachers were erected. Trucks brought in the elephants and other animals during the night. At dawn the performers arrived, 100 clowns, the trapeze artists, the lion tamers, the Big Top master of ceremonies, the tumblers, the horse trainers, and the high-wire act. The neighbors started to arrive at 10 A.M. When Paul awoke, the entire grounds had been transformed into a major performing circus.

He walked the grounds wide-eyed in amazement. The overnight transformation had changed his private and solitary playground into a land of clowns, funny cars, elephants, lions, tigers, monkeys, trapeze artists, beautiful horses with magic riders, and huge striped tents with people hustling and bustling everywhere. He held onto his parents' hands as they strolled the grounds.

The performance began at noon. The guest cars lined the driveway, all the way out onto the road. The chauffeur was transporting people in Livermore's three-seat electric car, which he and the boys usually used to roam the estate.

The circus went on all afternoon, and there was a big party in the Livermore house when it was done, with a giant 6-foot birthday cake and food and drink for everyone. It was emblazoned forever in Paul's mind. It was his biggest day.

Later, when he got older, he thought that his parents might have felt guilty for all the attention they lavished on his brother, Jesse, who was openly the favorite of both his parents. He knew this from a very early age and was able to cope with it, happy in his own world.

Neither of the boys saw much of their parents. They went to boarding school in the winter, camping in the summer. When they were young, they always had their own individual nannies, who were later replaced by maids, chauffeurs, private detectives, and the imposing, protective presence of Harry Edgar Dache, their favorite, who sometimes tutored them in math, languages, and life.

The servants all spoke French. Mousie thought it gave them culture to speak French in the house. Both Jesse and Paul could speak French. Paul was the best. He spoke perfect French. Their father never even tried; he stuck to English.

He was too busy with the market.

★ *chapter twelve* ★

Livermore's Money-Management Rules

Rule number one is don't lose money.
Rule number two is don't forget rule number one!

Warren Buffett

ONE AFTERNOON AT BRADLEY'S BEACH CLUB IN PALM
Beach, Livermore sat around a table in the gaming room playing
high-stakes bridge with Walter Chrysler; Ed Kelley, the head of
United Fruit; and T. Coleman Du Pont. They took a break from
their game to enjoy a lobster lunch, a specialty at Bradley's.

The Florida lobster is different from the Maine lobster. It is
really more like a giant crawfish than a true lobster. It was Bradley
who introduced this crustacean to the palates of the American
rich. The lobster salad was famous—large pieces of lobster on a
bed of greens, covered with a mustard sauce whose exact compo-
nents were the chef's most prized secret. The bridge players all
ordered the same thing, with two bottles of vintage Rogert champagne. Green turtle soup, another specialty of the house at $1 per
cup (a very high price for soup at the time), preceded the salad.

"You hear what happened last year with these lobsters?"
Chrysler asked.

"What?" Kelley replied.

"Bradley liked them so much he said he would take the whole
Bahamian crop. He didn't know that it could be as high as 10,000
lobsters. The Bahamians went nuts and were going to fish the hell
out of them, because they had a firm order to buy them all from
some crazy American."

Chrysler paused as the green turtle soup was served from a large
silver tureen.

"So?" Du Pont asked.

"So when Bradley realized he had made a giant blunder, he told
them he would still go through with the purchase anyway—you
know how he is about honoring a commitment—although he had
no idea what the hell he would do with that many lobsters."

"Don't tell me that he sold them to Flagler and had them
shipped to New York and made a fortune," Livermore said.

"No, the hurricane last year wiped out the Bahamas and the lobster fishing, so he skated out of the whole problem," Chrysler replied.

"What luck!" Kelley said with a smile. "He's got lucky horseshoes hidden somewhere."

They all laughed.

"Just like you, J.L., in your latest wheat trade. I've been hearing rumors on the Street about you. Tell us about it, entertain us at lunch."

"Nothing entertaining to tell. I just felt the demand for wheat in America was underestimated and the price was going to rise. I waited for what I call my *pivotal point* and stepped in and bought five million bushels of wheat, about seven million dollars worth.

"I watched the market closely after the purchase. It lagged. It was a dull market, but it never declined below where I bought it. Then one morning the market started upward, and after a few days the rise consolidated, forming another of my pivotal points. It lay around in there for a little while, and then one day it popped out on the upside with heavy volume.

"A good signal, so I put in an order for another five million bushels. This order was filled at higher and higher prices. This was good news to me, because it clearly indicated that the market line of least resistance was upwards.

"I liked the fact that it was much more difficult to acquire the second lot of five million bushels. I then had filled out my predetermined target position of ten million bushels, so I stepped back and kept my eye on the market. It formed a strong bull market and rose steadily for several months.

"When wheat rose 25 cents above my average price, I cashed in. This was a bad mistake." Livermore paused as the lobster salads were served and the second bottle of champagne was opened.

5

"J. L., how the hell could it be a bad mistake to make a profit of two and a half million dollars?" asked Chrysler.

"Because Walter, I sat back and watched wheat rise another 20 cents in price in three days."

"I still don't get it," Chrysler said.

"Why was I afraid? There was no good reason to sell the wheat. I simply wanted to take my profit."

"It still looks like a pretty good trade to me. I'm afraid you lost me, J.L.," Kelley added.

"All right, let me explain myself better. You remember that old joke about the guy who goes to the race track and bets on the daily double and wins, then takes all his winnings and bets it on the third race and wins. He does the same on all the other races, and wins. Then, on the eighth and final race, he takes his hundred thousand dollars in winnings and bets it all to win on a horse, and the horse loses."

"Yeah." Chrysler nodded.

"Well, he's walking out of the track and he meets a pal of his, who says, 'How'd you do today?'

" 'Not bad,' he answers, smiling. 'I lost two bucks.' "

They laughed. "That's a good story, J.L., but how does it apply to you and wheat?" Chrysler asked.

"Simple. Why was I afraid of losing the track's money? When I sold, I was simply acting out of fear. I was in too big a hurry to convert a paper profit into a cash profit. I had no other reason for selling out that wheat, except that I was afraid to lose the profit I had made."

"What's wrong with being afraid? These days it seems like the safest bet," Du Pont commented.

"So what did you do, J.L.?" Kelley asked.

"After I booked my profit in the wheat, I realized I had made a great mistake. I had not had the courage to play the deal out to the end until I got a signal to sell, a real definitive sell signal."

"So?"

"I reentered the market and went back at an average price 25 cents higher than where I had sold out my original position. It rose another 30 cents, and then it gave a danger signal, a real strong danger signal. I sold out near the high of $2.06 a bushel. About a week later, it sold at $1.77 a bushel."

"Well, you have more guts than me, J.L., and it sounds a little like greed to me."

"That's because you sell fruit, Ed. The way you know how to diagnose the market on fruit is the way I am supposed to know how to diagnose the stock and commodities markets, and the wheat futures market had shown no signs of weakness when I first sold it.

"The next time I sold the wheat it was different; I could see definite symptoms of weakness. It gave the clues, the hints, the telltale signs of topping out. The tape always gives plenty of warning time for the savvy speculator to heed."

"J.L., I like your story, but sometimes I think maybe you got a set of those lucky horseshoes too, just like Bradley," Chrysler added.

"Walter, a little luck never hurt anyone," Livermore paused and looked around at the group. "I'd say we all had our share of luck at one time or another."

They all laughed.

Money management was one of the three pieces of the financial puzzle that fascinated Livermore: timing, money management, and emotional control. Livermore had five main rules in managing his money. He attempted over the years to explain his entire trading theory to his sons, money management was a big part of it.

One day he called his two sons into the library at Evermore. He sat behind the massive desk; the two boys sat down in front of him. He leaned forward and took a wad of cash out of his pocket. He peeled off 10 $1 bills. He did this twice, then folded the bills and handed each boy a pack of 10 ones.

The boys sat looking at him, each holding their money. "Boys, always carry your money folded and in your left pocket. Go ahead, do it. You can keep the money."

The boys did as they were told and put the folded money in their left pockets. "You see, pickpockets always go for a person's wallet, usually in their back pocket. Or they will come up behind you and go for your right front pocket, because most people are right-handed. You all right with this so far, boys?" he asked.

The boys nodded.

He continued, "All right, that's why you keep your paper money folded in your left pocket. See, if a pickpocket gets into your left pocket, and he gets that close to your balls, you're going to know about it."

The boys looked at each other.

Their father continued, "Don't ever lose your cash, boys. That's the moral of this story. Keep it close to your balls, and don't let anyone near it."

Livermore had several other money-management tips.

Rule 1: Don't lose money.

Don't lose your stake. A speculator without cash is like a store-owner with no inventory. Cash is your inventory, your lifeline, and your best friend. Without cash, you are out of business. Don't lose your line.

"It is wrong and dangerous to establish your full stock position at only one price. Rather, you must first decide how many shares you want to trade. For example, if you want to purchase 1,000 shares as the full final position, do it like this: "Start with a 200-share purchase on the pivot point. If the price goes up, then buy an additional 200 shares, still within the pivot point range. If it keeps rising, buy another 200 shares. See how it reacts; if it keeps on rising or corrects and then rises, you can go ahead and purchase the final 400 shares.

"It is very important to note that each additional purchase must be at a higher price. The same rules, of course, would apply to selling short, only each short sale would be at a lower price than the preceding sale.

"The basic logic is simple and concise: Each trade, as it is established toward the total 1,000-share position, must always show the speculator a profit. The fact that each trade shows a profit is living proof, hard evidence, that your basic judgment was correct in making the trade. It is all the proof you need. Conversely, if you lose money, you know immediately that your judgment was wrong.

"The tough part for the inexperienced speculator is paying more for each position. Why? Because everyone wants a bargain. The psychological battle is not to fight the facts, not to hope, not to argue with the tape, for the tape is always correct. There is no place in speculating for hoping, for guessing, for fear, for greed, for emotions. The tape tells the truth, but often there is a lie buried in the human interpretation.

"Finally, the speculator may choose a different ratio of purchasing the stock than I use. You could, for instance, purchase 30 percent as the first position, 30 as the second, and 40 for the final purchase. It is up to individual speculators to decide the ratio that works best for them. I have simply outlined what works best for me. The main rule is, do not take your entire position all at once; wait for confirmation of your judgment. Pay more for each lot you buy. This goes against most traders' natural instincts.

"And remember to establish in your mind the total amount of shares you want to purchase before you begin the trade."

Rule 2: Always establish a stop.

"Just as you should decide the number of shares you want to buy, what percentage of your portfolio you will invest in any play, and your general upside price target, you should always have a clear price at which to sell if the stock moves against you.

"And you must obey your rules, no cheating by waiting! My basic rule was never to take a capital loss of more than 10 percent. Losses are twice as expensive to make up. "I learned this in the bucket shops, where I worked with 10 percent margin. I was automatically sold out if the loss exceeded the 10 percent limit. The 10 percent loss rule became my most important rule for managing money. It is also a key *timing* rule.

"Remember, a successful speculator must set a firm stop before making a trade and must never sustain a loss of more than 10 percent of invested capital. If you lose 50 percent, you must make 100 percent to get even.★

"I have also learned that when your broker calls you and tells you he needs more money for a margin requirement on a stock that is declining, tell him to sell out his position. When you buy a stock at fifty and it goes to forty-five, do not buy more in order to average out your price. The stock has not done what you predicted; that is enough of an indication that your judgment was wrong. Take your losses quickly and get out.

"Remember, never meet a margin call, and never average losses.

"Many times I would close out a position before suffering a 10 percent loss. I did this simply because the stock was not acting right from the start. Often my instincts would whisper to me: 'J.L., this stock has a malaise, it is a lagging dullard. It just does

★Table 12.1 shows an example.

TABLE 12.1   Livermore's 10 Percent Loss Table

Starting Position	Amount Lost	Remainder	Loss, %	Gain Needed to Recover Loss, %
$1,000	$80	$920	8.0	8.7
	100	900	10.0	11.1
	200	800	20.0	25.0
	300	700	30.0	42.8
	400	600	40.0	66.6
	500	500	50.0	100.0

not feel right,' and I would sell out my position in the blink of an eye.

"Perhaps this was my inner mind working, distilling things I had seen thousands of times before and sending subconscious signals, registering repeated patterns that were stored in my memory and then subliminally remembered. Whatever it was, I have learned over the years, through many market experiences, to trust these instincts.

"I absolutely believe that price movement patterns are repeated and appear over and over, with slight variations. This is because humans drive the stocks, and human nature never changes.

"I have observed many times that people often become *involuntary* investors. They buy a stock that goes down, and they refuse to sell and take their losses. They prefer to hold onto the stock and hope that it will rally eventually and climb back up. This is why the 10 percent rule is essential. Don't ever become an involuntary investor. Take your losses quickly. Easy to say, but hard to do."

Rule 3: Keep cash in reserve.

"The successful speculator must always have cash in reserve, like a good general who keeps troops in reserve for exactly the right moment and then moves with great conviction, committing the reserves for final victory after waiting until all the odds are favorable.

"There is a never-ending stream of opportunities in the stock market and, if you miss a good opportunity, wait a little while, be patient, and another one will come along. Don't reach for a trade, all the conditions for a good trade must be on your side. Remember, you do not have to be in the market all the time."

Livermore used the analogy of playing cards—in his case, gin, poker, and bridge—where it is only human nature to want to play every hand. This desire to always be in the game is one of the speculator's greatest hazards, and eventually will bring about disaster, as it did to Livermore several times in his early career.

"When playing the stock market, there are times when your money should be waiting on the sidelines in cash, waiting to come into play. Time is *not* money—time is time, and money is money.

"Often money that is just sitting can later be moved into the right situation at the right time and make a fast fortune. *Patience* is the key to success, not speed. Time is a cunning speculator's best friend if it is used wisely.

"Remember, the clever speculator is always patient and always has a reserve of cash."

Rule 4: Let the position ride.

"As long as the stock is behaving normally, do not be in a hurry to take a profit. You must know you are right in your basic judgment, or you would have no profit at all. If there is nothing basically negative, then let it ride. It may grow into a very large profit. As long as the action of the overall market and the stock do not give you cause to worry, have the courage of your convictions, and stay with it.

"When I was in profit on a trade, I was never nervous. I could have a line of 100,000 shares out on a single stock play and sleep like a baby. Why? Because I was in profit on that trade. I was simply 'using the house's money'—that is, using the stock market's money. If I lost all that profit—well, then I simply lost money I never had in the first place.

"Of course, the opposite is true as well. If I bought a stock and it went against me I would sell it immediately. You can't stop and try to figure out why a stock is going in the wrong direction. The fact is that it *is* going in the wrong direction, and that is enough evidence for an experienced speculator to close the trade.

"Profits take care of themselves, losses never do.

"Never confuse this approach of letting the position ride with the buy-and-hold-forever strategy. I do not, and never have, blindly bought and held a stock. How can anyone know that far into the future? Things change: Life changes, relationships change, health changes, seasons change, and people change—why shouldn't the basic conditions that caused you to buy a stock change? To buy and hold blindly on the basis that a stock is in a great company or a strong industry, or that the economy is generally healthy, is, to me, the equivalent of stock market suicide.

"Stick with the winners. Let them ride until you have a clear reason to sell."

Rule 5: Take the profits in cash.

"I recommend parking fifty percent of the profits from a successful trade, especially when the trade doubled the original capital. Set this money aside, put it in the bank, hold it in reserve, or lock it up in a safe-deposit box.

"Like winning in the casino, it's a good idea, now and then, to take your winnings off the table and turn them into cash. There is no better time than after a large win on a stock. Cash is the bullet in the chamber; always keep a cash reserve.

"The single largest regret I have ever had in my financial life was not paying enough attention to this rule."

Livermore agreed with his friend Bradley, the gambler. After timing and money management come emotions. It is one thing to know what to do; it is quite another thing to have the will to actually do it. This is true of the stock market. This is true of life. Who knew better than Livermore?

As he explained to his sons, "I believe that having the discipline to follow your rules is essential. Without specific, clear, and tested rules, speculators do not have any real chance of success. Why? Because speculators without a plan are like a general without a strategy, and therefore without an actionable battle plan. Speculators without a single clear plan can only act and react, act and react, to the slings and arrows of stock market misfortune, until finally they are defeated.

"It is my conclusion that playing the market is partly an art form; it is not just pure reason. If it were pure reason, then somebody would have figured it out long ago. That's why I believe that all speculators must analyze their own emotions to find out just what level of stress they can endure. Every speculator is different; every human psyche is unique; every personality is exclusive to that one person. *Learn your own emotional limits before attempting to speculate*—that is my advice to anyone who has ever asked me what makes a successful speculator. If you can't sleep at night because of your stock market position, then you have gone too far. If this is the case, then sell your position down to the sleeping level.

"On the other hand, I believe that anyone who is intelligent, conscientious, and willing to put in the necessary time can be successful on Wall Street. As long as they realize the market is a business like any other business, they have a good chance to prosper.

"I believe that irresistible forces are at work behind all major movements in the stock market. This is all the successful speculator needs to know—just be aware of the movements and act upon that knowledge. It is too difficult to match up world events or current events with the movements of the stock market. This is true because the stock market moves ahead of world events. The stock market is not operating in the present or reflecting the present, it is operating on what is yet to be, the future. The market often moves contrary to apparent common sense and world events, as if it had a mind of its own. Remember, it is designed to fool most of the people most of the time. Eventually, the truth of why it moved as it did will emerge.

"It is therefore foolish to try to anticipate the movement of the market based on current economic news and current events, such as the purchasing manager's report, the balance of payments, the Consumer Price Index and unemployment figures, or even the rumor of war, because these are already factored into the market.

"It is not that I ignored these facts or was ignorant of them; I wasn't. The truth is that I voraciously read every newspaper I could get my hands on, and I had done so since my youth. I was well aware of world events, political events, and economic events. But these facts were not facts I could use to *predict* the market. After the market moved, its movement would be rationalized by the pundits in endless post mortems. Later when the dust had settled, the real economic, political, and world events would eventually be brought into focus by historians telling us why the market acted as it had. But by that time it was too late to make any money.

"Trying to figure out the *why* of a market move can often cause great emotional strife. The simple fact is that the market always *precedes* economic news, it does not *react* to economic news. A good earnings statement is issued by a company, and the stock proceeds to fall in price. Why? Because the market has already factored in those earnings.

"One of the problems with looking too deeply into economic news is that it may plant suggestions in your mind, and suggestions can be dangerous to your emotional stock market health.

"I once proved this in a golf game with my old friend Ed Kelley, head of United Fruit. We were playing in a threesome with Walter Chrysler on the Lake Placid golf course behind my home one weekend. We always played for between one and two hundred dollars a hole.

"Kelley was the better golfer, a scratch handicap. On the fifteenth hole, I said to Kelley, 'Ed, you're by far the best golfer in our group. Have you ever thought about that big boulder on the left side of the fairway on seventeen?'

"He answered, 'Why would I think about that, J.L.? I've never come near it. It's you that always hits that, isn't it?'

" 'I've hit it a few times, yes, but I think today is your day to hit it, Ed.'

" 'Please, J.L.,' he laughed.

" 'No, Ed, suppose you hit it and your ball goes flying off into the lake.'

" 'Impossible. Then I'd look like you,' he said.

"We played on for a hole with no mention of the boulder. As we teed up on the seventeenth, I said 'You know I'm famous for my hunches, Ed, and I've got a feeling, a hunch, you're going to hit that boulder today. In fact, I want to make a wager that you do.'

" 'J.L., don't throw your money away, no matter how easy it is for you to make it. What do you want to bet, a hundred?' Kelley said.

" 'No, Ed, let's make it three hundred. Off the boulder and into the lake.'

" 'It's your funeral, J.L.,' Kelley said.

" 'Maybe it is my funeral, just don't you forget to miss that boulder.' I smiled and stepped back. Ed addressed the ball and took a mighty swing. The ball arched up like a rainbow and descended directly onto the rock, careening off like a demented pool ball directly into the lake.

" 'J.L. you jinxed me!' Kelley yelled. 'You made me do that. I never came close to that boulder in my life!'

" 'No Ed, it wasn't me,' I answered. 'It was the power of suggestion, the power of the subconscious mind, that made you do that. I know you're good at your business, Ed, but be careful if you ever try to play the market. You get that all the time in the market, the power of suggestion infiltrating the subconscious. Believe me, Ed, I'm an expert. I've been broke enough times, haven't I?'

" 'J.L., I'm speechless.'

" 'Ed, just thank me for the cheap lesson today.'

" 'J.L., I have no intention of playing the market. So I don't think I'll thank you for that cheap three-hundred-dollar lesson,' Kelley said. We all laughed."

Livermore told his sons that he never understood why people thought making money in the market was easy. "We all have our own businesses. I would never ask Kelley to tell me the secrets of the fruit business or Chrysler those of the automotive business. It just would never dawn on me. So I can never understand when people ask me how they could make some fast money in the stock market.

"I always smile and say to myself, 'How could I possibly know how you could make money in the market?' I always evade the question; it's like asking me, how someone could make some quick money performing brain surgery or defending some person in a murder case. I believe, from experience, that even attempting to answer these questions would affect a person's emotions because they would have to take a firm position and defend their thoughts, which could change the next day, depending on the conditions of the market.

"But I have always fully understood that I am not the only one who knows that the stock market is the world's biggest gold mine, sitting at the foot of the island of Manhattan. A gold mine that opens its doors every day and invites anyone and everyone in to plumb its depths and leave with wheelbarrows full of gold bars, if they can—and I have done it. The gold mine is there all right, and every day somebody plumbs its depths, and when the bell rings at the end of the day they have gone from pauper to prince, or gone from prince to supreme potentate, or gone stony broke. And it's always there, waiting.

"I believe that uncontrolled basic emotions are the true and deadly enemy of the speculator; that hope, fear, and greed are always present, sitting on the edge of the psyche, waiting on the sidelines, waiting to jump into the action, plow into the game."

He told his sons this was one of the reasons he never used the words *bullish* or *bearish*. These words are not in my vocabulary because I believe they can create an emotional mind-set of a specific market direction in a speculator's mind. The words *bull* and *bear* cause a trader to get a fixed mind-set. And there is a good chance the speculator will blindly follow that trend or direction for an extended period of time, even if the facts change.

"I have found that well-defined trends do not last for extended periods of time. When people ask me for a tip, I say the market is currently in an upward, downward, or sideways trend. Or I tell them that the line of least resistance is currently up or down, as the case may be, and that is all I say.

"This leaves me with the flexibility to change my mind, according to market behavior. I never try to predict or anticipate the market. I only try to react to what the market is telling me by its behavior.

"I firmly believe that there are always clues as to what is going to come next. The clues are buried in the behavior of the market—what the market actually does, the here and now—not what is predicted that it will do. In a way, you have to be like a detective and solve the puzzle using the facts that are given. But, like a good detective, a trader should always look for proof of those facts and reconfirm them if possible. This requires an unemotional analysis.

"And I am one of the few speculators who has never cared in which direction a stock was going. I simply go with the line of least resistance. For me it is simply a market play; the direction of the stock is not important. In fact, one of the reasons I was noted as the Great Bear of Wall Street was that so few other speculators had the courage of their convictions to play the downside, the negative side of the market.

"When stocks decline swiftly and abruptly, they are being driven by fear. When they rise, they are being driven by hope. If people are hoping a stock will rise, they are slower to sell. If they fear the stock will decline, they are usually quick to dump that stock. This is why declines produce faster, more abrupt market action. So traders who play the short side must react to faster, more drastic market patterns and conditions.

"I believe there are no good stocks or bad stocks; there are only *money-making* stocks. So there is no good direction to trade, short or long; there is only the money-making way to trade. I have observed that to sell short goes against human nature, which is basically optimistic. And I believe that fewer than 5 percent of speculators trade the short side. There is also no question that it is extremely dangerous to sell short, because the potential loss is unlimited. It takes strong control of your emotions to trade on the short side.

"I observed early on that the stock market moves up roughly a third of the time, sideways a third of the time, and downward a third of the time. Therefore, if you only play the bull side of the market you are out of the action two-thirds of the time, waiting, hoping, and wondering. For good or bad, I was never one who wanted to wait and hope and wonder. I wanted to play the game and win more times than I lost.

"I am fully aware that of the millions of people who will speculate in the stock market, few will spend their full time involved in the art of speculation. Yet, as far as I am concerned, it is a full-time job, perhaps even more than a job, perhaps a vocation, to which many are called and few are singled out for success.

"By far the hardest emotional battle for a speculator is dealing with tips. The main reason I moved uptown to Fifth Avenue was to get out of the reach of everyone who was trying to help me by giving me 'sure things' and 'inside information.' Beware of *all* tips!

"Tips come from all sources. One such tip was passed to me by the chairman of a major American corporation at a dinner party at my house in Great Neck.

" 'How are things going?' I asked him.

" 'Great. We've turned the company around—not that it was really in trouble, but it looks like clear sailing from here. In fact, our quarterly earnings are coming out in a week, and they are going to be terrific.'

"I liked him and believed him, so the next morning I bought a thousand shares to test it out. The earnings came in just as the chief executive had said they would. The stock rose nicely, the earnings continued to rise for the next three quarters, and the stock rose steadily. I was lulled into a feeling of security as the stock continued to rise. Then it stopped and started plummeting in the opposite direction, like a waterfall.

"I called the chairman and said, 'This fall in your stock price has me worried. What's going on?'

"He answered, 'I know the price has fallen J.L., but we consider it nothing more than a natural correction. After all, we have had a pretty damn steady rise in the price of the stock for almost a year now.'

" 'How's business?' I asked.

" 'Well, our sales are slightly off, and that news may have leaked out, I'm afraid. Looks like the bears got hold of that information and are hammering the stock. It's mostly short selling, a bear raid, we think. We'll drive them out on the next rally, squeeze them a little, eh J.L.?'

" 'Are you selling any of your holdings?' I asked.

" 'Absolutely not! Where would I put my money with more safety than my own company?'

"Sure enough, I later found out that the insiders were busy selling into the stock's strength the minute they got wind of the business going into a slump. On the bad news, known only to them, they were dumping as much stock as the market would take.

"I never got mad. It was my stupidity and greed. I knew that all key executives were basically cheerleaders and that they must remain positive, must be bearers of only good news. They could never tell shareholders or competitors that things were not as rosy as they appeared. In fact, it always made me smile to listen to their mendacity. The misstatements, the lies, were just a matter of self-preservation, an essential part of the job of a chief executive officer at every level of power.

"But it was my self-preservation I was interested in, not that of the top executives and shareholders of the companies I invested in. Therefore, after a while—and some substantial lost money—I never asked insiders about how their businesses were doing.

"Why waste my time listening to half-truths, shadowy statements, inaccurate projections, and just plain bold-faced lies? I could just look at the behavior of the stock. The story was clear in its action. The truth was in the tape for anyone and everyone to see.

"I have suggested to people who are interested in the stock market that they carry around a small notebook, keep notes on interesting general market information, and perhaps develop their own stock market trading strategy. I always suggest that the first thing they write down in their little notebooks should be: 'Beware of inside information—*all* inside information!'

"There is only one way to achieve success in speculation—through hard work, persistently hard work. If there is any easy money lying around, no one is going to try to give it to me, this I know. My satisfaction always came from beating the market, solving the puzzle. The money was the reward, but it was not the main reason I loved the market. The stock market is the greatest, most complex puzzle ever invented—and it pays the biggest jackpot.

"Always remember; you can win a horse race, but you can't beat the races. You can win on a stock, but you cannot beat Wall Street all the time. Nobody can.

"People always talked about my instincts, especially after the Union Pacific story and the San Francisco earthquake. But I never thought my instincts were that special. The instincts of a seasoned speculator are really no different from the instincts of a farmer like my father. In fact, I consider farmers to be the biggest gamblers in the world. Planting their crops every year, gambling on the price of wheat, corn, cotton, or soybeans. Choosing the right crop to plant, gambling on the weather and insects, the unpredictable demand for the crop—what could be more speculative? These same principles apply to all businesses. So, after twenty, thirty, or forty years of growing wheat or corn, raising cattle, or making automobiles or bicycles, a person naturally develops a sixth sense, an intuition, experienced-based hunches about the business. I consider myself no different.

"The only way I may have differed from most speculators is that when I felt I was truly right, dead right, then I would go all the way, shoot the works, as I did during the 1929 market crash, when I had a line of 1 million shares of stock out on the short side, and every rise and fall of a single point meant a million dollars to me. Even then, my biggest play, it was never the money that drove me. It was the game, solving the puzzle, beating the market that had confused and confounded the greatest minds in history. For me, the passion, the juice, the exhilaration was in beating the game, a game that was a living dynamic riddle, a conundrum to everyone who speculated on Wall Street.

"Perhaps it was like combat is to a soldier. It's a mental high that's also visceral. All your senses are pushed to the limit.

"I've always told you boys to stay in the business you're good at, and I was good at speculating. Over the years I took many millions of dollars out of Wall Street and invested them in Florida land, aircraft companies, oil wells, and new 'miracle' products based on new inventions. They were all abject failures, disasters. I lost every cent I ever invested in them.

"Just remember, without discipline, a clear strategy, and a concise plan, a speculator will fall into all the emotional pitfalls of the market and jump from one stock to another, holding a losing position too long, cutting out of a winner too soon for no reason other than fear of losing the profit. Greed, fear, impatience, and hope will all fight for mental dominance over the speculator. Then, after a few failures and catastrophes, the speculator may become demoralized, depressed, and despondent, and may abandon the market and the chance to make a fortune from what the market has to offer.

"Develop your own strategy, discipline, and approach to the market. I offer my suggestions as one who has traveled the road before you. Perhaps I can act as a guide for you and save you from falling into some of the pitfalls that befell me.

"But in the end, the decisions must be your own."

chapter thirteen

Livermore's Luck Sours

In war there is no substitute for victory.
General Douglas MacArthur

THE USUAL FOURSOME WAS GATHERED FOR LIVERMORE'S usual Monday night high-stakes bridge game: Walter Chrysler, Alfred Sloan, Ely Culbertson, and Jesse Livermore. There was a knock at the closed library door.

"Come in," Livermore said.

The butler entered, leading a cow with a big blue bow tied around her neck. Dorothy followed him in and said, "I hope I'm not interrupting."

"No, darling, of course not. Why would you think you were interrupting by bringing a living, breathing cow into the library while we're playing bridge?" Livermore responded.

"J.L., I did it for a reason. It's your coffee break now, and you're always complaining about how the cream is never fresh, especially for those solitary six o'clock breakfasts. I thought the cow would help."

The players broke up laughing. Dorothy and the butler left after the butler served the coffee. The cow was left behind. The foursome returned to their bridge hands and started to play, ignoring the cow, who was just standing there looking around when Chrysler said, "J.L. I think you better get that bovine out of here before she does her business on your twenty-thousand-dollar Persian carpet."

They cracked up again as they watched Livermore get up and personally escort the cow out of the library, yelling for Dorothy and the butler.

Dorothy was the perfect foil for Livermore. She was his mirror image, his perfect match, and he knew it. She was spontaneous, he was reserved; she blurted out whatever was in her brain, and no one ever knew what was really in Livermore's brain. Together they made larger people of each other, and they both knew it.

Livermore's greatest years, personally and in the market, were between 1920 and 1930. He entered the 1930s with great hope, but he was faced with increasingly severe personal problems. Dorothy was drinking heavily and they were fighting constantly. The boys were always sent away to school and summer camp. They felt alienated and distant from their parents and, as a result, shunned them.

Jesse Jr., a remarkably handsome, high-spirited boy, was growing into manhood and starting to get into trouble. He was having difficulty in school and fighting with both his parents when he was at home for the summer.

Livermore himself was always attracted to beautiful women. Showgirls were his Achilles' heel. He had a magnetic presence thanks to his power, money, and mysterious ways. Women were attracted to him like moths to a flame. Showgirls and actresses were a perfect setup for him. He could date them, go out, have a good time, then usually forget about them and move on to the next relationship.

But his liaisons were constantly filtering back to Dorothy. She hated it. She had been 18 when she married him, and she had no experience with men other than Livermore. She was frustrated and hurt. He was the love of her life, and she could feel him drifting away from her.

This all manifested itself in payback when Dorothy met a very handsome treasury agent, a prohibition specialist named J. Walter Longcope. She had an affair of her own. Longcope was semifamous for his undercover work in New York City in 1927. Handsome as a movie star, he had the good looks of a young Gary Cooper.

Longcope was part of a group of revenue agents who posed as thirsty college students looking for fun. They busted the flamboyant Texas Guinan, a famous woman of the 1920s, who ran one of the biggest speakeasies in New York.

Longcope was quoted as saying his undercover group spent $7,000 in expense account money, drinking and dining while obtaining crucial evidence for the famous raid he led on Guinan's 300 Club. There was a well-publicized trial after the raid in which Longcope served as a witness. Guinan was acquitted. She had many friends in high places.

Dorothy finally filed for divorce and took up temporary residence in Reno, Nevada, with her new lover, Agent Longcope. On Friday, September 16, 1932, she divorced the great financier on grounds of desertion. They had been married since December 2, 1918—14 years. Dorothy retained custody of the boys.

Judge Thomas F. Moran sat on the bench for the hearing. In order to have the divorce validated, Livermore had to take the stand himself and affirm that he had deserted his wife on July 15, 1931. As he spoke he looked over at Dorothy, who had matured but was still beautiful. He said what he was supposed to. Judge Moran granted the divorce decree.

Livermore and Dorothy left the courtroom a few minutes later, walking side by side, not speaking. She took one final look at him. They stood there in the lobby of the courtroom, face to face, in silence. Livermore shook his head and walked away.

Dorothy immediately walked over to Longcope, who stood in a corner. She took his arm and walked back into the courtroom. She smiled at Judge Moran, who smiled back at her before he began the wedding ceremony. She later told her sons that she was a single woman for almost 20 minutes.

It reminded Livermore of his first Reno divorce from Nettie Jordan on December 2, 1918, and his marriage the next day to Dorothy—history almost repeating itself.

Livermore followed the same settlement plan as he had in his first divorce. He gave Dorothy everything she wanted: the house, the jewels, and a $1 million trust fund for herself and each of the boys, as well as a $1 million handpicked stock market portfolio.

Livermore always believed he could make more money for himself. All he needed was a decent stake of cash to carry on in the market, so why not give his former wives what they wanted?

Dorothy's first act after her marriage to Longcope was to sell the $1 million stock portfolio Livermore had chosen. She bought railroad bonds. She was angry, very angry. Her drinking increased. Later, the "safe" railroad bonds would become worthless; the stocks Livermore picked for her would rise in price to over $50 million by the 1950s. She did not care. She wanted his memory gone. But he would never really be gone from her life. She spoke of him at least once every day for the remainder of her life.

Livermore left Reno and returned to New York. He sank like a stone. He disappeared into a deep, dark depression. The same dark cloud that had never been far from him all his life now totally enveloped him.

Soon after the divorce, Livermore met Harriet Metz Noble of Omaha, Nebraska. They met in New York through Alexander P. Moore, who introduced them at a cocktail party in his New York penthouse. Attracted to each other, they immediately began to go out at night, particularly to the Stork Club, where Livermore was very well known; he was a close friend of the owner, Sherman Billingsley. The Stork Club was the place to be and to be seen in the 1930s.

One evening, when Harriet and Livermore were there for late drinks, in walked Georgie Jessel, a great wit and master of ceremonies. He was always full of surprises. This evening he had a tall, startlingly beautiful black woman on his arm. She towered over Georgie by at least a foot. The unwritten law in the Stork Club was that blacks were not welcome. Jessel knew this. Nevertheless, he walked up to the maître d' and asked for a table. The maître d' went immediately to Billingsley and asked him what to do.

Billingsley rose from the table and walked up to Jessel and his date.

A silence fell over the room as Billingsley spoke. "Georgie, you have a reservation? The maître d' says no."

Jessel put his arm around his date and said, "Yes, Sherman, I have a reservation here at the Stork Club, and it was made by a very important man a long time ago."

"And who might that be, Georgie?" Billingsley asked.

"Abraham Lincoln. He made my reservation for me."

The room exploded into laughter. Livermore rose from his table and walked over to Jessel, who had been invited to parties at his home in Great Neck.

"Hello Georgie," Livermore said. "I have room at my table for you and your tall friend, so why don't you join us?"

"My pleasure, J.L. It's always my pleasure to join a gentleman." They walked to the table, and the room settled back to normal.

The next day Billingsley called and thanked Livermore for defusing the situation of the night before.

Harriet was a wealthy woman whose family owned the Metz Brewery in Omaha. She had been an accredited concert singer and New York socialite. After six months of dating, she and Livermore decided to get married.

On March 28, 1933, Livermore and the 38-year-old Harriet were married in Geneva, Illinois. There was no honeymoon.

It was Harriet's fifth marriage. All four of her previous husbands had committed suicide.

The newlyweds immediately moved into a beautiful suite of rooms occupying an entire floor of the Sherry Netherland Hotel on Fifth Avenue across from Central Park. The apartment consisted of a beautiful living and dining area, a library and two large bedrooms.

On May 30, 1933, Congress passed the Securities Exchange Act. The Securities and Exchange Commission (SEC) was formed in 1934, headed by Joseph P. Kennedy (the father of John F. Kennedy), who wrote the SEC rules. President Roosevelt had asked Kennedy to write the legislation, which would go on to withstand the test of time.

Roosevelt reportedly said to Kennedy, with a smile, "Joe, since you have probably done everything a person can do on the stock exchange to make money, I believe I can safely assume that you're the man to write the new rules." As a reward, Kennedy was later appointed ambassador to Britain, a highly prestigious post. Kennedy was a student of Andrew Carnegie, the great steel robber baron, who said, "Money always sanctifies itself in the second generation." Kennedy wanted to start in the first generation. He had several sons to make into presidents and many sins to sanctify.

These new rules changed the market complexion; now the issuers of stock had to work within the rules. The government's aim was to protect the buyers. The character of the market changed for a while, but human nature did not change for a second. Livermore studied the new rules and wondered if he would have to change his rules and strategies to adjust to the new rules. Later he said with a smile, "There were no serious changes necessary with the new rules coming into effect."

Dorothy, Livermore's former wife, had vowed she would never return to Evermore after the divorce. She wanted nothing more to do with the estate. The memories tortured her. But she did return to live there for a short time. She had several small dogs. She refused to take them for walks on the expansive estate. She did nothing to stop them from urinating and defecating on the priceless Persian rugs. When the rugs became too foul and the stench was too much, she had them rolled up and thrown into the trash.

The foundation for one of the rooms in the mansion had sunk about three inches. The room was sloped down on the water side. One day Dorothy and the butler walked into the room and leveled the antique furniture by sawing the appropriate legs. This included sawing the legs of a Louis XIV desk valued at $100,000, as well as several other pieces of that quality.

Finally, she collected up some of the furnishings, carpets, art, and mementos and moved them into her New York apartment.

When the taxes came due, she refused to pay them. She sent a letter to Livermore and told him to pay the taxes. He ignored her. She was advised that the house and contents would be sold at auction if she did not pay the tax bill.

"So? Let them sell the house and everything in it. Why would I care? They're all bad memories for me now."

Inside the house was one of the finest collections of antique furniture that had ever been assembled in America. Livermore had spent millions collecting it. The property, exclusive of the furniture, was appraised at $1.35 million in 1932. Livermore had spent over $150,000 on landscaping the property alone. The silverware was appraised at $100,000; there was $309,000 in jade ornaments; there was a $10,000 needlepoint screen; and there was Dorothy's custom Rolls-Royce, worth $22,000.

The auction hammer fell on June 22, 1933. The house and property went for $168,000; the needlepoint screen went for $800; and Mrs. Guggenheim of New York bought Dorothy's jet-black Rolls-Royce convertible, with the gold embossed letters D.L. on the doors, for $4,750. The total amount rendered at the auction for the property and all the furnishings was $250,000. The country was in the very depths of the Great Depression.

Early the next morning, ensconced in his office, Livermore read of the auction in the newspaper. He took a deep breath, folded the newspaper, and dropped it in the trash can. He sat still, lifeless, in his chair, staring at the green chalkboards and the secret markings that had always looked to him like the sheet music for a symphony performed only for himself. Today, it was just a jumble of glyphs.

He looked out the window at New York waking up. His eyes misted over. He took a deep breath as the door opened and Harry Edgar Dache walked in with the first of the chalkboard markers. They nodded at the boss. The board marker silently put on his alpaca jacket and headphones. He climbed the steps to post the London and Paris markets, which were hours ahead of New York. Livermore looked away from the board and back at the newspaper in the trash basket.

He still had his boys, his two beautiful boys.

Shortly after the house in Great Neck was auctioned, Dorothy had her friend, confidant, and employee, Lucien, drive to the entrance of her apartment in New York City in her 16-cylinder light gray Cadillac convertible.

She jumped into the back seat with a picnic basket and a few bottles of whiskey.

"Lucien, I want to go to Santa Barbara."

"Where's that?" Lucien asked.

"California."

"When, madam?"

"Now will be fine, Lucien. Let's get going."

"Why?" he asked.

"Because it as far away from that bastard Jesse Livermore as I can get. And I want the boys far away from him and his women!"

They were going through a nasty custody battle for the children. Livermore believed that Dorothy was drinking too heavily, and she believed his libertine attitude toward women was not healthy for the boys.

"I see," Lucien said. Well aware of the couple's battles, he put the car in gear and started driving.

"And Lucien, I heard from a friend it is the center of fun for those Californians who count," she added.

Lucien drove and drove and drove until they reached Santa Barbara, with Dorothy hardly ever leaving the back seat, keeping the top down as much as possible, enjoying her picnic lunches and drinks in the back. When they reached Santa Barbara, she went immediately to a real estate agent and rented the biggest furnished house she could find. She found one in Montecito—a big, obscene, pink stucco mansion.

There was more bad news for Livermore. He learned, through a private detective, that Boston Billy Monaghan wanted revenge for what he believed was an excessive sentence. He thought Livermore and the other powerful people he had robbed had lobbied the judge to put him away forever and set an example.

Livermore had never spoken to the judge. However, he was not sure about the other rich people who had been Monaghan's victims.

On September 23, 1933, in a seemingly unrelated incident, there was a murder on board a gambling ship, the *Johanna Smith,* anchored three miles off the Long Beach, California, coast. There had been a wild argument between Buell Dawson, a young, well-known gangster, and James Walsh, a recently released convict and former cellmate of Boston Billy Monaghan. The argument had been resolved when Walsh pulled a pistol and shot Dawson dead. The police found the murder weapon in a washroom and confronted Walsh with it. There were also several witnesses to the murder.

Walsh confessed and explained to the police that the shooting took place as a result of a fierce argument between the two men as to the best method of kidnapping Livermore and E. L. Doheny, a wealthy Californian in the oil business.

The news shook Livermore. It was one more thing that he did not need in his life.

On October 27, 1933, a breach-of-promise civil suit was filed in the New York Supreme Court against Livermore by Nadia Krasnova, an outstanding beauty and actress, who had been Livermore's long-term mistress. Her suit was for $250,000.

This suit upset his new wife, Harriet, who had known nothing of the long-term affair. She was a naturally possessive and jealous woman. This revelation of another woman, her new husband's lover, led to major discord in the marriage. They battled almost every day about the affair with Nadia. Harriet made him vow to call her every hour on the hour, no matter where he was, no matter what he was doing. "You have broken your trust with me! I doubt if I can ever forgive you!"

This was just one more thing that was not going right in Livermore's life. Perhaps the bigger question was why Livermore needed a mistress when he had a new wife. What was missing from his life?

Plus, Livermore knew he was losing his trading skills. His attention, discipline, and energy were all deteriorating. His passion for the market was waning, and he did not know why. Was it the divorce from Dorothy? Was it not seeing the boys very often? Was it his new wife driving him down? Had his success in the 1929 crash caused him to lose interest in the market? Could he not deal with success? Was it 1907 all over again, when he had lost his fortune? Where were the blackness, the despair, and the emptiness coming from? Where had they always come from? Was there nothing that would make his soul happy? Give him peace and real contentment?

On December 19, 1933, Livermore fell into the deepest depression of his life. He left the apartment he now lived in at 1100 Park

Avenue at 3 P.M. and did not return home. Harriet called the police: "He normally calls me every hour, on the hour. I fear something has happened to him."

A confidential wire was sent over the teletype system at 2:32 on the morning of December 20 reporting that the famous financier was missing. The teletype was terse and gave no information except a brief description of Livermore and his age, 56. It was later reported to the police that Livermore had failed to keep an appointment with a friend at the Waldorf-Astoria that afternoon. His chauffeur, who had been waiting outside, told the police that Livermore had told him that he would not be needed and then hailed a cab, disappearing into the city.

The news spread immediately down the corridors of Wall Street. City and state police were called in on the case. They investigated all the possibilities: amnesia, suicide, and kidnapping. They were sure that if it were a kidnapping, they would receive a ransom note any moment. The kidnapping possibility brought the Federal Bureau of Investigation (FBI) into the picture.

Livermore's attorney, James O'Gorman, spoke to the press. "I'm conducting my own private investigation, and I'm betting Mr. Livermore will be back within twenty-four hours."

At 6:15 Wednesday night, Livermore returned to his apartment through the private entrance on Eighty-ninth Street, 26 hours after he had departed. Reporters were gathered at the entrance. Livermore walked past them without speaking and went directly up to his apartment. There were detectives inside talking to Harriet.

He looked pale and wan, shaky. He sat down and spoke to them. "I just saw the papers and realized that you were looking for me."

"Where have you been?" Harriet asked. "I've been frantic with worry about you. I thought maybe you'd been kidnapped."

"No, I was in a hotel."

"What hotel?" asked Detective Captain Louis Hams.

"The Hotel Pennsylvania," Livermore responded. He handed the key to his wife, who handed it to the police.

"How did you get down there?" Hams asked.

"Taxi."

"What happened?" Harriet demanded.

"I don't know. I've been in a daze since I left yesterday. I awakened this afternoon dazed and confused, then I finally read the paper that was shoved under my door. I immediately came back."

"Was it amnesia, then?" Hams asked.

"I don't know. I blacked out."

Later, Captain Hams explained to the press that he had no idea what ailment Jesse Livermore was suffering from to cause him to disappear. "Livermore said he had no idea we were looking for him, and when he found out he rushed right home."

The police located the cab driver, Abe Kamarick, and questioned him. The driver told the police that when Livermore entered the cab he immediately threw up all over the back seat. He was sweating and his hands were shaking. He also said that Livermore paid him "real good" to clean up the awful mess.

The police investigated further at the Hotel Pennsylvania. They found that Livermore had been staying in the suite of J. L. Lord, a permanent guest of the hotel who kept a room year-round. The police tried to locate Lord with no success. They dropped the case, since they now knew Livermore was safe.

Had the police persisted in their investigation, they would have found out that J. L. Lord was an alias that Livermore used to rent the room. He had rented the room for years. It was in this very hotel that Livermore had conducted his dalliances during the time he was married to Dorothy, including his long-term liaison with the beautiful Nadia Krasnova, the Greta Garbo look-alike.

Livermore's spirit left him. His personality changed. Even his friends began to notice that the Great Bear of Wall Street had lost his claws. He was despondent, distant; his thoughts seemed blurry and disconnected. His all-consuming interest in the market was dying. He moved his offices to 120 Broadway and let his chalkboard markers go. He stopped seeing his core of old friends: Ed Hutton, Walter Chrysler, Ed Kelley, Alexander P. Moore, and William Durant.

He stopped his bridge games at the Metropolitan Club, something he had loved, and also dropped poker and backgammon. Even his appearance seemed to change—he was still a natty dresser, but he was now just slightly behind the fashions. He also had a vacant stare much of the time, a long-distance stare that perplexed his friends, who felt that he was staring off into space even when they were talking to him.

He was also having serious problems with his son Jesse Jr. He had found out that Jesse, a handsome lad who looked older than his years, had been having sex with some of the women in their Great Neck set, some of Dorothy's friends. He had started having sex with these women when he was 14. He had also discovered the liquor cabinet when he was 14, and he liked what liquor did to him.

Young Jesse was having trouble at his school, Choate, and he hated the fact that his mother had moved to Santa Barbara. "There is no place that I can think of that is further away from that man," she had explained to him and her friends after she moved.

Jesse had loved living in New York and being near his father, who doted on him, giving him whatever he wanted, whenever he wanted it. Jesse loved his father and vice versa. There was nothing Livermore would not do for Jesse, and it was ruining the boy. Dorothy knew this and took special pains to make it difficult for Livermore to see the boys. This worked very well for Livermore's new wife, Harriet, who hated the boys because they distracted his attention from her.

Paul, Livermore's other son, a sensitive and handsome boy, had a different temperament from that of his wild brother Jesse, who was full of mischief and cunning. Paul was a gentle person, calm and placid, happy to be by himself on the great estate, or playing with his brother Jesse on the beach in front of the Breakers. He had a highly creative mind, was good with his hands, and could fix or build anything, like his grandfather. Paul was aware that Jesse got all the attention, but he was not envious. He was content within himself.

In fact, Paul was slightly in awe of his brother and wondered how he could walk such a tightrope between their parents, often using their intense feelings for each other and for himself against them, manipulating them easily.

Things in general turned sour for Livermore. His financial fortunes snowballed downhill at a rapid rate. Articles started to appear in the press revealing judgments against him. The first article appeared on January 10, 1934, in the *New York Times,* outlining a $13,130 judgment in favor of John J. Tierney, a member of the New York Stock Exchange. Another appeared on February 2, 1934, reporting a judgment of $90,840 in favor of brokers Benjamin Block and Company. Ben Block was a friend of Livermore's. Livermore made no attempt to defend the suits, and they were all lost in summary judgments.

Livermore was finally leveled on March 5, 1934. He filed for bankruptcy in federal court. Samuel Gilman, the great trader's attorney, gave a statement to the *New York Times:* "On each of the three previous occasions on which my client has failed, he has ultimately paid one hundred cents on the dollar to all his creditors. I can assure you that Mr. Livermore will once again triumph over his present difficulties." The disputed breach-of-promise claim by

Nadia Krasnova was also included and settled in the bankruptcy. What no one knew was that Livermore, through his friend Alexander P. Moore, had secretly given her $5,000 to help her move to California.

On his lawyer's advice, Livermore had borrowed $100,000 from Harriet. The loan was secured by the interest from his $1 million trust fund—a trust fund that he had set up in such an ironclad way that he could never touch the principal. This trust fund survived the bankruptcy.

On March 7, 1934, the bankrupt Livermore was automatically suspended as a member of the Chicago Board of Trade. It was never disclosed to anyone what had happened to the great fortune he had made in the crash of 1929, five years earlier. He had lost it all.

Livermore was, of course, depressed and disoriented. He was on the brink of personal disaster, as well. On December 1, 1934, he set sail on the Italian ocean liner *Rex*. He said to the *New York Times* on his departure, "This is a long-belated wedding present for me and my wife. I intend to study the European commodity markets as a basis for my comeback."

"Do you think you'll come back this time Mr. Livermore?" a reporter asked.

"I have made comebacks before, but this one will take longer because world market conditions are worse," he answered. What he really meant was that it would take him longer to get back on his feet because he had lost his emotional balance, and he was not sure if he would ever get it back.

"What will you deal in?" he was asked.

"I expect I will deal in wheat and other commodities."

Rumors and stories were constantly spread about Livermore. He was always fascinating to the press and the Wall Street crowd. For

example, there was the "black cat" story spread by a Wall Street
stockbroker who said he knew how Livermore had called the crash
of 1929. The broker claimed he had found a cat with magical
powers. The broker took the cat home, and his luck changed. He
immediately made a big hit on the market, and every time the cat
had a litter of kittens, he would call Livermore, who would reverse
his position in the market—if he were long he would go short and
vice versa.

"That damn cat made Livermore a fortune," the broker said.
"Then one day a year ago my cat died, and it destroyed Livermore.
That's why he went bankrupt and lost his fortune!"

Livermore also languished under the cloud of being the Great
Bear of Wall Street. He had been blamed as one of the main causes
of the crash of 1929. But he found this ridiculous, because he
believed that no one person or group could ever change the overall direction of the market or even drive a stock down for a sustained period of time. He knew that it was ultimately the sales and
profits of a stock, the financial backbone of a company, that won
out in the end, even though there could be a bumpy ride in the
journey. Nevertheless, people still blamed him, sometimes yelling
at him in public.

"Companies that make money consistently rise consistently,"
Livermore told all who would listen.

For the public, the nonprofessional stock players, there was
always the famous gray *they* in the market. *They* were raiding Steel
today. *They* were behind General Motors all week, pushing it up.
They had a full-fledged bear raid going on with Standard Oil. *They*
were distributing stock right now because *they* knew the market
was finished. *They* were led by that bastard Livermore and his bastard friends.

The public believed there was a club, headed by a powerful person or group, that ran the market. The club supposedly consisted

of people like Livermore, James Keene, John "Bet-a-Million" Gates, Bernard Baruch, William Durant, Arthur Cutten, and the Fischer brothers. These people were believed to simply manipulate the market as they desired, so the small trader was always the sucker.

The public also had a strong view on price movements. Any influences that pushed the market up were "positive" influences and any influences that forced the market down were "negative" influences. This was based on the premise that it was always good for prices to rise, because when prices were rising, the brokers, customers, company executives, and investing public were happy and getting rich. But any person who was involved with the *decline* of stock prices or making a profit from that decline was therefore a monster, and most likely was unpatriotic to boot.

For Livermore, this attitude toward bears in the market was ludicrous. It ignored the facts of what really happened. Livermore said to the *New York Times:* "The public believes that this group of elite men can drive a stock far below its 'real value,' its basic value. If such a stock goes down, the public then erroneously presumes that there is a group of super-traders, super-speculators, super financiers who are severely punishing the stock, pushing it below its 'real value,' to create an 'absolute bargain.' The public wrongly assumes that smart speculators will not step in and buy it at the depressed prices."

There were people who firmly believed that if the bear in the stock market could be declawed and caged forever, the markets would go in only one direction—up, up, up!

No one has ever been able to prove that short selling damages markets. In fact, there is a strong belief among many speculators that a large short position actually represents a large reserve of buying power, because all that stock must be bought to cover the shorts at some future date.

There is also a contrarian theory that states that most investors are wrong most of the time in foreseeing the direction of a stock or the overall market. So if the short interest rises past a certain point, contrarian speculators believe that this is a valid signal that indicates it is the time to go long.

Livermore was an independent thinker. He believed that the market was set up to fool most of the people most of the time. Certainly there was no one who could call the market direction or the direction of a stock all the time. If that was possible, that person would already be the richest person on the planet.

Livermore believed in the free market system with limited government interference. He said: "In a free market system, prices fluctuate. They never go up all the time and they never go down all the time. This is good."

All this did not stop people from tarring Livermore with accusations of being a ravaging bear and having caused the Great Crash. He was ready for his trip to Europe. He needed it to regain his sanity.

But he did not know that his greatest personal tragedy was just ahead of him.

chapter fourteen

The Shooting of Jesse Livermore Jr.

He remembered poor Julian and his romantic awe of them.
And how he had started a story that began:

"The very rich are different from you and me."
"Yes, they have more money."
Ernest Hemingway, *The Snows of Kilimanjaro*

THANKSGIVING DAY, NOVEMBER 29, 1935. IT WAS LATE. They were both drunk.

Jesse Jr., 16 years old but looking 20, stood tall and defiant in the living room, unsteady on his feet, wavering slightly from drink. He looked athletic in his tan slacks and white shirt, with his white tennis sweater casually tied around his shoulders.

Dorothy sat pie-eyed drunk on the couch.

There had been a Thanksgiving party at Dorothy's rented pink stucco mansion in Santa Barbara, where she had moved permanently after her house in Great Neck had been auctioned. She had divorced Jim Longcope, the prohibition agent, in August and was now having a fling with D. B. Neville—who, like Longcope, was handsome, charming, and had a deep interest in her money. Some of her "companions" blatantly stole from her.

Both Jesse and Paul were home for the holidays and would be returning to school shortly. Paul would head back to the Hotchkiss School in northwest Connecticut, a tough, highly disciplined environment, and Jesse would be going to his new school, the exclusive Laguna Bianca, which he desperately did not want to attend. He had finally left Choate, where it was almost obligatory for every student to have his own horse for polo. For years, both his mother and his father had labeled him as incorrigible. He only laughed when they told him to straighten out.

Jesse did not want to return to school—*any* school. He told his mother that he wanted to go to Europe instead and have some fun. After the party, he took off in his 16-cylinder dual-exhaust Chrysler convertible, which was equipped with cutouts to bypass the mufflers. There was no mistaking when Jesse was behind the wheel and the cutouts were engaged. He could be heard throughout the quiet neighborhoods of Santa Barbara. Livermore had called his good friend Walter Chrysler to buy the prototype sports car and have it shipped to California for Jesse—nothing was too good for his favorite son. Jesse drove fast and skillfully, drunk or sober.

After the Thanksgiving party, Jesse had gone out for a drive to see a girl and stop at the Biltmore Hotel for a few drinks. Afterward, Jesse dropped the girl off and stormed into the house, blazing drunk, after midnight. His mother was in the living room, drinking with Neville, when Jesse walked in.

Her son saw her and her companion in the living room.

"You've been drinking," she said.

"You're drunk, Mother. So don't tell me I've been drinking."

Jesse walked over to the bar and raised a full bottle of whiskey to his lips. "I'll show you that a man, a real man, can outdrink any woman."

Dorothy jumped from the couch and smacked the bottle out of his hands. "I'd rather see my son dead than drinking himself to death."

Livermore bolted out of the room to the nearby small guesthouse on the property. He returned brandishing a shotgun. He handed the stock of the shotgun to his mother and said, "Here, go ahead and shoot me. I dare you!

Neville leapt from the couch and intervened. He wrestled the gun from Dorothy's hands. He quickly ran from the room to hide the shotgun. As he did, Jesse bolted up the steps and flew into his brother's bedroom.

Paul awoke and looked at his brother. "What's going on?" he asked.

"Your mother wants to kill me."

"Why?"

"Never mind why, where's your rifle?"

"In the closet."

"Ammo?"

"Right next to it. Twenty-two longs," Paul said, studying his brother. He watched as his brother quickly slipped a round expertly into the chamber and locked it. It was a bolt-action, single-shot rifle. Everyone in the family was a crack shot and knew all about guns.

Jesse turned as he reached the bedroom doorway. "Go back to sleep, Paul. There's something I have to do."

This was not the first dramatic drunken scene Paul had witnessed between mother and brother. Jesse flipped off the light switch, and Paul rolled over in his bed, pulling the covers over his head.

Jesse raced down the circular stairwell, rifle in hand.

His mother stood at the foot of stairs. She looked up at him. He flipped the gun around and thrust the stock of the rifle into her hands. She was adept with weapons; her small finger automatically wrapped around the trigger as the stock slipped down her forearm.

"Now's your chance, Mother! Your chance to kill me. But you don't have the nerve to pull the trigger." With her finger around the trigger, Jesse suddenly pulled the barrel toward himself. Fire shot from the muzzle. The bullet entered his chest one inch from his heart, traveled past his liver, and rested near the spine. He collapsed on the stairs and rolled bleeding to the floor.

Neville entered after disposing of the shotgun and found the boy slumped at the foot of the stairs.

Dorothy bellowed at the top of her voice over and over again: "Oh, my God, I've shot my son. I've shot my boy. I shot my boy, Oh God! God! God!"

Paul bolted out of bed at the sound of the gunshot. He ran down the stairs to see his brother in a heap, bleeding. He ran to get Lucien, Dorothy's friend and employee, who was asleep in the guestroom. Paul woke him and brought him to the living room. Lucien immediately called Dr. Neville Usher, who came immediately to the home. As he arrived, so did Deputy Sheriff Jack Ross. Dorothy was still shouting "I've shot my boy!" over and over.

An ambulance appeared just ahead of the doctor and the sheriff. Jesse was taken immediately to Cottage Hospital. As he was slipped into the ambulance, he whispered to the paramedics: "I'm all right. It's nothing. Don't blame mother."

At the hospital, he was still drunk and in great pain when they gave him a whopping dose of morphine to kill the pain. Before he was lost to the drugs, he told the police investigators: "It was an accident. That's all I wish to say about it. I'm too tired to talk now, anyway." He then slipped away into sleep.

Livermore was in Saint Louis, Missouri, with "Nina," as he called his new wife, Harriet, when he got the news. He chartered a plane to take him to Los Angeles. A chauffeur-driven Ford Phaeton was waiting at the airport to pick him up and speed him to Santa Barbara. The case was covered in great detail by the *New York Times* and the *New York Daily News*. In Los Angeles, he told the press with clenched teeth, "If anything has happened to that boy, I will see that she pays!"

Santa Barbara District Attorney Percy Heckendorf and Deputy Sheriff Jack Ross questioned Dorothy for two hours but found her dazed and in shock, not making any real sense. She was put in a private room in the hospital and given a shot to quiet her down and put her to sleep. When she awoke, she was placed under arrest and taken to the county jail for more questioning.

The next day the doctor issued a press statement: "Jesse Livermore Jr. is slightly improved, but little change in his basic condition is expected for several hours."

District Attorney Heckendorf made a statement of his own: "Pending the outcome of the boy's final condition, she will be charged with assault with intent to kill." He was implying that he was waiting to see whether Jesse would die. In that event, they were going to charge Dorothy with murder.

When Livermore arrived on the scene, he went directly to see the doctors and then his son. He looked down at him and said, "Fight, son. Please fight. I'm standing by you, my boy."

On December 2, 1935, while Jesse was still fighting for his life against incipient pneumonia and shock, Dorothy was arraigned on a charge of assault with a deadly weapon with the intent to commit murder. She pleaded not guilty, and the following Monday was set for a preliminary hearing. Her bail was set at $9,000. The authorities were convinced she would not go far from her son, even if she had shot him.

The story was big news, carried on all the wire services and in all the important papers in the country. The Boy Plunger, the Great Bear of Wall Street was in the news again, only this time it was a tragedy, a real tragedy.

Livermore checked into the El Mirasol Hotel in downtown Santa Barbara.

When Dorothy was released from jail, she went immediately to the hospital and pleaded with the doctors: "I want to see my son, my boy! I must see him."

But the surgeons refused.

"Just for a moment!" she begged.

"No, not even for a moment. His condition is very sensitive," the surgeons replied. They had decided not to operate to remove the bullet from where it was lodged near his spine until he was stronger. The bullet had missed his heart by scant inches.

The news spread like wildfire. Dorothy got a call from Edward J. Reilly, a famous lawyer who had defended Bruno Hauptman in the Lindbergh kidnapping case, wanting to represent her. But Harrison Ryon, vice chairman of the California Bar Association, was selected, and Livermore paid his fees. Ryon had acted for Livermore in his divorce from Dorothy.

When Ryon was asked if Livermore thought his wife was guilty of trying to kill her own son, Ryon was quick to point out that "It should be obvious that Mr. Livermore, by retaining my services, is himself interested and active in his ex-wife's defense on these charges. That speaks for itself."

Ryon was a powerful California lawyer. He said that he and Livermore had already designed her defense. "It's the 'unloaded gun' defense. It is clear to myself and Mr. Livermore that the discharge of the gun was purely accidental. The defense will prove that Mrs. Livermore did not do the shooting on purpose. Mrs. Livermore had no knowledge or suspicion that the gun was loaded."

Then Jesse's physicians announced that Jesse had said: "I don't want to see either my mother or my father. I want to lie here and think things over for a week or so. And I don't want to see the district attorney either."

The district attorney went along, "In deference to the boy's request, and his doctor's concurrence, I will agree to put off the questioning. I have plans to assemble more details of the shooting over the next few days."

Livermore took action. He sent an airplane to pick up Dr. Joseph d'Avignon, a gunshot-wound expert from Lake Placid. It was also announced that Dorothy would not be arraigned until after the Christmas and New Year's Day holidays. The final announcement informed the public that Livermore had filed suit to recover custody of both of his sons. He was given custody of Paul immediately on a temporary arrangement.

On December 6, 1935, there was a piece on the shooting in the *New York Times*.

The 16-year-old boy, Jesse Livermore Jr.'s physical wound is not the only wound. From the stories that have been told so far by the press it is plain that the boy was caught in a cross-fire between his unhappy and embittered elders. As a result, he has suffered intense spiritual hurt.

The various articles covering the shooting were read avidly by those on Wall Street.

Then a turn for the worse came on December 16, as the *Times* reported.

The condition of Jesse L. Livermore Jr., was reported as "exceedingly grave" at Cottage Hospital. After a week of slow but steady progress toward recovery from a bullet wound inflicted in a quarrel by a shot fired by his mother, the youth took a turn for the worse yesterday. He spent today under an oxygen tent while the doctors studied new X-ray photographs and made lab tests of the fluid from the wound area in his lower chest.

It was not until January 6, 1936, that Jesse was declared out of danger. But for months, it was still necessary for his doctor or an attending nurse to tap his chest for fluid every other day to prevent infection. Later in his life, Jesse would tell his wife Pat that the doctors and nurses would come into his room, ream out the wound using an antiseptic and a Q-tip, and then drain it. Every time, he would scream in pain at the top of his lungs, cursing his mother for shooting him and his father for ignoring him all his life. Even the morphine did not help.

Finally, on March 5, 1936, Dorothy was exonerated of all charges before Ernest Wagner, a justice of the peace. It was Judge Wagner who had ordered the complaint charging Dorothy with assault with intent to kill after the preliminary hearing in January.

Jesse testified that he would assume all blame for the shooting, which had followed an argument over his drinking. Dr. Neville Usher, who was first on the scene and attended Jesse through his long convalescence, testified that Dorothy had been under the influence of alcohol and was incapable of remembering anything she might have said at the time.

When specifically questioned about her having said: "I have shot my boy! I've shot my son," the respected physician replied he could not recall that he had ever heard her say that.

Months later, on March 25, the bullet lodged near Jesse's spine was finally removed at Post-Graduate Hospital in New York City. Dr. John Moorhead, chief of surgeons at the hospital, performed the operation. But Jesse would always have a scar and a slight curvature of the spine, which he did his best to hide. He was also, because of this wound, rejected for military service in World War II.

Livermore was given permanent custody of both boys.

In 1935, Livermore had moved into the Sherry Netherland Hotel on Fifth Avenue across from Central Park. The Sherry Netherland was an exclusive elegant hotel-residence for some of the most prominent people in the world. Livermore took an entire upper floor. The apartment suite was spacious, furnished with Livermore and his new wife's favorite things. There was a kitchen, living room, dining room, den, and two bedrooms, including one for Paul when he was home, which was rarely. A maid who also cooked came every day—and, of course, there was always room service available to provide anything they wanted.

Paul lived with his father and Harriet when he was not at boarding school or away at summer camp. Paul hated living there and called his father's new wife "the Bitch-Witch." He found her a dark and depressing presence. He could feel her hatred for him and his brother. She wanted his father's undivided attention.

One afternoon, he was playing soccer on the fields of Hotchkiss, his boarding school in Lakeville, Connecticut, when one of his friends came up to him. He said, "Paul, isn't that your mother coming up the drive?" The boy pointed at a black Rolls, his father's Rolls. Dorothy often borrowed Livermore's Rolls and chauffeur to drive her to visit Paul.

Paul ran over, and out of the car stepped Harriet, his step-mother, a surprise visit. She scared him so deeply that he ran across the soccer fields to his dormitory, screaming.

His father later made him call and apologize to Harriet. But that did not stop his fear of her. She was very possessive of his father and insisted on summer camp for Paul so he would not be in the apartment with them during his summer vacation. Paul always brought home a school chum over holidays in order to insulate himself from her. He also needed the company for the long periods of time he would otherwise be alone in the apartment.

On July 31, 1936, Dorothy Livermore Longcope sued Livermore in a New York court. She wanted a summons issued against him to obtain money for the hospital expenses Jesse had incurred after the shooting. The judge refused to issue a summons and advised her to carry out other legal remedies. He threw the case out of court. Livermore was informed of the action and could only shake his head in astonishment.

When Jesse was well, fully recovered, Livermore sent him on the trip to Europe he had wanted.

Livermore himself stayed at home.

Livermore's next battle was with the Internal Revenue Service, after he was hit with an $800,000 tax bill. He negotiated and settled the claim with the IRS in the same year.

In the summer, he was ready for a fishing excursion. He chartered the *Ranger,* a deep-sea fishing boat that ran out of Montauk Point. In the early afternoon, trolling off Montauk slightly into Long Island Sound, he hooked into a broadbill swordfish. Locked into the fighting chair, he fought the fish for over an hour using only 36-pound-test line. The fish ran long and hard, jumping, sounding, but with an expert captain, John Sweeting, at the helm, it was an equal battle between human and fish.

Finally, the fish was brought alongside the boat. It was hoisted out of the water with a block and tackle and weighed at the dock. It weighed 486 pounds and remains a record as the second-largest swordfish ever caught off Montauk Point on rod and reel.

Two years later, on November 14, 1937, at the age of 18, Jesse married Evelyn Sullivan, the daughter of Hen Bletzer, who for years promoted prizefights and operated a bar in Baltimore. Evelyn gave her age as 20, and it was reported that she had been married before, four years prior to this wedding. Dorothy was at the wedding to give her blessings. In fact, she assisted in obtaining the license and witnessed the marriage ceremony. Jesse was particularly happy to be out of the oppressive presence of the dour and gloomy Harriet.

Livermore did not attend. As a wedding present, he bought his son the Pepsi-Cola bottling franchise for Connecticut.

In 1938 and 1939, Livermore sank lower and lower in his depression. He was still playing the markets, but not like in the old days when he would be consumed with energy and passion to get to work, to beat the game, to apply all his energies on the stock market, the grain markets, the overall market.

Those high times of the 1920s and the pure fun of living were gone. He had ruined it with his affairs and carrying on. Sure, Dorothy drank, but her drinking only got worse after the affairs, the humiliation, and the desertion.

Dorothy was complimentary mirror image to his personality. He was repressed and cerebral; she was outgoing and instinctive. And she was beautiful. He missed her more as time passed. The fun, the joy, the laughter were gone from his life.

He started having recurring nightmares for the first time in his life.

In late 1939, Livermore's son Jesse suggested that he write a book about his experiences and techniques in trading in the stock and commodity markets. This brought a flash of life back into Livermore: a mission, a goal, and a purpose. He began at once, thinking perhaps it would rekindle his spirit. The book was completed and published by Duell, Sloan, and Pearce in March 1940. It was titled *How to Trade in Stocks.*

The book did not sell well. The world war was underway, and the general interest in the stock market was low. His methods were still new and controversial at the time, and they received mixed reviews from the stock market gurus of the period.

They remain controversial today.

Livermore said that his basic theories were just the beginning, as Sigmund Freud's and Carl Jung's were in the study of the human mind. In his book he said, "I know people will take these thoughts I offer to new and better heights. Don't worry, I won't be jealous. I wish them all well. I agree with Virgil: '*Exoriare aliquis nostris ex ossibus ultor.*' Let someone arise from my bones as an avenger."

chapter fifteen

Facing the Grim Reaper

There is a reaper whose name is death.
And with his sickle keen,
He reaps bearded grain at a breath,
And the flowers that grow in between.
                    Longfellow, *The Reaper and the Flowers*

ON WEDNESDAY, NOVEMBER 27, 1940, THE 63-YEAR-OLD Livermore and his wife, Harriet, whom he had nicknamed "Nina," were at the Stork Club, Livermore's favorite club. The house photographer came up and asked if he could take a photo.

"Of course you can," Livermore said. "But it's the last picture you will take, because tomorrow I'm going away for a long, long time."

Nina was shocked. She asked Livermore, "Laurie, what do you mean?"

"Only a joke, darling, only a joke." He smiled back at her.

The flashbulb fired. Several people came by from time to time to join them, and Nina had a few dances with friends. Livermore looked on, a faraway stare in his eye. His food went untouched; he had long since lost his appetite. He looked thin and wan.

The next day, November 28, at noon, he wandered up from his offices in the Squibb building at 745 Fifth Avenue and entered the Sherry Netherland Hotel. He stopped to say hello to Eugene Voit, the manager. He had lived in the hotel for years before moving to Park Avenue. He often stopped by for a cocktail on his walk home from work.

At 12:30 he sat down for lunch alone, which was not unusual. He was well known to the staff and a favorite regular at the hotel bar and restaurant. He sat near the bar and accepted his old-fashioned, which the bartender automatically made when he saw him enter. He spoke to no one during lunch. He appeared to the waiter to be distraught and intense.

Throughout his lunch, he would whip out his favorite small leather-covered memorandum book and extract the gold pen attached to the chain on his vest to write. He wrote hurriedly, a page or two at a time, like someone who had a lot to say but could only say a little at any moment. Each time he replaced the notebook in his pocket. He did this several times through lunch. He smoked cigarette after cigarette as he sat there. At 2:30, he left the hotel and returned to his office.

He came back to the Sherry Netherland at 4:30 in the afternoon and went directly to his favorite table near the bar. As usual, he was handed an old-fashioned as he sat down. Livermore smiled at the waiter but said nothing. He sat there for an hour, taking his notebook out and writing in it, then replacing it. He ordered one more old-fashioned during the hour he sat there.

He finally rose from his table and walked out of the bar into the lobby.

To get to the men's washroom in this hotel, it was necessary to enter the lobby and walk about 120 feet, through swinging doors that obscured the view, to an area which then led into the banquet room, the cloakroom, and the washrooms.

At 5:33, Livermore walked through the swinging doors and slipped through the closed door of the dim, dark, cloakroom. He took a seat on the stool at the end of the cloakroom. He withdrew a .32-caliber Colt automatic pistol and slid the barrel back, popping a round into the chamber. The clip was full. He had bought the gun in 1928 when he was living at Evermore.

He placed the barrel of the gun behind his right ear and pulled the trigger.

The bullet ripped through his brain. He died instantly.

A few minutes later, the assistant manager, Patrick Murray, was making his hourly rounds when he opened the door to the cloakroom. He saw Livermore slumped in the chair. At first he thought he should not disturb him, that Livermore was asleep. Then he saw a pool of blood on the floor and the gun.

He ran back to the reception desk and called the police. The news spread like wildfire. Reporters and newspaper photographers

crowded into the hotel lobby. Two radio cars sped up to the
entrance; four patrolmen were stationed in the lobby and entrance.
Inspector Patrick J. Kenney, who ultimately led the investigation,
arrived in an unmarked car along with Captain Edward Mullins
of the East Sixty-seventh Street station. Inspector Kenney, after
appraising the situation, phoned the Livermore apartment on Park
Avenue to notify Mrs. Livermore that her husband had shot himself.

"What? What are you telling me? He's been ill lately.
Maybe . . ."

"I'm sorry ma'am, but I'm afraid your husband is gone from a
bullet wound."

There was a dead silence on the other end of the phone. He
heard a thump on the floor. Inspector Kenney was a seasoned officer. He had known people to faint on the phone before from the
news he had given them. He sent a squad car over to make sure she
was all right.

The police phoned Jesse Livermore Jr. to give him the news. He
arrived by taxi at 6:45, shaking and visibly upset. He was accompanied by Harry Edgar Dache, Livermore's office manager. Livermore's body had not been moved. Jesse was led into the
cloakroom. He walked to the far end where his father was slumped
dead on the stool, the gun on the floor in the pool of blood. He
identified the body and collapsed, slumping down in the far corner. He was raised to his feet by a police officer and Dache.

He would not leave the body. He waited in the lobby until the
medical examiner, Inspector Raymond O. Miles, arrived at 9.
They left the body untouched until the medical examiner came,
examined the scene, and released the body. The medical examiner
verified the police verdict of suicide.

Dache made immediate arrangements to remove the body to
the Campbell Funeral Chapel at Madison Avenue and Eighty-first
Street.

At 8:30 that same night, Paul Livermore was studying in his room at the Hotchkiss School in Connecticut. There was a knock on the door. "Paul, you're wanted in the headmaster's office," a student told him.

Paul walked down the long halls to the headmaster's office. He knocked on the door. "Come in," was the response.

Paul stood in front of the headmaster. He was 17, slim, a good athlete and student, and movie-star handsome, like his brother. He would later actually become an actor in movies and various television series. "Yes sir?" he said.

"Young man, I'm afraid I have something to tell you, and there is no easy way to do it." He stepped out from behind his desk. "I'm sorry to have to tell you that your father killed himself this evening in New York. He shot himself. A car and chauffeur have been sent from New York to drive you to the city. The car is waiting outside."

Paul stood numb for a second and actually doubled over, as if he had been punched in the stomach. He went down on one knee, dizzy. He felt a wave of nausea sweep over him. He grabbed for the edge of the headmaster's desk. The headmaster circled the desk and helped him to his feet. He gave him a glass of cold water, and after a few short minutes, he walked him to the waiting Packard town car in the driveway, where Frank, the chauffeur, waited, out of uniform. Frank helped him into the back seat.

Paul Livermore sat alone in the dark silence of the rear seat of the Packard as the lights flashed by him on the parkways that led back to New York City. He was too numb, too dazed, and too confused to cry.

The police revealed that there was a suicide note of eight small handwritten pages in Livermore's personal notebook. It was reported in the November 30 *New York Tribune*.

The press wanted to know what it said. Tersely, the police

responded. "There was a leather-bound memo book found in Mr. Livermore's pocket. It was addressed to his wife." A police spokesman read from the notebook: " 'My dear Nina: Can't help it. Things have been bad with me. I am tired of fighting. Can't carry on any longer. This is the only way out. I am unworthy of your love. I am a failure. I am truly sorry, but this is the only way out for me.' He signed the eight-page note, 'Love Laurie,' which we presume was a nickname, maybe from his middle name, Lauriston."

The police went on to explain that this theme of failure, desolation, and despair was repeated throughout the book, with the identical words used over and over again. They said it was not an incoherent note, just repetitious, and obviously had been written under great emotional stress.

A little after 10 that night, the Packard rolled up in front of the private entrance and elevator to the Livermore apartment at 1100 Park Avenue. Frank rang the bell.

"Is that you, Frank?" Harriet asked.

"Yes ma'am," he replied.

"Paul with you?"

"Yes ma'am."

"Good, send him in. You wait there for me. I'll be down in a few moments," she said through the speaker as she buzzed him in.

When Paul walked in, he saw Harriet, fully dressed, moving quickly about the apartment. There were three paper bags by the door. They were full to the top with cash, cash enclosed in bank wrappers.

She saw him as he entered. "Hello Paul," she said, stopping her movement, her hands full of cash.

"Hello," he said.

"Paul, come and sit on the couch." He did as he was told. "The school told you about your father?"

"Yes."

"Look Paul, I just talked to a friend, a lawyer, who told me the police often investigate suicides like they do homicides. They came already, a uniformed officer in a squad car, to see if I was all right. I'm afraid they might come here and search the apartment and I could not explain certain things. Your father kept too much cash in the house. So I'm going to go for the evening. Besides, I'm very upset, but I have to try and think straight. I must think straight. You understand?"

"Sure."

"Okay, I'm in a hurry. They could arrive any moment. I'm not going far, just to a hotel. But you tell the police that I've gone to see a friend if they come, okay? I'll send Frank back to be with you after he takes me to the hotel."

"I'm okay. I don't need Frank."

"You sure?"

"Yes."

"Alright then, I have to go."

Paul waited as she went to the safe in the living room. He watched as she swept her jewels out of the safe into the paper shopping bag, using her forearm. She disappeared into the bedroom. He could hear her opening and closing bureau doors, dumping more jewelry into the last shopping bag. She came out with a shopping bag half full of jewelry and stuffed a sweater in on top.

"See, Paul, I use these shopping bags because nobody would ever suspect what was in them," she said. "I'll take care of everything in the morning."

Paul walked her to the door as she slipped on her coat. She swept up the other shopping bags with the cash and left. He watched her take the private elevator down to the waiting chauffeur.

Later he was to estimate that she had about $3 million in cash and at least another $1 million in jewelry—the boy's inheritance. It was never spoken of again. Paul spent the night alone in the 12-room apartment.

The next morning, November 29, when Paul awoke around 10, Harriet had already returned to the apartment.

"Good morning," she said to Paul. "I've notified Jesse Jr., Alexander Moore, and Reverend Crossland to meet us at Campbell's at noon." Paul just looked at her and nodded in stunned acquiescence.

From Campbell's they drove directly to the Ferncliff Crematorium in Hartsdale, New York, where they entered a small, spartan, furnished room. The casket was removed from the hearse, rolled into the room, and rested against a wall with floor-to-ceiling black crepe curtains.

The Reverend Edgar Crossland stood, Bible in hand, and said a few brief words over the closed casket. Paul and his brother Jesse sat together by the side of the casket in iron chairs. Across from them sat Harriet and Moore.

When Reverend Crossland was done, the attendant pulled back the black floor-to-ceiling curtains to reveal an iron furnace door. The door was opened, and flames could be seen hissing inside. The boys were startled and looked at each other. They did not know what to expect. They all rose as the two attendants grasped the casket handles and rolled the casket on conveyor wheels through the open door into the flames.

As the casket hit the flames, they heard a great whoosh. After the casket was completely inside, the iron door was clanged shut. Moore, Jesse, and Paul just stood there numb, in stunned, silent bewilderment. The great Lone Wolf of Wall Street, the Boy Plunger, was gone forever. He had shot himself just the evening before, and his body was cremated by noon, with only four people to mourn his passing.

Back at the apartment on Park Avenue an hour later, Harriet talked to Paul. "Here Paul, take this." She handed him a $20 bill. He sat dumbfounded. "Your mother called from Brooklyn and wants you to come over and see her. She wants you to stay with her. I think it's a good idea, Paul."

"All right," he said.

"Fine. Well, that's settled. Frank is downstairs waiting with the car for you."

She walked him to the door and said goodbye. He went directly to his mother, Dorothy, who was waiting for him at her home in Brooklyn. She had not been invited to the funeral, nor had anybody else. He walked silently into his mother's open arms. They cried together. These were the first tears that he had shed.

On February 1, 1941, Livermore's estate was settled; a report was published in the *New York Times*. Harriet Metz Livermore was the sole executor. The total estate was valued at $10,000 in assets and $361,010 in liabilities. There was no mention of Livermore's personal $1 million trust fund or of the money Harriet had taken from the Park Avenue residence.

Paul went on to finish school at Hotchkiss. He then joined the Army Air Forces for wartime service. He spoke perfect French, so he was assigned to train pilots in the Free French air force to fly P-51 Mustangs. When he got out of the service, he was called by Harriet to come for a visit. "It is important," he was told.

When he arrived, Harriet offered to leave him her entire fortune if he would just stay with her as a companion. "I'm so lonely," she said to him.

Paul refused to give up his life this way. Instead, he went to

Hollywood, where he got roles and acted in several movies and television series. He later went to Hawaii to surf, where he eventually married Margaret Seely, with whom he had two sons, Chad and Scott. He and Margaret later divorced.

Paul wound up owning the Embers nightclub and restaurant in Honolulu, where he met and married Ann MacCormack, a beautiful, talented nightclub singer who had sung with Frank Sinatra, Tony Bennett, and many big bands. They remain happily together.

Jesse's life was a different story.

Patricia Schneider Freiberg was a tall, slender, blonde beauty, highly educated, a New York socialite, and the daughter of a prominent real estate developer in Cincinnati, Ohio.

When she was introduced to Jesse by her friend Timmy Houston, he whispered to her: "Pat, Jesse Livermore is one of the most famous playboys in New York. For God's sake, don't get involved with him!"

Patricia ignored her friend's advice and enjoyed herself as Jesse swept her off her feet with lavish romantic candlelit dinners in New York's finest nightclubs, dining at the best restaurants, trips to the country, surprise gifts of clothes and jewelry, and the use of the Livermore name, which still got the best tables in places like the Plaza Hotel and Sherman Billingsley's exclusive Stork Club.

Their relationship seemed sealed when Patricia's black poodle, Hefner, who had a broken leg and was not a normally friendly dog, ran down a flight of stairs to meet and greet Jesse, who loved animals and had a way with them. In particular, he loved Dobermans and always had at least one dog.

Jesse was already separated from his first wife, Evelyn Sullivan. He had a son with her, Jesse III, who was born on December 7, 1941. He rarely saw his son.

Jesse had run the Connecticut Pepsi-Cola franchise his father had given him into the ground. It finally had to be sold to avoid bankruptcy. He then convinced Charles Revlon to hire him, and he eventually became the sales promotion manager for Revlon.

Jesse lived in the Metropolitan Club, an elegant men's club in midtown Manhattan. His father had also been a well-known member. Jesse was a major backgammon and gin player and would often play through the night, drinking and gambling for high stakes.

Jesse lived as he was brought up to live. He had no regard for money. He had always had money, and he believed it would always be available to him. His father, who made sure Jesse had the finest cars, the finest clothes, and plenty of spending money, had opened every door in the country to him. One time Jesse showed his father his report card from Choate when he had done poorly in English composition.

"What's this, son, this poor grade in English comp?" his father had asked.

"I'm not a very good speller, Dad, that's the problem."

"That's not a problem, son. You'll always have a secretary. She'll do the spelling for you."

Jesse married Patricia in March 1965. His divorce from Evelyn Sullivan had cost him his Park Avenue apartment and whatever cash and assets he had. He was broke except for his trust fund, which was administrated by his mother, "Mousie," as he called her, as his father had. He still had problems with the gunshot wound. Patricia never knew whether the problems were psychosomatic or real. He occasionally complained to her of intense chest pain, and still had a slight curvature of the spine.

The couple moved into a house at 214 East Seventy-second Street.

Dorothy, Jesse's mother, was living in Long Island at Bright Waters with Willie K. Thompson, her fourth husband. Thompson

JESSE LIVERMORE: WORLD'S GREATEST STOCK TRADER

was a mob figure. He was directly hooked up with Frank Costello, a major boss in New York City. When they sold their house on Long Island, Dorothy called Patricia and Jesse. She asked if it would be okay if she and Thompson moved into a nearby building. The couple said okay. Soon after they moved into the building, Thompson suffered a heart attack and died.

After only a year of marriage, Jesse's drinking and carousing increased. His strange relationship with his mother became more and more intense. His mother still had control of Jesse's trust fund and doled the money out to him as she saw fit.

Before he asked for money, usually at dinner, Jesse would often first feign pain, grabbing his chest, grimacing, moaning, and slumping forward in his chair. Jesse made sure that his mother never forgot that she had shot him. Dorothy never failed to give him the money. When things got especially tight, she would often give him some pieces from her still-large jewel collection to hock. They would never be seen again. Dorothy and Jesse had an intense love/hate relationship. Jesse often stormed out in a rage after his mother gave him the money.

It was in their second year of marriage that Jesse took up with other women. He, Dorothy, and Patricia were also imbibing plenty of alcohol, which did not help the situation. Their house on East Seventy-second Street had four floors, with the dining room, living room, and kitchen on the first floor; a library and bedroom on the second; two bedrooms on the third floor; and two bedrooms on the fourth floor.

Dorothy moved into the house. Her bedroom was on the third floor, directly over the library. Patricia and Jesse's bedroom was also on the third floor, and William, the live-in butler, had quarters on the fourth floor. There was a spare bedroom on the fourth floor that eventually became Jesse's bedroom for his sexual liaisons.

Things deteriorated fast once Jesse's affairs came into the picture. Jesse made no effort to conceal his affairs, once telling Patricia, "It's no fun having an affair if you aren't married!"

Jesse got involved with all kinds of women: showgirls, socialites, hookers, and shop clerks. Eventually he started bringing the women home and taking them to the bedroom on the fourth floor, which eventually became his permanent bedroom.

"He's like a cat with his trophy, dragging those women in here," Patricia told Dorothy.

One night Jesse brought home one of his favorites, an English hooker and frequent visitor, whom he introduced before climbing the stairs to the fourth floor.

He said, "This is my English friend, Pamela. We are going upstairs to have a visit."

As he climbed the stairs, his mother screamed: "I curse my son! I curse my son! Oh my God!" and she broke down crying in the living room.

Things eventually turned violent, and Jesse started beating Patricia. One night he beat her up so badly that the neighbors called the police. Both of them were drunk when the police came to the door.

Jesse was fast on his feet. He told the police, "We've both been drinking and I was just restraining her from attacking me."

"Ma'am, do you want to press charges?" the police asked Patricia.

"No, I just want to go to my sister's house." The police helped her get to her sister's house.

She was warned to leave him by everyone close to her, but she could not do it. She loved him no matter what.

Jesse resented his mother more and more. He resented the fact that she had "pissed away" his real inheritance through her foolish acts, such as not paying the taxes on the properties; letting her jewels go for 10 cents on the dollar; converting her $1 million stock portfolio, handpicked by his father, into railroad bonds that failed; and generally being whimsical and stupid about money. He also resented the way she handed out his trust funds to him. His and his brother's trust funds had been solidly set up. Every time Jesse tried to break the trust to get at the principal, he was rebuffed by his mother and Morgan Guaranty, which administered the trust strictly according to the dictates of the law and the exacting provisions his father had instructed the attorneys to write into them.

Jesse's violence increased along with his drinking and carousing. Patricia gave up drinking in 1967. She believed this saved her life. One night Jesse came in roaring drunk and found Patricia in the bathtub. He attacked her, slapping her over and over and then holding her head underwater with both hands, until she nearly drowned.

His periods of making up, his self-recriminations when he was sober, the tears of repentance, his apologies were works of art. He could be as kind and charming as he was cruel and unfeeling. Patricia's love for him was so great that she always forgave him.

When he was sober, they all had plenty of good times. Dinner parties and meeting in the library every night for cocktails was often great fun, with lots of laughter and good cheer.

Patricia called her mother-in-law by her nickname, "Mousie." She considered her "the funniest woman on the planet, who could take over any dinner or social occasion. She would light up the room. And the biggest part of her charm was that she didn't know she was being nonstop funny."

One night Patricia asked Jesse why his father had killed himself.

"Pat, for my father the game was over as he knew it. The players had changed, the SEC rules had changed, and times had changed." He paused, "But maybe it was more than that, maybe his spirit was broken. Like a dog—you know how you can break the spirit of a dog, and the dog is no good anymore? Maybe that's what happened. He told me once that he only lost money when he stopped following his own rules.

"I think he had stopped playing the game correctly, and that bothered him most of all. He was off his form, his mind was fuzzy. After he divorced Mom and moved out of Evermore, things went bad for him. It was like she was his good luck, and when she was gone, his good luck was gone. He had nobody to go to, no friends, and nowhere to go, no place to get any peace.

"And Nina was a killer bitch. She smothered him, devoured his spirit with her negativity. I told her to beat it within days of having to live with her after the shooting. It's one of the reasons Dad sent me to Europe and I married Evelyn. I wanted to be on my own. She hated Paul and me; anything that got between her and Dad, she hated. She pushed him deeper and deeper into the blackness."

"What else?" Patricia asked, after a pause.

"Yeah, when Mother shot me I think he began to think his life was a total failure. How could it be that a mother would shoot her own son? How the hell could that happen? How could it be his wife, the beautiful young girl he had married so many years before, would sink so low as to shoot her own son? A Greek tragedy that happened to involve him as a principal player.

"And he was with me all the time—by my side through all that pain and agony when my life was on the line. He must have had time to think about it. In fact, that was the only time he was really *ever* with me for any length of time.

"Finally, I think he just had one of those dark personalities. There was always something unreachable about him, a kind of detachment from humanity, from the rest of us. He slipped into the darkness, and there was nothing to pull him back. His real passion was the market. When he lost his interest in the market, he lost it all."

Patricia was interested in astrology. She had never met Livermore, but one day she read his chart. Her conclusions were clear.
He was a very strong Leo, with his planets in Leo. Patricia concluded that he never did it for the money; he did it for the game,
for the sake of winning. And he never wanted to *break* anyone. He
wanted to *best* everyone. He wanted world recognition as being
the best there ever was, like a superb athlete who climbs to the
highest level and receives the world's accolades. Even though he
was not boastful—in fact, he was quiet and secretive—he still
wanted world recognition. He wanted the world to know that he
was the best stock market trader who ever lived. But he wanted the
world to come to this realization on its own. He did not want to
promote it himself.

Near the end of her relationship with Jesse, Patricia's father, an
Austrian gentleman whom she loved very much, called her to
Cincinnati. He was suffering from the beginning stages of
Alzheimer's disease. Her parents had been separated for years, but
every Christmas he would show up for dinner.

"Pat," he said to her, "I don't ever want your mother to control
my life. It's something she's always wanted to do. Promise me you
won't let her control my life."

"Daddy, I'll do everything I can." Patricia answered.

A month later, her father shot and killed himself. Patricia was
devastated.

Jesse became meaner and meaner. At one time he had two
Dobermans. He and a couple of his neighbors would go for a walk
in Central Park to exercise their dogs. Once in the park, they
would free the dogs to wake up the homeless people who were
sleeping in the park in droves at that time. They would walk down
to the far end of the park and watch as the homeless people
streamed out of the park, screaming, running, and tripping over
each other as they fled, with the dogs in hot pursuit.

By 1975, the violence, drinking, gambling, and womanizing was out of control.

At 1:15 A.M. on March 23, 1975, Jesse called on one of the three telephone lines in the house. Unknown to Patricia, Jesse had been drinking for two days straight.

"Hello, Pat," he said. "I want you to listen to this." Jesse went on to quote Shakespeare for several minutes. Pat could not tell he was drunk. He spoke clearly. She wondered if he had been smoking pot.

There was a silence on the line, then he said, "Pat I'm going to kill my dog and then kill myself."

There was a dead silence on the phone and then a click as the line went dead. This was not the first time that Pat had heard him threaten to kill himself. The phone rang a second time. "Pat, you there?"

"Yes, Jesse. I'm here."

"I mean it. I'm gonna kill my dog, and then I'm gonna kill myself." For the second time there was a click on the phone and then the buzz of a disconnection.

Two shots rang out in the house. Pat leaped out of bed and put on a robe. She was tying the robe when Jesse appeared in her doorway, a smoking chrome-plated .32-caliber Colt revolver in his hand.

"Cesare is dead. It's your fault that my dog is dead. Come with me and bring Alexi."

Patricia stood dumbfounded, locked in fear. She picked up her standard white poodle, Alexi, and took the dog in her arms. She was positive that she and her dog would die that night. Jesse staggered slightly, framed in the door jamb, eyes glazed from drink. There was no question he was as drunk as a person could be and still stand.

"You follow me. I've been in the library," he said, and he led the way down the stairs. The library occupied the second floor. There was a balcony in front of the library that overlooked the large living room downstairs. When Jesse got to the library door and entered, Pat ran for her life down the stairs to the floor below. She ran through the kitchen and out the back door, breathing hard, clinging to Alexi.

In total panic, she ran to the building next door and shoved Alexi, the frightened poodle, into the arms of the doorman, who let her use the phone. She called Robert Cohen, the family lawyer.

"Bobby, it's Patricia. Jesse's killed his dog and he wants to kill me and kill Alexi," she blurted.

"Where are you?"

"Next door with the doorman. I'm hiding in the lobby. I'm afraid he's gonna shoot me through the windows if he gets a glimpse of me."

"Stay there. I'll call the cops and I'll be there in minutes. Don't move!"

Cohen and the police arrived simultaneously. The police came from the Sixty-seventh Street station. The station sent an emergency service special response team of 10 officers led by Lieutenant John Weeks. These officers were specialists in dealing with dangerous hostage and suicide cases.

Attorney Cohen and Patricia asked to go back into the house with the police. The police led them into the dining room and told them to keep out of sight, unless called.

Lieutenant Weeks and Officer Charles Brezny took the lead. The other officers took up strategic shooting positions. Weeks and Brezny climbed the stairs to the library. When they reached the top, they positioned themselves on opposite sides of the door to the library. They saw Jesse sitting casually in an easy chair, his 85-pound dog Cesare lying in a pool of blood at his feet. There were two chrome-plated .32-caliber Colt revolvers in his lap.

Patricia had told the police to be careful, because Jesse was a deadeye shot. "He must be very drunk to have to use two shots to kill his dog," she told them.

Brezny got the nod to try to enter the library. As he passed through the door, Jesse fired a shot in his direction. The bullet hit the wall. Brezny darted back outside the doorway.

The officers were well trained, and they did not return fire. Instead, they talked to him, chit-chatted for an hour, calming him down. He told them he was going to kill himself. He read to them from his long suicide note.

After a full hour of chit-chat, Brezny said: "I'm thirsty. I could use a drink. Could we have a glass of wine?"

"Sure. Sure you can," Jesse answered.

As he poured the wine, the two police officers rushed him, with other officers following.

Jesse was able to get one of the guns up from his lap. He rammed the barrel of the revolver into Lieutenant Weeks's chest and pulled the trigger.

The gun only clicked.

The police were instantly on top of him. They subdued him. Brezny, 29 years old, suffered a broken wrist in the scuffle.

The two guns were confiscated, and Jesse was charged with attempted murder of a police officer, reckless endangerment, possession of a deadly weapon, resisting arrest, and attempted suicide.

He was in serious trouble. New York Governor Nelson Rockefeller had just signed a law mandating life imprisonment for anyone convicted of attempted murder of a police officer.

The police also explained to Patricia that people who attempt suicide often want the police to kill them, so they provoke the police into shooting. It was never explained whether the second gun, the gun Jesse jammed into Lieutenant Weeks's ribs, was actually loaded.

There was no question for Patricia. She believed that Jesse really did not have the courage to kill himself and had intended to provoke the police into doing the job for him. He was very smart.

Dorothy emerged from her room on the third floor above the library after Jesse had been taken away. "What happened, Pat?" she asked, having quietly feigned sleep through the entire incident.

She left for Long Boat Key, Florida, the next day, unable to cope with the events.

Jesse was arraigned and denied bail. He was taken to Rikers Island, where he was kept in isolation. His jailers were sure that his unbridled arrogance would get him killed quickly if he was allowed to enter the general prison population.

The police had a dilemma: If something happened to Jesse while he was in jail, it would make headlines. So they came up with the idea of giving him bail on the proviso that he leave New York and reside in Florida. "Let him kill a Palm Beach cop—get him out of New York!" was their attitude. He could come up from Florida for his trial.

After 54 days in prison, they released him. He looked awful. He had dropped from a trim 155 pounds to 125. When he had been arrested, more than 200 people called to inquire about him. When he was released from Rikers, there were only two. He immediately started drinking on his release.

As a condition of his bail, he had two weeks to pack up and leave for Florida. Pat, still afraid for her life, left the house and stayed with a friend in Pleasant Valley, New York, until he left.

He went down to Palm Beach by himself. As a condition of his bail agreement, he had to get psychiatric help. His mother called him and told him not to bother, he was fine.

"You don't need a psychiatrist, son, you just need some rest."

Patricia always believed Dorothy said this to her son for selfish reasons, not wanting him to relive the Santa Barbara shooting as he got more deeply into therapy.

Therapy was a condition of his bail, however, so he went to a doctor in Palm Beach. The doctor did all he could, diagnosing Jesse as a manic-depressive, paranoid, suicidal alcoholic. But he was dealing with a determined patient.

The trial was postponed each time Jesse came to New York. His lawyer told him he would beat the rap, but he did not believe it. On the day before the trial was to begin, Jesse called Patricia from Palm Beach. "I can't go to prison, Pat. I just can't go."

"Jesse, your lawyer says you can beat it."

"I don't believe that moron. I can't go to jail," he said, and hung up.

He went to some friends in Palm Beach, Saint John and Alretta Terrell, and borrowed a shotgun from them. But he was unable to use it.

Instead, he opened the oven door and turned on the gas. He took a handful of pills and collapsed. He was found dead the next day.

Pat flew to Palm Beach immediately, that same afternoon. The next day, Jesse's body was quietly taken to a crematorium in Palm Beach. A minister said a few words, and the body was turned into ashes. No one was in attendance except Patricia and the minister.

Much later, it dawned on Patricia just how afraid of his mother Jesse really was. Yet, he stayed so dependent on her for company and money. His mother knew that he never got over the shooting, and, no matter what she did, she could never make it up to him. Somehow they were hooked together, connected by a karmic umbilical cord that had become inextricably tied when she fired that shot into his chest.

"What a tragedy! Three lives destroyed in one flash of a gun barrel. What is the matter with us all?" Pat thought to herself.

After Jesse's death, Dorothy moved back in with Patricia for a while, but she eventually moved down to Sanibel Island, Florida.

In 1985, Dorothy fell ill, and she called her son Paul and his wife Ann to come and visit her. Ann and Paul arrived on Sanibel and found the nurse waiting for them.

"Your mother asked me to come here to the house and wait for you," she said.

"Where's my mother?" Paul asked.

"She went to the hospital two days ago, and I'm sorry to tell you she passed away that same day," the nurse said.

"Where is she now?" Ann asked.

"She's in the mortuary, I'm afraid." The nurse let a silence fall. "She left specific instructions to be cremated tomorrow with no ceremony."

At that moment, Caesar, Dorothy's cat, appeared in the living room and rubbed up against Ann. She picked up the cat, who was a very old, treasured member of the family. The cat had been very close to Dorothy. Ann played with the cat as he settled in her lap.

"Mrs. Livermore, I wouldn't get too close to the cat if I were you," the nurse said.

"Oh?" Ann said.

"Mrs. Livermore left very clear instructions that the cat was to be placed in the casket and cremated with her."

Ann gasped and held the cat closer to her. "Paul?" she said, pleading with her eyes to keep the cat. Paul also wanted to keep the cat, but he felt obligated to honor his mother's will.

She had left everything in perfect order—her will, her bankbooks, car keys on the table, written instructions on how to dispose of her estate, and instructions for her funeral. It was unlike Dorothy to be so organized; in fact, she was famous for being disorganized and careless. Later, when they moved the dresser, they found a gold chain and a beautiful watch that had fallen on the floor.

"She never did keep good track of her jewelry," Paul said.

"What she had left, you mean," Ann said.

Over the years, Dorothy had given over $500,000 in jewelry to her son Jesse, who had hocked it.

The next day, they took the cat to the vet and had him put to sleep. They drove to the crematorium and placed the cat in the casket.

Dorothy "Mousie" Livermore entered the flames of eternity with Caesar the cat to join her husband and son.

Livermore's Laws and Trading Secrets Revealed

To know is to do!   Socrates

A SUCCESSFUL SPECULATOR REMAINS A CONSTANT STU-
dent of three things:

- *Market timing.*   You must learn when to enter and when to exit a market trade—when to hold and when to fold, as Ed Bradley used to say.
- *Money management.*   Don't lose money, don't lose your stake. A speculator without cash is like a storeowner with no inventory. Cash is a speculator's inventory, lifeline, and best friend. Without it you're out of business. Don't lose your line!
- *Emotional control.*   Before you can successfully play the market, you must have a clear, concise strategy and stick to it. All speculators must design intelligent battle plans, customized to suit their emotional makeup, before speculating in the stock market. The biggest thing speculators have to control is their emotions. Remember, reason, logic, and pure economics do not drive the stock market. It is driven by human nature, which never changes. How can it change? It's our nature.

You can not tell if your judgment about the market is right until you place a bet, purchase a stock.

If you don't put your money on the table, you can never test your judgment, because you can never test your emotions. Livermore believed that emotion, not reason, dictates the direction of the stock market, just as in most important things in life: love, marriage, children, war, sex, crime, passion, religion. It is rarely reason that drives people.

This is not to say that things like sales, profits, world conditions, politics, and technology do not play a part in the ultimate price of a stock. These factors eventually come to bear, and the price of the stock market and the individual stocks may reflect these factors, but it is always *emotion* that carries the extremes.

Livermore believed in cycles, life cycles and market cycles. They are often extreme, rarely balanced. Cycles come like a series of ocean waves, bringing the high tide when things are good, and the low tide as conditions recede. These cycles come unexpectedly, unpredictably. Good or bad, they have to be weathered with temperance and patience. Remember, the skillful speculator knows that money can be made no matter what the market conditions, if a speculator is willing to play both sides of the market.

Livermore realized early on that the stock market is never obvious. It is designed to fool most of the people most of the time.

Livermore's rules are often based on thinking against the grain:

- Cut your losses quickly.
- Be sure to confirm your judgment before you take your full position.
- Let your profits ride if there is no good reason to close out the position.
- The action is with the leading stocks, which change with every new market.
- Keep the number of stocks you follow limited in order to focus.
- New all-time highs are to be bought on breakouts.
- Cheap stocks often appear to be bargains after a large drop. They often continue to fall, or have little potential to rise in price. Leave them alone!
- Use pivotal points to identify changes in trends and confirmations in trends.
- Don't fight the tape!

The stock market is a study in cycles; when it changes direction, it remains in that new trend until the momentum weakens—a body in motion tends to stay in motion. Remember, don't buck the trend. Don't fight the tape.

In a free market system, prices fluctuate. They never go up all the time, and they never go down all the time. This is good for the alert speculator, since either side of the market can be played.

MARKET-TIMING RULES

Never sustain a loss of more than 10 percent of your invested capital. Livermore learned this in the bucket shops, where he worked with 10 percent margin and was automatically sold out if his loss exceeded the limit. This is also a money-management rule.

The big money is made by the *sitting,* not the *thinking.* Once a position is taken, the hardest thing to do is to be patient and wait for the move to play out. The temptation is strong to take fast profits or cover a trade solely out of fear of losing the profit on a correction. This error has cost millions of speculators millions of dollars. Be sure you have a good clear reason to enter a trade, and be sure you have a good clear reason to close your position. It is the big swing that makes the big money for you.

Play the market only when all factors are in your favor. No one can play the market all the time and win. There are times when you should be completely out of the market.

The speculator must know the overall trend of the market—the line of least resistance—before making a trade. Be sure you know whether this line of least resistance is upward or downward. This applies to both the overall market and individual stocks. The basic thing you need to know before making a trade is which way the overall market is headed: up, down, or sideways. You have to decide this before making a trade. If the overall trend of the market is not in your favor, you are playing at an extreme disadvantage.

Remember, go with the flow, bend with the trend, do not sail into a gale, and—most of all—don't argue with the tape!

The only thing to do when you are wrong is to be right by ceasing to be wrong. Cover your losses quickly, without hesitation. Don't waste time—when a stock moves below a mental stop, sell it immediately.

Stocks often act like human beings, expressing different personalities: aggressive, reserved, hyper, high-strung, direct, logical, predictable, unpredictable. Study the stocks as you would study people; after awhile, their reactions to certain circumstances become predictable and useful in timing the stock's movement.

Stocks are never too high to begin buying or too low to begin selling short.

Failure to take the opportunity to get out of large illiquid positions when the opportunity presents itself can cost you dearly.

Failure to take advantage of a serendipitous act of good luck in the stock market is always a mistake.

In a market moving sideways in a narrow channel where stock prices are essentially stagnant, there is a great danger in trying to predict or anticipate *when* and *in what direction* the market will move. You must wait until the market or the stock breaks out of this sideways channel in either direction. Don't anticipate! Wait for confirmation! Never argue with the tape. Follow the line of least resistance.

Do not spend a lot of time trying to figure out what moves the price of a particular stock. Rather, examine the tape. The answer lies in *what* the tape says, not in trying to figure out *why* the tape is saying it. Behind all major movements in the stock market there is an irresistible force which will most likely be revealed later. This is all the successful speculator needs to know.

The stock market goes up, down, and sideways. You can make money on the up side or the down side—you can buy long or sell short. It should not matter to you what side of the market you are on. You must be impersonal. When the market goes sideways and you are confused, take a vacation.

A danger signal to watch out for: the *one-day reversal,* when the high of the day is higher than the high of the previous day, but the close of the day is below the low of the previous day, and the volume of the current day is higher than the volume of the previous day. Beware!

If the stock you traded is going in the opposite direction from what you expected, sell it quickly. This means your judgment was wrong. Cut your losses.

Wait, be patient, until as many factors as possible are in your favor. It's the patience that makes the money.

Study the action of a stock that has made a severe break in price, a precipitous drop. If the stock does not rebound quickly, it will most likely fall away further. There is an inherent weakness in this stock; the reason will be revealed at a later time.

The market is operating in future time. It has usually already factored in current events.

It is the inception of a basic movement, the *pivotal point,* a change in trend, which indicates whether to buy or sell. It is this change in trend that, if caught, yields the most rewards.

There are two kinds of pivotal points. The *reversal* pivotal point is defined as the perfect psychological time at the beginning of a major market move, a change in basic trend. It does not matter if this is at the bottom or the top of a long-term trending move.

The second pivotal point is called the *continuation* pivotal point. The reversal pivotal point marks a definite change in direction; the continuation pivotal point confirms it.

Be alert—major pivotal points can often be accompanied by a heavy increase in volume.

Pivotal points provide an essential timing device, a trigger that reveals when to enter and when to exit the market.

At the end of a bull market, watch for *wild capitalization*—good stocks selling at 30, 40, 50, or 60 times their annual earnings. These will be the same stocks that had previously traded at much lower multiples.

Beware of wild speculative stocks that take off for no real reason, except that they are trendy, currently favored stocks.

New highs are very important for timing. A new all-time high can mean that the stock has broken through the overhead supply of stock, and the line of least resistance will be strongly upward. Many people, when they see that a stock has made a new high, sell it immediately, then go to look for a cheaper stock.

Group action is the key to timing your move. Stocks do not move alone when they move. If U.S. Steel climbs or drops in price, then sooner or later, Bethlehem, Republic, and Crucible will follow along. The premise is simple: If the basic reasons why U.S. Steel's business should come into or go out of favor in the stock market are sound, then the rest of the steel group should also follow for the same reasons.

Trade the leading stocks in the leading groups. Buy the market leader of an industry group.

Watch the *market leaders,* the stocks that have led the charge upward in a bull market. When these stocks falter and fail to make new highs, it is often a signal that the market is turning. As the leaders go, so goes the entire market.

Confine your studies of stock market movements to the prominent leaders of the day. If you cannot make money out of the leading active issues, you are not going to make money out of the stock market. That is where the action is and where the money is to be made. It also keeps your universe of stocks limited, focused, and more easily controlled.

You should have a clear target price at which to sell if the stock moves against you, a firm stop. And you must obey your rules!

A successful market trader must bet only on the course of highest probabilities. Buy small positions, and probe to test your judgment before you commit to a large position. Do not establish your full position all at one time. Use probes to confirm your judgment and timing, and to find the line of least resistance.

The trader must react quickly to the unexpected. If it is a windfall, grab it. If it is bad news, hit the road, and don't look back or hesitate—sell out the position.

Beware when volume gets heavy and stocks churn after a long upward trend. This is a clue, a warning that the end of the move is near. This is an indication that stocks are going from strong hands to weak hands, from the professionals to the public. The public often views this heavy volume as the mark of a vibrant, healthy market going through a normal correction, not a top or a bottom.

The public tends to believe that the insiders are feeding out their stock on the upward rise of a stock. They are often wrong. They are often being fed the majority of the insider or pooled stock after the stock has crested at new highs and is rolling over, churning, and starting its decline. This is the time of the highest volume. This is often the reason why a stock cannot make a new high—there is simply too much supply hanging over the market. This is *distribution*—is not always from insiders, but usually from larger shareholders, such as mutual funds in today's markets.

MONEY-MANAGEMENT RULES

Establish stops! You should have a clear target price at which to sell if the stock moves against you. And you must obey your rules! Never sustain a loss of more than 10 percent of your invested capital. Losses can be twice as expensive to make up—if you lose 50 percent, you must gain 100 percent to get even (see Table 12.1). This is also a key timing rule.

Never meet a margin call, and never average down in your buying.

Turn paper profits into real money periodically. Take a percentage of your winnings and put them in a safe place, like the bank, or bonds, or an annuity. Cash was, is, and always will be king. Always have cash in reserve. Cash is your ammunition. Livermore's biggest mistake was not following this rule more often.

Examine and understand the dimension of time: Time is *not* money, because there may be times when your money should be inactive. Time is time, and money is money. The successful investor is not invested in the market all the time. There are many times when you should be completely in cash. Often, money that is just sitting can later be moved into the right situation once it has revealed itself. If you are unsure of the direction of the market, then stay out, and wait for a confirmation of the next move. This is how to make a fortune. Patience, patience, patience is the key to success. Don't be in a hurry.

Take some winnings off the table after the completion of a successful trade.

Use probes to establish your full position. After an initial probe, do not make a second move until the first probe shows you a profit. Do not establish your full position all at once—wait until your first trades, your early probes, have shown you a profit, then go ahead and fill out your full position.

To be precise: First establish 20 percent of your planned position on the first purchase, 20 percent on the second, and 20 percent on the third. Wait for a confirmation of your judgment, then make your final purchase of 40 percent.

Each of these purchases, or probes, is a crucial factor in establishing your overall position. If at any time the stock moves against you, close out all your positions, never sustaining a loss of more than 10 percent of invested capital.

Sell the losers; let the winners ride, provided all the factors are positive.

EMOTIONAL-CONTROL RULES

Emotional control is the most essential factor in playing the market.

Don't anticipate! Wait until the market gives you the clues, the signals, the hints, before you move. Move only after you have confirmation. Anticipation is a killer. Don't make a decision based on anticipation. The market always gives you time. If you wait for the clues, there will be plenty of time to execute your moves.

Do not spend a lot of time trying to figure out *why* the price of a particular stock moves. Rather, examine the facts themselves. The answer lies in what the tape *says,* not in trying to figure out why. Most important, never argue with the tape. It can't hear you.

Stock traders can be convinced to move away from their own convictions by listening to the advice of other traders, persuaded that their judgment may be faulty. Or, in the least damaging case, listening to others may cause indecision and bad judgment. This indecision may cause a loss of confidence, which may well mean a loss of money.

"Tips come from all sources—from relatives, loved ones, friends who have just made serious investments themselves and want to pass on their good fortune. They also come from hucksters and criminals. Remember: All tips are dangerous. None should be taken.

Remove *hope* from your trading lexicon. Hoping a stock will do something is truly gambling. If you do not have good, solid reasons for holding a stock position, then move on to another more logical trade. Wishing a stock up or down has caused the downfall of many stock market speculators. Hope walks hand in hand with greed.

Be aware of your emotions at all times. Don't get too confident over your wins or too despondent over your losses.

Nothing ever changes in the market. The only thing that changes are the players, and the new players have no financial memory of the previous major cycles—like the panic of 1907 or the crash of 1929—because they have not experienced them. It may be new to the speculator, but it's not new to the market.

Always have a method of speculating, a plan of attack. And always stick to your plan. Do not constantly change your plan. Find a method that works emotionally for you, and stick to that method. Stick to your own customized game.

Speculators are not investors. Their object is not to secure a steady return on their money over a long period of time. Speculators must profit by either a rise or a fall in the price of whatever they have decided to speculate in.

Play a lone hand. Make your decisions about your own money by yourself. Be secretive and silent in your stock trading. Do not disclose your winners or your losers.

The successful investor is not invested in the market all the time. There are many times when you should be completely in cash. If you are unsure of the direction of the market, wait.

Never lose control of your emotions when the market moves against you. And never become elated with your successes to such a degree that you think the market is an easy way to make money. Never fight the tape; the tape is the truth. Seek harmony with the tape.

Stay in the business you're good at.

It takes four strong mental characteristics to be a superior market trader:

- *Observation*—The ability to observe the facts without prejudice
- *Memory*—The ability to remember key events correctly and objectively
- *Mathematics*—The ability to calculate numbers easily; being at home with digits
- *Experience*—The ability to learn, to retain knowledge gained through experience and call upon it at will

Subliminal messages, apparent impulses, are nothing more than the subconscious mind talking to you, calling up years of trading experiences. On occasion, Livermore let his inner mind lead him, even if he did not know the reason at the time. He agreed with Aristotle: "We are the sum total of our experience."

Emotions must be understood and harnessed before successful speculation is possible:

- *Greed* is a human emotion present in all people, defined by Webster's dictionary as the excessive desire for acquiring or possessing; a desire for more than one needs or deserves. We do not know the origin of greed, all we know is that it exists in every person.
- *Fear* lies ready to appear in a single heartbeat, and when it does, it distorts reason. Reasonable people act unreasonably when they are afraid. And they become afraid every time they start to lose money. Their judgment becomes impaired.
- *Hope* lives hand in hand with greed when it comes to the stock market. Once a trade is made, hope springs alive. It is human nature to be hopeful, to be positive, to hope for the best. Hope is important to the survival of the human species. But hope, like its stock market cousins ignorance, greed, and

fear, distorts reason. Hope clouds facts, and the stock market only deals in facts. It is like the spinning of a roulette wheel— the little black ball tells the outcome, not greed, fear, or hope. The result is objective and final, with no appeal.

Beware of ignorance. The market must be studied and learned, not in a casual fashion but seriously and deeply. The stock market, with its allure of easy money and fast action, induces people into the foolish mishandling of their money like no other entity. The reverse of ignorance is knowledge, and knowledge is power.

The stock market is never obvious. It is designed to fool most of the people most of the time. These rules are often based on thinking against the grain.

You should not be in the market all the time. There are times when you should be out of the market, for emotional as well as economic reasons.

When the tape doesn't agree with your decision to buy or sell, wait until it does. Never try to rationalize your position with what the tape is saying.

Do not give or receive stock tips; just remember: In a bull market stocks go up, in a bear market they go down. This is all anyone needs to know, or all you need to tell them.

Stock speculators sometimes make mistakes, and know that they are making them, but proceed anyway, only to berate themselves later for breaking their own rules. Do not break your rules.

Never become an involuntary investor by holding a declining stock.

Never think about buying a stock on reactions, or shorting a stock on rallies.

Do not use the words *bullish* or *bearish*. These words fix a firm market direction in the mind for an extended period of time.

Instead use *upward trend* and *downward trend* when asked the direction you think the market is headed. Simply say: The line of least resistance is upward, or downward, at this time.

Speculation is a business, and like any other business it takes hard work and diligence to succeed.

CONCLUSION

There is nothing new on Wall Street or in stock speculation. What has happened in the past will happen again and again and again. This is because human nature does not change, and it is human emotion that always gets in the way of human intelligence.

Jesse Livermore

Sources

A great deal of the information in this book was derived from extended interviews with Paul Livermore, Jesse Livermore's younger son, and Patricia Livermore, wife of Jesse Livermore Jr. Their first-hand knowledge of Jesse Livermore was integral in learning many new aspects of Livermore's trading techniques and secrets, as well as learning the facts about Livermore, the man.

BOOKS

Fisher, Kenneth L. *100 Minds That Made the Market* (Woodside, Calif.: Pacific Publishing Group, 1995).

Galbraith, John Kenneth. *The Great Crash of 1929* (New York: Time, 1962).

Klingaman, William. *1929: The Year of the Great Crash* (New York: Harper & Row, 1989).

Lefevre, Edwin. *Reminiscences of a Stock Operator* (New York: John Wiley & Sons, 1994).

Livermore, Jesse. *How to Trade in Stocks* (Greenville, S.C.: Traders Press, 1991, 2001).

Wyckoff, Richard D. *Jesse Livermore's Methods of Trading Stocks* Windsor Books (Bright Waters, N.Y.).

NEWSPAPERS

New York Times, Various articles from 1922 to 1940.

Palm Beach Post, Palm Beach, Fla.

PERIODICALS

American Mercury, November 1926.

Brooks, John. "Annals of Finance," *The New Yorker,* 6 June 1959.

Cunningham, Thomas N. "The Life and Career of Edward R. Bradley" (thesis), Florida Atlantic University.

Harper's Weekly, 20 December 1913.

Newsweek, 9 December 1940.

Saturday Evening Post, 4 January 1930; 11 January 1930.

Time, 9 December 1935.

Bibliography

CHAPTER ONE   THE GREAT BEAR OF WALL STREET

Klingaman, William. *1929: The Year of the Great Crash* (New York: Harper & Row, 1989).
"Livermore Not in Bear Pool," *New York Times,* 22 October 1929.
"Livermore Now a Bull," *New York Times,* 13 November 1929.
"Stocks Driven Down as Wave of Selling Engulfs the Market," *New York Times,* 20 October 1929.

CHAPTER THREE   THE SAN FRANCISCO EARTHQUAKE RUMBLES IN NEW YORK

Baruch, Bernard. *My Own Story* (New York: Holt, 1957).
Fisher, Kenneth L. *100 Minds That Made the Market* (Woodside, Calif.: Pacific Publishing Group, 1995).

CHAPTER FIVE   THE COTTON KING

"Cotton 'King' a Bankrupt," *New York Times,* 18 February 1915.
"Jerome Arraigned for Seizing Auto," *New York Times,* 22 September 1915.

CHAPTER SIX   BACK ON HIS GAME

"Exit the Swashbuckling Trader of Wall Street," *New York Times,* 13 May 1917.

"Jerome Is Held on Bail," *New York Times,* 7 September 1917.

"Jerome Free in Auto Case," *New York Times,* 23 September 1917.

"Livermore Even on Two $1,000,000 Deals," *New York Times,* 2 February 1917.

CHAPTER EIGHT   STOCK POOLS AND SCANDALS

"Livermore Makes Denial," *New York Times,* 8 March 1924.

"Not Mex. Pete, Goat, Says Livermore," *New York Times,* 29 June 1922.

"Stock List Timeless on Oil Revelations," *New York Times,* 16 February 1924.

CHAPTER NINE   BOSTON BILLY

New York Times and *New York Daily News.* Numerous articles on the Boston Billy gang robbery from May 31, 1927, through December 27, 1929.

CHAPTER TEN   THE CRASH OF 1929

Galbraith, John Kenneth. *The Great Crash of 1929* (Boston: Houghton Mifflin, 1961).

Mizner Development Corporation advertisement, *Palm Beach Post,* 15 May 1925.

CHAPTER ELEVEN WHEN TO HOLD AND WHEN TO FOLD

Livermore, Jesse. *How to Trade in Stocks* (Greenville, S.C.: Traders Press, 1991, 2001).

CHAPTER FOURTEEN THE SHOOTING OF JESSE LIVERMORE JR.

Hemingway, Ernest. *The Snows of Kilimanjaro* (New York: Scribner and Sons, 1964).
"Livermore Goes Abroad," *New York Times,* 6 December 1935.
"Livermore Kills Himself, 'Failure' at 63," *New York Tribune,* 29 November 1940.

Traders Press, Inc.®
PO Box 6206
Greenville, SC 29606

Serving Traders Since 1975

- **Publishes books exclusively for market traders and investors**
- **Publisher of the largest catalog collection of financial classics in the U.S.**
- **Founded in 1975 by an active trader in stocks, options, and futures**
- **Owned and operated by the founder, Edward Dobson, still an active trader**

Readers of this book are invited to contact TRADERS PRESS, INC. ® for a free copy of our current Traders Catalog, as well as a free book.

Our 100 page Traders Catalog describes hundreds of books, gifts, and courses of interest to traders and investors. It normally sells for $10 but as a reader of this book, you may obtain a copy at no charge, as well as a free copy of any of the following three books: *Understanding Bollinger Bands* by Edward Dobson, *Understanding Fibonacci Numbers* by Edward Dobson, or *Safe Sex on Wall Street* (please specify choice when contacting us):

Contact:

TRADERS PRESS, INC. ®
800-927-8222
864-298-0222

Tradersprs@aol.com
http://www.traderspress.com